The Indian Renaissance
and
Raja Rammohan Roy

Prof. (Dr) Hari Hara Das
Dr. Sasmita Mahapatra

Pointer Publishers

Jaipur 302 003 (Raj.) India

Distributed by
Prem C. Bakliwal
Aavishkar Publishers, Distributors
807, Vyas Building, Chaura Rasta
Jaipur 302 003 (Raj.) India
Phone : 2578159
e-mail : aavishkarbooks@hotmail.com

2023

ISBN 978-81-7132-101-8

Published by
Mrs. Shashi Jain for
Pointer Publishers
Vyas Building, Chaura Rasta
Jaipur 302 003 (Raj.) India
Phones : 2578159
e-mail : pointerpub@hotmail.com

Printed at
Trident Enterprises (UP)
Noida

Preface

The East India Company which was a trading company came to India for the purpose of carrying on trade and commerce. But in the course of time due to internecine war and rivalry among the heads of the ruling dynasties, the British got the opportunity to set one ruler against the other and achieved their sinister designs. The Company's rule over India was responsible for allround decline and degradation. It resulted in economic exploitation, political prostration, social stagnation and cultural decadence throughout the country. India's political subjugation to the British rule ruined her economy, indigenous industries, agriculture and impoverished the Indians. The British were interested only in the perpetuation of the political authority. They did not bother about the socio-economic development of the people of India. They looked down upon the Indians and preached the obnoxious theory of the Whitemen's burden to rule over the coloured people. In their political game, since they were only interested to continue in power, they followed the policy of non-interference in the socio-religious practices of the people. From the time of the Battle of Plassey in 1757 upto the First War of Indian Independence in 1857, there was no major challenge to the exploitative imperialist policy followed by the British in India.

The Eighteenth Century in Indian History was a period of allround decline.[1] It had become a fertile field of operation for English imperialism and colonialism. It presented a spectacle of thorough economic decline, political prostration, social stagnation and cultural decadence. From the death of Aurangzeb in 1707 to 1818-19 when Maratha Power was crushed for ever and British hegemony was recognized all over the sub-continent, for a little over hundred years, India was continually divided into numerous warring camps and suffered badly from the concomitant ravages and destruction.[2]

The expansion of British Power in India was "marked by a few characteristics that largely determined the course of modern Indian history particularly during the 19th century".[3]

India's political subordination to British caused incalculable harm to her economic interests.[4] The British mercantile interests had their full play in ruining the indigenous industries and impoverishing the country further. British administration while in some cases adopted many oppressive measures, in other cases, 'lack of knowledge of the country and its people rendered the official economic policy-decision faulty and difficult to execute'.[5] The permanent settlement of land revenue started by Lord Cornwallis was the example of a miscalculated step. It became a lucrative source of income and luxury for the landlords and an instrument of oppression of the peasants. From 1814 onwards the company government in India, as the instrument of industrial classes of England, imposed heavy duties upon Indian goods imported into England while British goods were forced on Indians without the payment of any duty.[6]

The British were interested in having a permanently firm footing in India. This they achieved by gaining the support of a prominent class of absentee landlords. They became the sole masters of land in collecting revenue from the peasants. The land policy of the British government reduced the Indian ryots to landless paupers. It created a hierarchy of class division, wherein the rich became richer and the poor, poorer. Money was invested in purchasing zamindari and other means of production. The era of capitalist enterprise was thus ushered in, the immediate results of which broke the moral backbone of the people.

Crushed down by political and priestly tyrannies and economic privations, the people of India were hardly in a position to rise and assert themselves morally and intellectually.[7] India in the 18th and 19th centuries presented a very dark and dismal picture of social and cultural degeneration with many retrograde and abhorrent practices. Religious bigotry and ritualism had eclipsed the spiritual endeavour of man and social life was tormented by priestly tyrannies, casteism and class-conflict.

Everywhere the emphasis was on rituals and ceremonies. Corruption and priestly tyranny were at their height, especially in the centres of pilgrimage all over India. Worship of numerous local and village deities became popular and worst form of idolatry was practised everywhere.[8] Temples maintained Devadasis and nautch girls which spread debauchery and sexual immorality at high places in the name of religion.[9] The condition of Hindu pandits was far from satisfactory. They were rapacious and would not be reluctant to commit any fraud for some pecuniary gains. The 'Sadhu community' was divided into innumerable factions. Instead of preaching unity, peace, non-violence and compassion, they themselves were torn asunder by discord, and disunity. Hinduism was divided into many sects and subsects.[10] All of them professed corrupt practices either overtly or covertly under the authority of their 'sacred books'.[11] A Brahman was regarded as an embodiment of knowledge and wellversed in the scriptural learning. But most of them had no insight into the sacred literature of Hindus.

Apart from the religious conditions, the social conditions too were distressing. Christianity and Islam had been making their way through the Hindu society, due to internal weakness of Hinduism itself.[12] Infant marriage, enforced widowhood, caste vanity and various other superstitions prevailed in the Hindu social system. The sale of female children under the pretence of marriage was practised by nearly two-thirds of the Brahmans of Bengal and Tirhut. These practices continued unhindered by the British government. "Even cruel and immoral rites, such as hook-surlinging, practised in the worship of deity and the burning of widows, were carried out under the British supervision".[13]

Rigid caste system was prevalent. The Old Varna Vyavastha[14] or caste system prescribed by the scriptures, had completely broken down.

Despite his erudition, there was absolutely no chance for a low-caste person to become a Brahman. "No king, however, powerful, can make or unmake a Brahman, no genius however transcendent, no services however conspicuous, no virtues however pre-eminent, can avail to raise a Hindu from a lower caste to the Brahman's estate".[15] It was considered defiling to be within a certain distance of a member of some low castes. A man violating the rules of his caste was excommunicated. The word meant "the snapping of cherished domestic ties, upsetting of close social relations for an essentially home loving people, the forfeiting of everything that makes life bearable."[16]

The system of infant marriage had taken root in the soil. Girls whose husbands died in their infancy were to become helpless and rot in misery for the rest of their life. The belief in witchcraft was prominent in many parts of India.

False religious notions and hypnotic control over society of corrupt Brahmans were described as causes responsible for the social and religious decadence in India during 18th and 19th centuries. The decadent ideas which hastened decline of Hinduism, according to Ranade, were "isolation, submission to outward force or power more than to the voice of inward conscience, perception of fictitious differences between man and man due to heredity and birth, and a general indifference to secular well-being, almost bordering on fatalism".[17] Bhandarkar condemned caste system as the root of all social evils. Healthy growth of society was prevented by numerous maladies of the caste system.

Social reformers of early 19th century were moved to action by a desire to pull out their countrymen from the abyss of superstition, obscurantism and stagnation into which Hindu society had fallen.

While the people languished under deep rooted priestly tyrannies and social maladies, the British Government under East India Company followed a policy of passive non-interference in social and religious affairs of Indians. It refrained from taking any reformative measure to remove social and cultural despondency. The conservative answer to the question of general welfare of the Indian people and initiating socio-cultural reformative measures, in its essence, was to leave things as they were. It was the notion that the British masters should content themselves with the patronage of art, literature, and even religion without, interfering with the established customs of the land.[18]

Subsequently however, the radicals, utilitarians and liberals triumphed over the conservatives in influencing the government to accept concrete proposals for initiating and implementing some definite measures for the benefit of the people of India. Lord William Bentinck, the Governor General (1828 to 1835), was mainly responsible for initiating, directing and implementing the policy of reform in India.[19] In 1813, the wind of change started blowing with the abolition of Company's monopoly of trade, opening of the country to missionary activities, and sanction of an annual sum of Rs. 100,000 for the promotion of learning among the people of India.

The immediate result of the last clause was significant and far reaching in the history of British India. It led to the formation of the Committee of Public Instruction and a favourable atmosphere particularly in Bengal was created for the introduction of English education. English education supplied a potent stimulus for allround awakening in India during 19th century. It was as Chandavarkar noted, "accomplishing silently what no law could have accomplished — unsettling people's minds, raising controversies and thus forwarding the cause of social progress".[20]

Social reformers like Raja Rammohan Roy played a prominent role in the introduction and spread of English education in India. English education and learning helped in inculcating a new spirit of intellecutal quest with the use of reason as the standard of judgement over various social, religious and political problems.

The vision of a renascent new India was cherished by the Indian intelligentsia of the time. The reform movements began with individual revolts against existing customs. It took shape under the influence of Western methods of organisation and propagation and recruited the supporters from men who were English educated or who had imbibed Western ideas indirectly.[21] The work of J. S. Mill left spectacular influence on the minds of modern Western educated reformers like Rammohan Roy, Vidyasagar and others. His work on 'Liberty', which showed that social tyranny might be more oppressive than political subjugation had tremendous impact particularly on social reformers like Rammohan Roy, who played the greatest role in the process of the new awakening of the 19th century.

A remarkable outburst of Christian missionary activities during 19th century was another major stimulating factor to lodge the country on the path of reforms. Ronald W. Scott, concluded that modern Indian religious and social reforms have been in large part, a response to the ethical challenges of Christian doctrine and to the "conception of human personality as expressed primarily in the Christian religion".[22]

Christian missionary enterprises in the 19th century contributed in several ways to arouse passion for carrying out social and religious reforms in the 19th century. They initiated the movement for abolishing the unhealthy practices of Sati, female infanticide, and untouchability. They worked for the uplift of the backward classes and for the amelioration of the women in India. They were very critical of the practices like polygamy, early marriage and the 'Kulinism' which brought the women to a degraded position. They therefore, sent a petition to the Government for removing these evils.[23] They preached the ideal of 'Fatherhood of God and Brotherhood of Men'.

In India, however, the humanitarian work of the missionaries was 'a direct result of their fervent desire to promote Christianity'.[24] The missionaries were trained primarily for the work of proselytization. But it would be unfair not to recognise the stupendous influence that was effected by missionary ideas and activities on the minds of early 19th century social reformers of India. Their fierce attacks on Indian religious and social evils served eventually to rouse the Indian people from their slumber, and made them aware of their own backwardness and degeneration.[25] Soon a series of national leaders with deep knowledge of both Western and Indian education and culture emerged, "whose supreme task in the early 19th century was the defence of the Hindu society and culture from the challenging West."[26] These arose many indigenous organisations like the Brahmo Samaj, the Arya Samaj, the Prarthana Samaj, the Theosophical Society and the Ramakrishna Movement etc., to spearhead reform movements against the prevalent religious and social maladies that had for a long period of time crippled the spirit and dwarfed the moral and intellectual stature of the people of India.

It is interesting to note that due to degradation in the society and lack of unity and national consciousness among the people, the British who had come to India for carrying on trade and commerce, found themselves wanted to rule over the country. By the dawn of the 19th century the British had become the unquestioned masters of the entire sub-continent.

During the period when the British were busy consolidating their position in India, it was passing through one of the darkest periods in its history. The extremely stratified society with its hierarchies and socio-religious customs and conventions, rules and regulations had completely subjugated the individual and he was feeling helpless and restless. This resulted in the isolation, exploitation and oppression of the masses in the hands of the privileged classes. Rabindranath Tagore rightly pointed out at a later stage that these main points of artificial differences among masses prevented the proper growth and spread of national consciousness in the country. The social and religious superstitions and blind adherence to rigid socio-religious regulations and customs were responsible for the continued perpetuation of the extremely stratified social system. Promotion of unity among the people and the development of national consciousness, required the elimination of social inequality and deprivation suffered by the vast majority of people.

It may be pointed out in this connection that the spread of English education in India freed the minds of the educated men from the bondage of superstitions and they refused to accept things as sacrosanct, merely because they were declared with the authority of the socalled scriptures. They started to question the validity of every custom and socio-religious practice and anything that did not pass the tests set by rational mind was not acceptable. English education convinced the educated class about the need for rapid transformation of the social order.

Thus the concept of social democracy in terms of removal of social and religious superstitions and evils and provision of equality of opportunity for all, irrespective of the differences of caste or class dawned in India, much prior to political consciousness. The social urge which was predominant in the whole of the 19th century became an integral part of the national movement in India. The social reformers urged that, social evils have to be destroyed for preparing the base for progressive forces like liberty and democracy.

The legacy of the socio-religious reformers was a formidable factor in the organisation and the working of the Indian National Congress during its formative period. The material prosperity of the subjects was considered more important than the political rights and the liberties of the people. For social and religious reformations and for promoting the material prosperity of the subjects no agitation was ever thought necessary. This could only be achieved with the sympathy and support of the British. Although in the beginning the Rule followed a policy of non-interference, at the later stage it helped and promoted reformist activities, particularly when there was support from the educated class.

The Renaissance and Reformation of the 19th century aroused a new awakening, which aimed at the purification of the society and the Hindu religion by destroying the socio-religious prejudices, superstitions and the caste barriers.

There were two clear trends in the approach of the people, who wanted to emancipate India from one of the darkest periods of her history. One group of people was cosmopolitan and eclectic and tried to emulate the Western model and assimilate the good aspects of other religions and cultures in order to reform the Indian society. The other group of people aimed at the revival of the great Indian culture and heritage and wanted to purge Indian society and Hinduism from the evils that had crept into it due to Brahmanical influence. It was highly nationalistic and conservative in its approach. As a result of these movements, even the orthodox elements in the society, were roused from their slumber and were forced to give up their self-complacency. Raja Rammohan, the leader of the cosmopolitan group, who was highly influenced by the Western civilization, organised the Brahmo Samaj.

The Brahmo Samaj Movement started by him played a pioneering role in the sphere of socio-religious reformation in India. The Brahmo ethics and religion preached against idolatrous polytheism, religious ritualism, and practice of other superstitions like Casteism and Brahminical supremacy. Rammohan started a vigorous movement against the practice of Sati, female infanticide, and other discriminatory practices against women.

In the political sphere Rammohan followed retrograde and conservative ideas. He could never imagine the assertion of India's independence in isolation from British hegemony. He was a cosmopolitan universalist who had pinned all his faith in the greatness of British culture and civilization and the 'providential role of British' in governing India. He, therefore, argued in favour of prolonged continuance of British rule over India. Thus Rammohan Roy, who followed the principles of socio-religious progressivism, had to follow the policy of political conservatism due to his ideological compulsions. In any case, it can be concluded that Rammohan Roy made a significant contribution to the socio-religious and political resurgence of the 19th century. He has, therefore, been rightly called, the 'Father of Indian Renaissance' and the 'Precursor of the Modern Age'.

– Hari Hara Das
– Sasmita Mahapatra

Footnotes

1. V. A. Narain, *Social History of Modern India*, 1972, p. 1.
2. *Ibid.*
3. D. C. Gupta, *Indian National Movement*, Vikas Publishing House, Delhi, 1970, p. 2.
4. Dr. Tarachand, a distinguished Indian historian has expressed the view that the economic policy of the British proved disastrous for the Indian people. See his book, *History of the Freedom Movement in India, Vol. (1),* 1961, p. 338-392.
5. Jadunath Sarkar, *Economics of British India*, Calcutta, 1916, pp. 175-176.
6. D. D. Basu gives detailed tables of the duties imposed on different goods imported into England from India. See his book, *Ruin of Indian Trade and Industry*, Calcutta, 1935, pp. 38-51.
7. R. G. Bhandarkar, Social History of India, in *Indian Social Reform* (edited by C. Y. Chintamani), Part I, pp. 25-26.
8. K. K. Dutta, *Survey of India's Social Life*, (1961), pp. 8-9.
9. Cf. R. V. Naidu, *Social Purity and Anti-Nautch Movement.*
10. The following were the popular sects of Vaishnavism, Ramanujees, Kabir Panthis, Kabir Maluk Dasis, Rai Dasis, Vallabhacharis, Sadhan Panthis etc. Sects of Shaivism were divided into Dandis, Yogis, etc. – H. H. Wilson, *Religious Sects of Hindus*, pp. 15-16.
11. See R. C. James, *Missions in Hindustan,* 1853.
12. R. S. Pareek, *The Contribution of Arya Samaj in the Making of Modern India*, p. 23.
13. J. N. Farquhar, *Modern Religious Movement in India*, London, 1929, p. 9.
14. Brahman, Kshatriya, Vaisya and Sudra constituted the old Aryan Varna Vyavastha.
15. V. Chorol, *Indian Unrest*, London, 1910, Ch. III, p. 32.
16. Opinion of Behramji M. Malabari, Bombay, 23rd Oct. 1884 – *Infant Marriage and Enforced Widowhood in India – A Collection of Opinions for and Against* – Bombay, 1887, pp. 4-5, Quoted in R. S. Pareek, *Contribution of Arya Samaj in the Making of Modern India*, p. 24.
17. Mahadev Govind Ranade, *Miscellaneous Writings.*
18. H. Sharp (ed.), *Selections from Educational Records*, Part–I, p. 17.
19. R. C. Mazumdar, *Glimpses of Bengal in the Nineteenth Century*, Calcutta, 1960, p. 23.

20. N. G. Chandavarkar, *The Speeches and Writings*, Bombay, 1911, p. 17.
21. C. H. Heimsath, *Indian Nationalism and Hindu Social Reform*, Princeton University Press, Princeton, 1964, p. 46.
22. R. W. Scott, *Social Ethics in Modern Hinduism*, p. 18.
23. '*On the Polygamy of the Kulin Brahmins*'. Calcutta Christian Education, pp. 10-12.
24. K. Ingham, *Reformers in India*, 1793-1833, p. 96.
25. N. Macnicol, *The Making of Modern India*, p. 50.
26. Hairdas Mukherjee and Uma Mukherjee, *The Growth of Nationalism in India*, (1857-1905), pp. 22-23.

Contents

1
Socio-Religious Decadence in India and the Dawn of New Awakening

Indian cultural system, through the ages, has displayed its unique characteristic of 'Unity in Diversity'. The fundamentals of the cultural unity are to be seen essentially in the flexible nature and assimilative character of Indian culture. The history of our culture is a unique effort at the elimination of conflict and establishment of social equilibrium. It has been exposed all the time to alien people and their culture through endless series of invasions followed by periods during which the invaders were assimilated into the vast cultural complex which they encountered. The incoming ideas and groups found accommodation not as they were, but as they were accepted and in the process became integral part of Indian history and culture by gradually losing touch with their foreign roots. This happened in the case of militant Islamic invasions that for centuries kept India in a state of constant turmoil. The Mughals, who represented the acme of Islamic power in India, were thoroughly Indianized.

The stresses and strain in the Hindu culture came to appear with the advent of British rule which as the conquering power having its seat of power located thousands of miles away, showed no inclination to be assimilated into the Indian culture. On the other hand, it produced certain peculiar effects upon the life and thought of India. In the reaction to this impact may be sought the genesis of the great Indian Renaissance that began in the later half of the 19th century and, at the dawn of the twentieth century. This was also responsible to a great extent for the first truly modern nationalist upsurge in India.[1] By and large, the British impact was left in the political, administrative, economic and intellectural unification of India that proved conducive to the birth and growth of modern Indian nationalism.

Indian culture, based essentially on religion, felt a deep stirring as it was drawn into the vortex of reform and revivalist activities. The principles of rationalistic secular approach, characteristic of European Reformation Movement found accession into the minds of Indian intelligentsia through Western contact and English education and motivated them for new thinking and greater social action. The early socio-religious reformers of modern India can be credited with setting in motion the secularisation of social and economic philosophy resulting from a naturalistic and not a religious explanation to society. European Reformation Movement influenced the evolution of Modern Indian thought in this regard.

Tawney has aptly observed that:

> "The social functions matured within the church, and long identified with it, are transferred to the state, which in turn is idolised as the dispenser of prosperity and the guardian of civilisation. The theory of hierarchy of values, embracing all human interests and activities in a system on which the apex is religion, is replaced by the conception of separate and parallel compartments between which a due balance should be maintained, but which have no vital connection with each other."[2]

Thus the new intellectual movements in India, which were expressed in the social and religious movements such as the Social Reform Conference, Brahmo Samaj and Prarthana Samaj were conspicuous for their catholic attitude towards religious and social life and for their reliance on western principles of reason, science and doctrines of social equality and humanism. It is interesting to note that the cooperation of legal administration, was extended to these various organisations, to correct numerous aberrations of Hindu religion and social life.

But in the later decades of the 19th century revivalistic socio-religious movements such as the Arya Samaj, Ramkrishna Mission, Theosophical Society, etc., preached religious nationalism. These movements started a true Hindu Protestant reformation movement and helped the regeneration of pride among Indian intellectuals in their national civilisation, Hindu culture and heritage. This was of cardinal importance in the 19th century renaissances of Hinduism and the rise of Hindu nationalism.

It may be emphasized that both the reformers and the revivalists were trying to forge a new society through different approaches. In matters of social reform and organisation of social life revivalists were equally modernists like the radical reformers, in their crusade against caste barriers and untouchability, advocacy for widow remarriage, women education and equality for women. The revivalists were "loud in their cry for the preservation of what was best in the historic traditions of the race, they were equally passionate in their zeal for the wide diffusion of modern scientific knowledge among their countrymen."[3]

The social reform movement of the 19th century was an intellectual phenomenon and it "was limited in its avowed leadership and most of its following to educated Indians. Educated men defined the ideals of reform, and those ideals accordingly reflected the particular needs and desires of their supporters."[4] Both the reformers and the so-called revivalists wanted to bring social transformation and create a new awareness in the society without bringing any reorganization in the structure of society at large. Most of the social reforms advocated by the reformers or the revivalists, had no meaning for the lower caste groups. The proposed social reforms were only concerned with the customs and norms of life of the upper castes, who in India established the traditional social norms. These high caste people were supposed to set the ideals for the people of the lower castes in the society. Thus most of the reformers essentially followed a conservative and gradualist approach to social change. In the words of Chandavarkar, "The customs and institutions with which the social reformer proposes to deal, are common to the higher classes of the Hindu society from whom the lower classes take their standard."[5] The efforts of the reformers, who were trying to bring some social change, were devoted to "adjusting the ideas and behaviour of high-caste, educated men and their families to the requirements of the Westernized culture which they desired to create for themselves."[6] It is to be admitted that the reformers, despite the Western influence, did certain commendable things in spreading social awareness regarding the social evils and taking steps in eradicating these evils from the society.[7] Western influence was itself responsible for creating certain other kinds of social evils in the form of blind imitation of the Western values and life style which in the long run led to a counter movement — the revivalist movement. The social reformers were "advocates of alterations in social customs which would involve a break with traditionally accepted patterns; they were those who, convinced themselves that altered ways of thinking and behaving were positive values, sought to convince others to modify or entirely transform their ways of life."[8] They fought against the obnoxious caste regulations and wanted the elimination of outworn customs. It was easier to implement changes in the direction of some minor social changes but major social change in the form of the breakdown of the caste system was difficult to achieve. However, they rendered yeoman service by advocating the welfare of the Indian society and the themes of universal ethics. They also preached the doctrine of equality of all men and the principles of universal ethics and the potentialities of all human beings.[9] On most of these issues and themes affecting social change there was not much difference in either the attitude or the approach of the reformers or the revivalists. They basically and predominantly differed on the issues of Indian traditions and heritage and the co-relation between religion and politics. These differences were natural and formed a genuine part of the social process. The overenthusiasm on the part of some of the reformers who were influenced by Christian Missionaries like William Carry, 1761-1834; Joshua Marshman, 1768-1837; John Clark Marshman, 1794-1877 and William Ward, 1769-1823, was bound to produce its reaction.[10] It is, however, true that the movements for social change and reconstruction were started mostly under the impact of Western culture, although revolt against caste laws and orthodoxy in religious beliefs could be noticed in some of the religious movements of India. Buddhism which was a protestant reformation movement tried to revolt against traditional social standards and religious practices existing in Hindu India. Hindus could exclude themselves from normal social and religious requirements by becoming ascetics or 'Sanyasis'. "Social and religious rebellions against the traditional authority of Brahmin priests and other higher castes created new movements whose doctrines and practices differed from orthodox Hinduism; the medieval bhakti, or devotional, movements represented that form of rebellion, as did Sikhism in its early stages. Social revolts with more indirect impacts periodically emerged throughout India in the form of efforts to improve the positions of certain castes in their relations to other castes. Mobility within the caste system has always existed as a result of rebelliousness and a group's desire for change and betterment."[11] The social reform movements and the various methods adopted by the reformers reflected the 'intellectual temper of the age'. The organised reform movements in the religious and political fields and the views and attitudes of the contemporary period were greatly influenced by these reform movements. In reality the Renaissance and Reformation movements of the 19th century in India were the products of Western education.[12] These movements led to the new awakening, which aimed at the purification of the society and the Hindu religion by destroying the socio-religious prejudices, superstitions and the caste barriers.[13]

The socio-religious movements of the 19th century represented a combination of reformation and revivalism and greatly influenced Indian nationalism. It has been rightly observed that, "None of these spiritual movements had any direct political aims, but they brought together men who were seeking fresh interpretation of old faiths, and who naturally passed thence into state affairs."[14] The socio-religious movements played a revitalising and revivifying role and helped the spiritual regeneration of the Indian society. The reformers and the revivalists equally criticised the superstitions and baneful practices like caste barriers, oppression of women and wasteful rituals and ceremonies which were responsible for the decadence of the Indian society. These movements aimed at making the people conscious of their social, cultural and economic degradations.

There was, however, a basic difference in the attitude and approach of the reformers and the revivalists, who wanted to purge the society or more particularly the Hindu society of the various evils. The reformers wanted to create a society "rational and scientifically minded, based on a broad humanism and the rejection of all sectarian barriers."[15] The reformers were obsessed with the Western model and wanted to reconstruct the Indian society on that basis without due consideration for India's traditions and heritage. They wanted that all the Indians irrespective of caste and creed, religion and beliefs, should come together to form a nation based on principles of pragmatism, rationality and equality. Raja Rammohan made a pioneering contribution in developing these basic tenets of the reformation movement which ushered in the Indian Renaissance or the new awakening among the people. Rammohan used reason to stress that religion should bring people together. He was of the opinion that the best form of religious practice was "the union of human hearts with mutual love and affection, without distinctions of caste or creed, race or colour."[16] He helped in the expansion of the Indian mind in the direction of the Western ideas and institutions. This process had been started due to the impact of the Western civilization and the spread of the English language, which brought the Indians in contact with the liberal writings of the European and American writers and thinkers.[17]

The revivalists, while being critical of the evils and shortcomings in the Hindu society, were not prepared to surrender their rich cultural heritage and glorious spiritual tradition in favour of an absolutely Western model of the society. They wanted to purify the society according to a nationalistic and purely indigenous model acceptable to the Indian masses and provided a spiritual base to politics for the purpose of inspiring the people with a sense of sacrifice and extreme dedication in the service of the Motherland.[18] The Indians were infused with a sense of pride in their glorious heritage and developed the spirit of self-confidence. It is needless to say that in revival of Hinduism as a vital and powerful force "produced striking religious and social reforms long before it issued in a movement for political emancipation.[19]

In the process of the social reform movement a crucial development took place during the later part of the 19th and the early part of the 20th century ending with the First World War in which the inherent strength and the greatness of Indian culture and traditions were re-emphasized and the blind imitation of the West was deprecated. "Corporate social values suited to the national society began to take precedence over the values of limited groups claiming to represent the nation, and Indian society (in fact, Hindu society), not transplanted Western society, was recognised as the proper vehicle for individual self-realization. An intellectual development was beginning in which social reform began to mean a regeneration of the traditional spirit of the nation – a regeneration, political as well as social, which was founded on religious revival."[20]

The reform movements of the early 19th century did not contribute any new political or social ideas. 'There was only the acceptance of European ideas by India's leaders.[21] However, they helped the process of secularization of social and economic philosophy resulting from a naturalistic and not a religious explanation of the social phenomenon.

On the other hand the so-called revivalist movements, which energed as a reaction against the too much Western orientation of the reformers, instead of the naturalistic explanation, gave a theological, spiritual and mystical view of the history of the world and of India in particular. But even these movements, which have been considered by some people as reactionary[22] by applying the European criterion of evaluation, have "questioned some of the irrational notions and superstitions of the immediate past and tried to reconstruct society on the basis of the so-called traditions of an idealist and distant past, which perhaps never existed and which were not far removed from the ideas of the modern period. The reformers and revolutionaries in many parts of the world had often used religion and the appeal to the past to bring about changes in the social and political spheres."[23]

Marxist scholars like R. Palme Dutt found fault with both the reformers and the revivalists and considered both the groups equally reactionary as they failed to organise the working class and the mass of the peasantry, but their wrath was more vigorously directed against the radicals.[24] Referring to the radical leaders like Bal Gangadhar Tilak and Aurobindo Ghosh, Palme Dutt was of the view that, "they build the national movement on the basis of still massive forces of social conservatism in India, on the basis of orthodox Hinduism and affirmation of the supposed spiritual superiority of the ancient Hindu or 'Aryan' civilization. They sought to build, the national movement, the most advanced movement in India on the basis of the most antiquated religion and religious superstitions. From this era dates the disastrous combination of political radicalism and social reaction."[25] These allegations were equally directed against the revivalist movements like the Arya Samaj, the Ramakrishana Mission and the Theosophical Society of India. As a matter of fact the Arya Samaj was the spiritual progenitor of the Radicals or the Extremists as the Brahmo Samaj was the intellectual progenitor of the Moderates.[26]

Palme Dutt and many other scholars who followed his line of approach, "failed to understand the significance of the interrelation between religion and politics in the country."[27] They were trying to evaluate Indian political leaders and socio-political movements with the help of European liberal and socialist doctrines as the model with which they were required to conform. They were considered reactionary as they did not conform to the Marxist standards set by Palme Dutt and the other scholars of his time. K. M. Panikkar was also of the view that the Extremists represented a combination of political radicalism and social reaction. He observes that, "Hindu nationalism, especially in Maharashtra and Bengal, was coming definitely to the fore, and with their new-found consciousness of religious greatness, their nationalism was not only more extreme, but was in spirit revivalist and not liberal... Tilak... desired to found the national revival on Hindu Dharma.[28]

Even Jawaharlal Nehru was no exception to this Marxist intellectual influence in his analysis of the national movement and the political role of the Radicals or the Extremists. Referring to the revivalist trends in Indian Politics, he analyses as follows:

> "There was a spiritual and religious element about all this, and yet there was a strong political background to it. The rising middle class were politically inclined and were not so much in search of a religion; but they wanted some cultural roots to cling on to, something... that would reduce the sense of frustration and humiliation that foreign conquest and rule had produced. In every country with a growing nationalism there is this search apart from religion, this tendency to go to the past."[29]

Most of the authors who took such a stand did not have the proper perspective for the analysis of the socio-political movements and were more or less obsessed by the liberal and socialist doctrines of the West. It may be pointed out that "these authors were cut off from the superstructure of ideas and institutions which modern India had inherited from an earlier period."[30] By the end of the 19th century the socio-religious movements became conscious of the innate potentialities of India's culture.[31] During this period the "criticism of society, frequently as harsh as in the earlier stages, was based on the failure of national social life to realize its own innate potentialities and not on its inferior performance in comparison to Western societies."[32]

The classification of the intellectual movements of the 19th century into two broad categories, such as the 'reformist' and the 'revivalist' movements is superficial, while calling the religious and social movements of the later 19th century as revivalist and reactionary, they have not taken into account some important aspects of the programme of action of the leaders of these movements, "which were directed towards making the country more modern and democratic than envisaged by the early leaders of the Congress."[33] It is needless to say that the Moderates and the Extremists in the Congress represented to a great extent the basic principles and doctrines of the Brahmo Samaj and the Arya Samaj respectively. Despite their fundamental difference pertaining to Hinduism and India's culture and traditions, they accepted rational principles as guide to individual conduct and social policies.[34] The educated leaders were greatly influenced by English education and had high regards for Western rationalism.

The Christian Missionaries and the Marxist scholars of the Western countries have unjustifiably maligned the Indian socio-religious movements and the extremist leaders for their spiritual and mystical attitudes and commitments, due to their failure in properly understanding the role of religion in Indian politics. They were trying to analyse the socio-political phenomena which were completely alien to them. But despite their intellectual inadequacy and limitations the books written by these foreign scholars became trend-setters and even to-day many writers turn to these works and follow the frame-work provided by the writers of the above categories :

> "The framework of thinking of many Indian scholars who followed them was western partly because they were inferred with Western education and dominated by the intellectual powers of Western scholars. So such words and phrases as 'modern', 'revivalist', 'progressive' and 'reactionary', occur to them exactly as they did to the Western scholars. They, like their Western masters, were confused by their own conclusions that Tilak was both a reactionary in social matters and a radical in regard to political questions; or Aurobindo Ghosh and Gandhi were political revolutionaries and religious revivalists. Instead

> of trying to find out the unique features of the Indian situation, these writers satisfied themselves with the explanations that Tilak and his colleagues appealed to the religious superstitions of the people, because they were not aware of the advanced and scientific political theories.[35]

This interpretation was out of context and was completely biased. Tilak and his colleagues went back to their historical and religious past to assert their self-confidence.

This analysis was incorrect, because Tilak and his colleagues who were unjustifiably branded as the "revivalist leaders", were not unaware of the scientific notions or the advanced ideas of the time. These leaders were, more than the Moderates, conscious about the important role religion played in the life of the Indians in general and political developments in particular. They knew better than the Moderates that nothing tangible could be done in India in the social or the political field without giving due importance to the historical and cultural traditions of the country. The extremists superseded the Moderates as political leaders, because they represented the spirit of the time and enjoyed the confidence of the people. They were rooted in India's culture and traditions unlike the Moderates who had sold themselves to the religion, culture and traditions of an alien country. "Still a vast section of the people of India often chose those political leaders who connected religion to politics because in their minds these two could not be separated. This was the same reason for the religious and social reform movements making political impact on the country.[36]

The social and religious reform movements of the early 19th century and late 19th century had their necessary historical concomitants. The Social Reforms Conference, Brahmo Samaj and Prarthana Samaj were highly anglicized in nature and adored the Western civilization, culture, way of life and the ethical and moral principles of Christianity. These organizations, no doubt had some followers, but they became suspect in the eyes of the Hindus, who had deep regard and commitment for their rich culture, traditions and religion. Even most of the Brahmo Samajists were aware of this and they tried to hide their Christian leanings. Keshab Chandra Sen, an ardent Brahmo Samajist asserted that to be an effective social reformer, one should not only have to work within the religious sphere, but should have to work within the fold of Hinduism itself. For this purpose Keshab Chandra, although he had become a Christian did not have the courage to express the same before others. In a letter to his disciple Pratap Chander Majumdar, he wrote :

> "I have my own ideas about Christ, but I am not bound to give them out in due form, until the altered circumstances of the country gradually develop them out of my mind."[37]

When Max Muller put him the question as to why he did not declare himself as a Christian, Keshab Chandra gave out the truth for hiding his Christian identity : "Suppose that thirty years hence people find out that I was a disciple of Christ, what would be the harm ? Only were I to profess a Christian now, all my influence would be gone at once."[38]

Socio-religious reforms should come from within the main body of the society and should enjoy the support of the society as a whole. Without this, the reforms, may for the time being catch the imagination of the people, but they would not have any lasting importance. Religious reforms have close connection with social and political regeneration of the country. The socio-religious reforms in order to be effective "had to be undertaken largely within the framework of the existing popular religions of the country."[39] Insisting on too much Westernization or Christianization was going to ruin the objective of the reform movements. Raja Rammohan Roy and M. G. Ranade were also conscious of this fact, which is evident from their writings. They have tried to justify the socio-religious changes for providing political advantage and social comfort to the Hindus rather than arguing for purging the society and the Hindu religion of their evils as seen through the Western eyes. Rammohan wrote to a friend, "It is, I think, necessary that some change should take place in their (Hindu) religion, at least for the sake of their political advantage and social comfort.[40] Similar view was expressed by M. G. Ranade : "You cannot have a good social system, when you find yourself low in the scale of political rights, nor can you be fit to exercise political rights and privileges unless your social system is based on reason and justice... If your religious ideas are grovelling, you cannot succeed in social, economic or political spheres. This interdependence is not an accident, but is the law of nature."[41]

Surendra Nath Banerji also had expressed the same view regarding socio-religious reforms in India. He therefore argued to take the help of religion and history in order to fight effectively against superstitions and irrational social conventions. In defence of his argument, he said :

> "You cannot think of a social question affecting the Hindu community that is not bound up with religious considerations, and when sanction, in whatever form, is involved in aid of a social institution, it is enthroned in the popular heart with firmness and fixity, having its roots in sentiment rather than in reason."[42]

Surendra Nath, however, agrees that people like Chaitanya, with forceful and commanding personality, were bound by no conventions and traditions or religious formulae and were able to transform the society. He was looked upon as an 'avatar' and the Indian masses were highly responsive to real greatness.

Swami Vivekananda, the great Indian saint and reformer had abundantly realised this truth. He also insisted that for the success of social reforms and political action, an appeal should be made to the religious instincts of the people :

> "We know that to the Indian mind there is nothing higher than religious ideals, that this is the key-note of Indian life, and we can only work in the line of least resistance... In the case of India it is the only possible means of work; work in any other line, without strengthening this, would be disastrous."[43]

The late 19th century reform movements in general and the Arya Samaj in particular realised the fundamental necessity of recognising the inherent and innate values of India's culture, traditions and religion. They were strongly opposed to the Western-phobia and obsessions of the English educated people who were carried off their feet by the influence of the Western ideas and looked at the past culture and traditions of India with hatred and disdain. "The British rulers were trying to convince the world that Indians were savages and they had come to India not to fleece it but to civilize, educate and modernize."[44] The views expressed by Justice Ranade, represented the attitude of the people who were influenced by the Brahmo ideology, "India's future would have been cramped and crippled for lack of the British connections. The British connection with India was providential in character and was, therefore, almost a Divine Dispensation."[45]

It is due to this obsession with the West, the earlier reformers believed that they could reconstruct Indian society by mechanically introducing Western ideas and institutions. The Arya Samaj, the Ramakrishna Mission and the Theosophist movement, emerged as a protest against this servile attitude of the early reformers, who found every thing wrong with India's culture, religion and heritage and painted an exalted and rosy picture of everything Western. Their spirit was expressed through the statement of Bankim Chandra Chatterji : "I think that we ought to disanglicise ourselves, so to speak, to a certain extent, and to speak to the masses in the languages which they understand."[46] The supporters of the later reform movements realised the strength of traditions and culture of India and the great innate strength of the Hindu religion. They insisted in maintaining the continuity of social life while introducing reforms in the socio-religious spheres of life. The common culture religion and historical traditions had given the Hindus a unique sense of pride and unity and this unity should be preserved at any cost. They were of the opinion that nothing should be done in hot haste that would either destroy or give the feeling of aiming at the destruction of the Hindu character of the society. This aspect of common cultural identity has been nicely described by the eminent historian Dr. R. C. Majumdar in the following words :

> "The common heritage of a great culture and rich historical tradition imbued the Hindus with an idea of common nationality. The revelation of India's past, supplemented by the bond of common religion, served to bring them together, and their mutual intercourse was facilitated by the use of English as a lingua franca and easy means of communication through railways, steamers, cheap postage and telegraphs. Nationalism was thus founded on the bedrock of common religion, culture and historical tradition. But this gave it a Hindu character which it has retained, consciously or unconsciously eversince."[47]

The reform measure proposed by the earlier reformers did not take into consideration these important features of India's historical tradition and culture. "And the necessary result was that our highest patriotic activities", admitted B. C. Pal, the one time ardent Brahmo Samajist, "whether in the field of religion, or social or political reconstruction, were without the historic continuity, which alone could furnish strength and vitality to them."[48] Even one of the ardent early reformers like Mahadev Govind Ranade realised the strength of traditions and the importance of maintaining continuity of social life while introducing reforms :

> "The true reformer has not to write upon a clean slate. His work is more often to complete the halfwritten sentence. He has to produce the ideal out of the actual, and by the help of the actual ... We cannot break with the past altogether, for it is a rich inheritance and we have no reason to be ashamed of it."[49]

The realisation that the traditions of a society cannot be altogether ignored while trying to reform it, also had some impact on Debendranath Tagore, an ardent Brahmo Samajist. He also pleaded for caution against any speedy action in the direction of bringing social reform :

> "We are in and of the great Hindu community and it devolves upon us by example and precept to hold up as a beacon to the highest truths of the Hindu Shastras. In their light must we purify our heritage of customs, usages, rites and ceremonies and adapt them to the needs of our conscience and our community. But we must be aware of proceeding too fast in matters of social change, lest we be separated from the greater body whom we would guide and uplift."[50]

The controversy between reformism and revivalism continued as a live intellectual debate for quite some time. It has been pointed out earlier that the aim of the social reformers was to reorganize Indian society on the basis of rational, scientific and modern ideas. But they had to face several difficulties in implementing their programme. Apart from the distinctions of creed and race, among the Hindu community itself, the customs of one province did not obtain in another. The caste organisations were based upon different principles in different provinces. Thus in the India of the 19th century it was also not possible for the reformers to implement extremely radical social reforms. The gap between the theory and practice of the Brahmo Samajists was the evidence of the reality of the existing situation. The reformers those who advocated unconditional application of European ideas to India, were ignorant about the strong hold of traditions on the life of the Indians. They also ignored the necessity of rapid economic changes, which provided the base for effective social changes. Finally those who acted boldly to implement the Western ideas became divorced from the masses of the people and could not effectively influence the masses. "It is significant that the refusal of the Brahmo Samaj to move away completely from Indian traditions was one of the sources of its strength."[51]

Although there were a few Brahmo Samajists who recognised the glory and importance of the Hindu traditions, there was no doubt that in their general approach and attitude they were inspired by alien ideologies.[52]

The Brahmo Samaj suffered from the lapses of ideological advance and organizational weakness. The devoted Brahmo Samajists were called upon to popularise ideas borrowed from the West, which were not only much ahead of the times but also led to a counter movement of resistance. "The reaction against the West had arisen because the first generation of English-educated Indians, the Indo-Anglians, were black Englishmen who were ashamed of India in their hearts and were anxious to consider England their spiritual home."[53]

Many educated Indians during the early days of the spread of English education, became excessively Westernized. They started criticizing ancient Indian culture and civilization indiscriminately. Under the impact of Western progressive ideas, the Indians thought "reforms were the important ingredients leading to the betterment of society."[54] Thus the growth of the spirit of revivalism became inevitable. The contact of Indian culture with a rationalistic and politically dominant foreign culture was further responsible for the growth and development of revivalism. It was partly as a reaction against the excessive westernization of some educated Indians that other Indians tried to defend the ancient traditions, culture and civilization of India with almost a fanatical spirit.

This process of revolt against too much westernization which took the form of extreme revivalism has been very aptly described by Rabindranath Tagore in his novel Gora. Reacting against the prostylizing activities of the Christian Missionaries and the social reformers like the Brahmo Samajists, who blindly imitated the west, Tagore's character Gora emphatically declared as follows :

> "We must refuse to allow our country to stand at the bar of a foreign court and be judged according to foreign law. Our ideas of shame or glory must not depend on minute comparisons at every step with a foreign standard. We must not feel apologetic about the country of our birth."[55]

Bipin Chandra Pal who was an Extremist admitted the shortcomings of India's culture and religion as he believed that India presented "the curious spectacle of a highly rational and spiritual people like the Hindus subjecting themselves to material symbols in the religious and irrational institutions in the social life."[56] It is also a fact that some of the reformers despised Hindu culture without even understanding it and blindly imitated the English way of life, habits and manners. Referring to this thoughtless imitation Lajpat Rai said : "He took his dress, he took his cheroot and pipe and also his cup and beefsteak. He began to live in houses built and furnished in the English way. He detested Indian life and took pride in being anglicized. Everything Indian was odious in his eyes."

The Arya Samaj was often associated with the revivalist trends in the Indian religious reform movements. The prominent leaders of the Arya Samaj were engaged in the work of social reconstruction based on progressive and rational principles and cannot be branded as reactionary. Compared to the ideological basis of the Brahmo Samaj and the Prarthana Samaj, the Arya Samaj was definitely less progressive and modern as far as the implementation of the social reform measures were concerned, but the Arya Samaj was in a position to have the support of a large number of followers and tremendous impact on Hindu life and institutions, because it had a better understanding of the Hindu psychology and realized the importance of maintaining the continuity of social life while introducing reforms.[57]

It may be pointed out that although most of the revivalists attacked the social reformers, they were themselves not pure revivalists for they also wanted to change and purify Hindu society. However, they always avoided the uncharitable and highly biased opinions of the social reformers as regards Hindu society.[58] They condemned idolatry, animal sacrifices, ancestor worship, pilgrimages, priestcraft, offerings in temples, the caste system, untouchability and child marriages like the Brahmo Samajists and helped in process of renaissance. But the Arya Samajists were also responsible for having a narrow view about other religious faiths and insisting on the infallibility of the Vedas, on Karma and rebirth, the sanctity of the cow, the efficacy of the 'homa' and the importance of 'Sanskaras'.[59]

Rabindranath Tagore in his later writings criticised all those who regarded everything Indian to be spiritual and praiseworthy and everything western as material and unethical.[60] Like the extreme view of the social reformers, the extreme ideas of the revivalists were far away from the realities. Tagore emphasized on the combination of the dynamic spirit of the West and the ancient wisdom of the East in order to create the ideal civilization. "Tagore was confident that through the conflicting movements of extreme revivalism and extreme Westernization, Indians would ultimately be able to effect a proper balance between the ideals of the East and those of the West."[61]

After going through the whole analysis it would be wrong to presume that all the social reformers were "modernists" and those who insisted on Indian traditions and continuity of social life while implementing social reforms, were "revivalists". "Broadly speaking, this is true because the modernist movements such as the Brahmo Samaj, the Prarthana Samaj and the Aligarh School appeared earlier than the Arya Samaj, the Ramakrishan Mission and the Theosophist movement. As was noted earlier, each of these movements cannot, however, be exclusively grouped in one category, revivalist or modernist. A movement like the Arya Samaj did spread some of modern ideas, although it had strong revivalist tendencies. It is equally true that movements like the Brahmo Samaj were not without elements of revivalism in them."[62]

Some of the progressive policies followed by the British in India whether consciously or unconsciously, quickened the process of modernizing the social and economic life of the country. The so-called social reformers and the revivalists were equally influenced by these modernist and rationalist principles. They however, differed in their approach and orientation. Under the influence of Western rationalism, modernism, liberalism, new legal system and judiciary and an efficient state apparatus, the social and religious reform movements of the 19th century started a process of re-examination in India. The following were the broad objectives of the various movements of the 19th century :

> "In the social sphere, there were movements of caste reform or caste abolition, equal rights for women, a campaign against child marriage and a ban on widow re-marriage, a crusade against social and legal inequalities. In the religious sphere, there sprang up movements which combated religious superstitions and attacked idolatry, polytheism and hereditary priesthood. These movements in varying degrees, emphasized and fought for the principle of individual liberty and social equality and stood for nationalism."[63]

Despite their various differences, most of the important reform movements like the Brahmo Samaj, the Social Reforms Conference, the Arya Samaj, the Ramkrishna Mission, and the Theosophical Society all propagated the ideals mentioned above.[64]

There was, however, no doubt that Swami Dayananda Saraswati and the Arya Samaj subscribed to some revivalist ideas, if that nomenclature has to be accepted and did create an exclusive and narrow attitude. But these may be taken as natural and spontaneous reactions to the indiscriminate imitation of western life and the principles of Christian ethics. This is evident from the following comment of Dayananda Saraswati on the Brahmo Samaj :

> "They are not good in all respects. How can the principles of those who are unaware of the Vedic lore be all good. They saved many men from the clutches of Christianity, they removed idolatry also to a certain extent, and they protected people from the snares of certain spurious scriptures. These are all good points. But they are lacking in patriotism. They have borrowed much from

> Christianity in their ways of living. They have also changed the rules of marriage, etc. Instead of praising their country and glorifying their ancestors, they speak ill of them. In their lectures they eulogise Christians and Englishmen. They do not mention the names of old sages, Brahma, etc. But they say that there was never a learned man like the English People from the very creation of the world, that Indians have all along remained ignorant, and that they never made any progress. Not only do they not respect the Vedas, etc., but they do not desist from condemning them. The books of the Brahmo Samaj include among the saints Christ, Moses, Muhammad, Nanak and Chaitanya. They do not mention even the name of the rishis and sages of ancient India. This shows that their religion also derives its tenets from the prophets whose names have been mentioned in their books."[65]

It may be pointed out that it was not only the Arya Samaj, but also other organisations like the Theosophical Society and the Ramakrishna Mission which took up the banner of protest against the Anglicization of India's culture and way of life. The Theosophical Society was an association which was founded outside India,[66] but took keen interest in the upliftment of India's culture and religion. It greatly succeeded in arousing the pride of the Indians in their ancient past.[67] Referring to the degeneration caused by western impact and the role played by the Theosophical Society, Annie Besant, one of its distinguished Presidents, makes the following observation :

> "Scepticism and materialism had eaten out the life of the nation. The crowds of the so-called English-educated class were followers of Huxley, Mill and Spencer, and had entirely forgotten their literature; were contemptuous of the past and hence hopeless for the future; they were copying English ways, English manners, filling their houses with English furniture to the destruction of Indian arts and crafts. They had lost all national spirit. De-spiritualisation had brought

> about national degeneracy. There was no activity of national life, no pulsing of the national heart... Colonel Olcott and Mme. Blavatsky saw that not until India recognised the value of its ancient faith could there be any bond of unity among the Indians, separated by provincial jealousies and hatreds. So they began with the revival of religion; they pointed out the value of Hindu teachings; they held up the Vedas as the glory of India, proclaimed the value of Indian thought and the priceless heritage of the Indian people; until at last the Indians began once more to pride themselves on their past, and to realise that the Hindu scriptures were not the babblings of children or the fancies of savages, but were the foundation of a mighty system, the glory of the past and the life of the future."[68]

Unlike the Arya Samaj which had a mass appeal and was popular among large sections of people, the Theosophical Society influenced only a small number of people. Despite its positive aspects, it had some shortcomings and failures. Swami Vivekananda criticized the works of the Society as the "Indian grafting of American spiritualism with only a few Sanskrit words taking the place of spiritualistic jargon–Mahatma missals taking the place of ghostly raps and taps and Mahatmic inspiration that of obsession by ghosts."[69]

It is interesting to note that Vivekananda and the Ramakrishna Mission founded by him, played a unique role in the history of religious reform movements in India. Ramakrishna Paramahamsa was a mystic, a realised soul and he was a rebel like Kabir and Rajjab.[70] His influence was purely spiritual and was concerned with inner-purity and universalism of spiritual realization. But Vivekananda, the most ardent disciple of Ramakrishna was no mystic and his activities were not confined to religion only. He was aware that the socio-economic conditions were hindering the progress of India. He, therefore, visualised a new order of society based on the spirit of equality, social awareness and the pragmatism of the West, blended with the best Indian traditions.

Vivekananda was large-hearted, broad-minded, modern in his outlook and highly rational in his approach. With all his revivalistic love for India's culture, heritage and tradition, he did not hesitate to condemn some of the evil practices and lapses on the part of the Indians. He insisted that the Indians should grow according to their nature.[71] He believed strongly that Indian traditions should be taken into account, while attempting to reform society. But it is quite surprising that while ardently believing that "India had a mission to perform in this world", he emphatically proclaimed that "We cannot do without the world outside India; it was our foolishness that we thought we could, and we have paid the penalty by about a thousand years of slavery."[72]

The significance of the contributions of Swami Vivekananda in contrast to that of the Brahmo Samaj is analysed by Romain Rolland in the following words :

> "... Herein lies the difference between the awakening of Ramakrishna and Vivekananda and that of Rammohan Roy and the Brahmo Samaj—in these days India refuses allegiance to the imperious civilization of the West, she defends her own ideas, she was stuped into her age-long heritage with the firm intention, not to sacrifice any part of it but allow the rest of the world to profit by it, and to receive it in return for the intellectual conquest of the West. The time is past for the pre-eminence of one incomplete and partial civilization. Asia and Europe, the two giants, are standing face to face as equals for the first time."[73]

Thus it may be observed that the reform and the revivalist movements of the 19th and early 20th century, were influenced by the liberal thoughts in England, which were very popular during this period. The British administrators, under the influence of these outstanding champions of liberal policies, who ushered reforms in several spheres of life in England, pursued policies, to widen the mental horizons of the Indians. India's indebtedness to the West has been aptly described by D. P. Mukherji in the following words :

> "All are agreed that India entered into a base of life in the nineteenth century. The spirit of vitality came from the West through various channels like commerce and trade, increased facilities for communication, Western learning,

> administration, unity, etc. For the first time, historians assert, an alien civilization impinged upon every detail of Indian life, changed its patterns and created new values. Thus India's wealth ceased to become treasure; money became capital, goods became commodities, land became a source of monopoly-rent, and the self-sufficiency of rural economy was transformed into the interdependence of urban and world economy. Similarly the vision of the average Indian, so long closed like a frog in the well,was enlarged... The broad march of the English Constitution, the glory of the French Revolution, the finality of the American War of Independence, the romance of the Italian, and the cold, ruthless realism of the German unity brought enlightenment into the dark nooks of the Indian mind thus far denied of any sense of history and politics. At the same time, Western philosophy and science introduced reason into daily habits and made Indians realise the meaninglessness of many ancient customs and privileges."[74]

The British East India Company became the supreme political power in India in 1818, after the defeat of the Mahrattas. Although the company was basically an exploiting agency, some of its officers under the impact of the liberal current in England, took a changed view of the functions of government. The East India Company introduced some social reforms like the banning of 'Sati' i.e., the practice of the Hindu widow burning herself to death on the funeral pyre of her husband, was indicative of the Company's desire to organise Indian society on the basis of reason and enlightenment. The sense of responsibility on the part of some of the administrators of the company; for the welfare of the people of India cannot be altogether ruled out. Steps like the introduction of Western education and the withdrawal of restrictions on the Press in 1835, helped the release of liberal and progressive forces in the country. The British were interested to encourage the development of the power of reason in the Indians so as to enable them to regulate the conduct of life and to develop a critical attitude towards socio-religious beliefs and practices. The British wanted to promote only such aspects of liberalism in India, which did not lead to conflict between the British administrators and the educated Indians. They did not, however, want the Indians to apply the same critical and liberal approach to the problems of government. But the social and religious reform movements, which were the product of the political, administrative, educational and legal institutions, introduced into India by the British masters, served as the prelude to the political awakening in the country. A detailed analysis of the socio-economic transformation that the country underwent as a result of its contact with the West, is furnished in the succeeding pages.

India Under East-India Company's Administration

In 1757, the Battle of Plassey had laid the foundations of the British Empire in India.[75] With Bengal first passing into the hands of the British, the transformation of the East India Company from a commercial concern into a territorial power was phenomenal. However, it revealed the inherent weakness and the incapacity of the trading body to carry on the administration of a vast country.[76] The administration by the East India Company, lay in graft and extortion. A consistent policy of exploitation of Indian economy for the prosperity of Britain was followed. Heavy duties were imposed on Indian goods imported into England, while British goods were forced on Indians without the payment of any duty.[77] This resulted in speedy ruining of the indigenous industries and impoverishment of the Indian economy and the people. British administration while in some cases adopted many oppressive measures, in other cases, 'lack of knowledge of the country and its people rendered the official economic policy decision faulty and difficult to execute.'[78] The Permanent Settlement of land revenue started by Lord Cornwallis was the example of a miscalculated step. It became a lucrative source of income and luxury for the landlords and an instrument of oppression of the peasants. A prominent class of absentee landlords was created. They became the sole masters of land in collecting revenue from the peasants. The land policy of the British government reduced the Indian ryots to landless paupers. It created a hierarchy of class division wherein the rich became richer and the poor, poorer. Money was invested in purchasing Zamindari and other means of production. The era of capitalist enterprise was thus ushered in, the immediate result of which broke the moral backbone of the people. Lecky has rightly observed that, "Never before had the natives experienced a tyranny which was at once so skillful, so searching and so strong... Districts which had been populous and flourishing were at last utterly depopulated, and it was noticed that on the appearance of a party of English merchants, the villages were at once deserted and shops shut and the roads thronged with panic-stricken fugutives."[79]

The policy of economic exploitation of India by the East India Company and its illegal interference in the affairs of the Indian States were carried out in a planned manner. But due to the Company's Misrule and the rampant bribery, favouritism, corruption and inefficiency among its employees it was in grave financial difficulties. Gradually the Indian and British opinion was articulated against the East India Company's mismanagement and tyrannical rule. The British government through parliamentary measures progressively began to assert its rights to interfere in the Company's rule over India.

The British parliament passed the Regulating Act of 1773 which provided that the Governors-in-Council of Bombay and Madras should pay due obedience to the orders of the Governor General of Bengal.

The Pitt's India Act of 1784 further diminished the power of East India Company by bifurcating the Company's commercial and political functions. The Court of Directors managed the commercial affairs while the Board of Control looked after the political matters.

The other important Acts passed by the British parliament during this period were the Charter Acts of 1793, 1833, and 1853.[80] According to the Charter Act of 1793, the Governor General and the Governors were required to exercise power, if necessary, to override the decisions of their respective Councils. According to the Charter Act of 1813, the Monopoly of the East India Company to trade with India was lost and it was thrown open to all British traders.

The Governor-General of Bengal became the Governor-General of India by virtue of the Charter Act of 1833. The Governor-General-in-Council was given the powers to make laws for the whole of India and the Governors of Madras and Bombay Presidencies were deprived of this power. This led to a highly centralised government in India. The Charter Act of 1853, provided for the separation of the executive and the legislative functions. The transfer of the administration of India from the hands of the Company to the Crown was finally completed with Queen's Proclamation being passed in 1858 following the Great Revolt of 1857.

The direct take over of India's administration by the Crown from the hands of the Company in the year 1858 did not result in any substantial change either in the attitude of Imperial Government or the policies followed by it. However, the British government could not afford to be as callous and irresponsible as the servants of the Company were. Queen Victoria giving expression to the sentiment of concern, wanted that the Proclamation of 1858 "should breathe feeling of generosity, benevolence and religious toleration, and point out the privileges which the Indians will receive in being placed on an equality with the subjects of the British Crown, and the prosperity following in the train of civilization."

At the same time British Imperialism preached the obnoxious doctrine of the whitemen's burden to rule over the coloured people. They did not bother about the socio-economic development of the people of India.

Knowles in his Economic Development in the Nineteenth Century points out "The English are not an assimilating race, their motives of expansion are wholly economic."[81]

The feelings of racial superiority and the consequent inequal treatment meted out to the Indians was wide spread. Lord Elgin wrote in his Journal on 21 August 1857 : "It is a terrible business, this living among inferior races. I have seldom from man or woman, since I came to the East, heard a sentence which was reconcilable with the hypothesis that Christianity had ever come into the world."[82] The British bureaucrats in India opposed from the very beginning any measure for the liberalisation of the Indian government.[83] It was observed by the Anglo-Indian newspapers, the Telegraph and Courier that it was not possible to introduce into the East the Anglo-Saxon political institutions and they doubted whether the tree of liberty would at all flourish after its transplantation in an alien soil.[84] The First War of Indian Independence of 1857 embittered Indo-British relations to an extreme degree. In 1866 G. Trevelyan wrote : "It was tacitly acknowledged that mercy, charity, the dignity and sacredness of human life— those great principles which at ordinary times, are recongized as eternally true—must be put aside till our sway was restored and our name avenged."[85] In fact the Anglo-Indian paper, 'The Friend of India' wrote on 8 September 1858 : "Any relaxation of our military control, any attempt to cover the steel hand with a velvet glove must be temporarily abandoned. The Asiatic, true to his training of 3,000 years, respects only the strong and his rulers must prove that their armed strength is irresistible."[86]

The most logical and consistent presentation of the imperialist case and the case for continuing an absolute, non-representative and paternal form of government in India was made by Sir James F. Stephen who was the Legal Member of the Supreme Council from 1869 to 1872 and was a judge of the High Court from 1879 to 1891. Sir James stated his views in a letter to The Times on 1 March 1883.[87] He wrote :

> "British Government of India is essentially an absolute Government, founded, not on consent, but on conquest. It does not represent the native principles of life or of government. ... It represents a belligerent civilization, and no anomaly can be so striking or so dangerous as its administration by men who, being at the head of a Government, founded upon conquest, implying at every point the superiority of the conquering race, of their ideas, their institutions, their opinions. ... and having no justifications for its existence except that superiority, shrink from the open, uncompromising, straight-forward assertion of it, seek to apologize for their own position, and refuse, from whatever cause, to uphold and support it."[88]

Thus the theory of superiority of the conquering race was eloquently stated by Sir James.

The Indian government was carried on in a spirit of highly conservative despotism.[89] The British administration had neither time nor the inclination to teach Indians the art of self-government or of political democracy[90] and representative institutions were considered by British Statesmen such as Burke, as "something peculiarly British, as an inherited national privilege."[91]

The systematic oppression, racial discrimination and economic exploitation were the characteristics of the British imperial administration which generated hatred and illwill for the British in the minds of educated Indians and led to the growth of national consciousness in India.

It is also important to note that some of the steps taken by the British for promotion of their imperial interest, inadvertently helped the cause of national unity, and the growth of national consciousness. Institutions of all India services like the Indian Civil Service, Indian Police and Indian Army on a non-political and non-caste basis, promoted equality among the Indians, eventhough "wide inequality existed between the Indians and Europeans."[92] The British organised a vast communication system in India to help the export of raw materials and to facilitate the better distribution of the British finished products. The vast network of roads and railways helped leaders and people from different parts of the country come closer to fight for a common cause by overcoming the barrier of distance.

Socio-Religious Renaissance and Indian Nationalism

Crushed down by political and priestly tyrannies and economic privations, the people of India were hardly in a position to rise and assert themselves morally and intellectually.[93] The awakening of the Indian spirit manifested its creativism first in the realms of philosophy, religion, culture, education and political self-consciousness came as an inevitable consequence.[94] The emergence of Indian National Congress and the spirit of nationalism are indeed the logical results of the genuine work of Indian uplift, a political consequence of the Indian Renaissance. Sir William Wilson Hunter in 'a vindication of the (Congress) Movement' (1888) said " ... I believe the political movement in India is an indestructible part of that great awakening in India which is showing itself not only in the intellectual progress of the Indian people, but in India's commercial development and in many signs of a new national life."[95]

The Indian resurgence can be viewed in the context of the resurgence taking place in the other Asian countries. Asian resurgence in the nineteenth century and afterwards as an event is "more explosive than the atom bomb". Asiatic countries resurged to free themselves from political prostration and economic exploitation by the Western Colonial Powers. Beginning of a re-examination of numerous forces of social stagnation and cultural decadence had been most spectacularly marked since the middle of the nineteenth century. Rise of Asian nationalism is seen as an inevitable sequel to the social and cultural reawakening of the people of Asia. Asian nationalism is of a different character than its European counterpart. It did not appear, as it did in Europe, as a result of resistance to foreign aggression and domination. It is rather a product of Western impact. The Nationalist resistance movements in the Asian countries were inspired by the Western political idealism of the 19th century. The influence of the English liberal philosophers, the French revolution, the American Declaration of Rights, the Irish Struggle for Home Rule, the struggle of Garibaldi and Mazzini for the independence of Italy and many other historical events played a considerable part in firing the patriotic fervour of the Asian nationalist leaders like Sun Yat-Sen, Tilak, Gandhi, Nehru and Kamal Pasha.

Renaissance in Europe had created a new awakening among the people by the spread of knowledge based on principles of rationalism and scientific pragmatism. People were no longer prepared to accept dogmatic preaching. They questioned all kinds of prejudices and superstitions. They developed a questioning spirit and were not prepared to accept anything as sacred or inviolable merely because it was supported by a class or group which derived benefit, notwithstanding its social and religious influence or political power. Thus for the first time in human history people started questioning and challenging many socio-religious practices which they were forced to follow as these were supported by so-called religious norms and longstanding customs and practices. Renaissance opened the flood-gates of rational and liberal thinking.

Socio-Religious Condition

In order to appreciate the nature and development of Renaissance in India one is required to have a comprehensive idea of the prevalent conditions of Hindu religion and society. India in the 18th and 19th centuries presented a very dark and dismal picture of social and cultural degeneration with many retrograde and abhorrent practices. Religious bigotry and ritualism had eclipsed the spiritual endeavour of man and social life was tormented by priestly tyrannies as well as casteism and class conflicts. Christianity and Islam had been making their way through the Hindu society due to internal weakness of Hinduism itself.[96]

Hindu religion had lost its originality amidst vast array of superstitions, dogmatic practices and amidst the false religion practised by corrupt Brahmins. It was against the religious evils of idol worship, polytheism and hereditary priesthood, that the voice of socio-religious reform movements and their leaders became most vociferous.

Hereditary Priesthood and Idol Worship

Everywhere the emphasis was on rituals and ceremonies. Corruption and priestly tyranny were rampant and the evil impacts were felt almost in all spheres of life. Hindu priests or the Brahmins represented God himself, and were the sole exponents of the divine wishes and commands. A Brahmin was born so and it was his authority as a priest that ruled and controlled the whole system of Hindu life, its pantheon of Gods and Goddesses, its dogmas, its philosophy, its rituals, its social economy and all that pertained thereto.[97] The Hindu pundits and Brahmins were rapacious and did not hesitate to commit any fraud for their financial benefit. The Sadhu Community was also divided into innumerable sects and sub-sects.

The simple and spiritual religion of the Vedas and the philosophical teaching of the Upanishads, had been superseded by what was only an "affair of temples and material sacrifices, of shows and processions, of festivals spread over the whole year in honour of innumerable deities."[98] Worst form of idolatry was the order of the day.[99] Dayanand associated idol worship with the economic religious and social degeneration of India. "Millions of rupees are spent in erecting temples which leads to poverty and indolence."[100] People lost unity of faith as they worshiped idols of different forms and names. Dayanand writes in Satyarth Prakash, that they (idol worshipers) are robbed of their independence and reduced to the conditions of a subject race, suffer in a hundred different ways like the pony of the baker and the donkey of the potter.[101] Idol worship encouraged mutual jealousies and competitions among people. One saint appeals to one set of people and another to another. This also leads to differences till 'people come to blows.'[102]

The most dreadful accompaniment of idol worship is superstition. Raja Rammohan Roy found "Hindus in general more superstitious and miserable, both in performance of their religious rites and in their domestic concerns, than the rest of the known nations on the earth."[103] They were the believers in the "most extravagant description respecting futurity, antiquity, and the miracles of their deities and saints."[104] The superstitious practices of maintaining Devadasis and nautch girls in temples was responsible for spreading debauchery and sexual immorality at high places in the name of religion.[105]

Against these evils of idolatrous polytheism of orthodox Hindu religion the voice of revolt was heard from the beginning of 19th century, from the social reformers like Raja Rammohan Roy. Hindu revivalists like Dayanand Swaraswati took up the cause in the later half of the 19th century. They preached the tenet of Upanishadic monotheistic worship of one resplendent, formless God. Early decades of the 19th century witnessed the efforts of Brahmo Samaj, religious reform movements and its leader Rammohan Roy to eliminate vast accumulation of degraded customs and untruths and to build India's essential spirit afresh on foundations of Western rationalism, scientific knowledge, and socio-religious ethics.[106] But in the late 19th century the clarion call of the religious movements, notably Arya Samaj and its leader Dayanand Saraswati, was to regenerate a purified Hindu society based on a spiritual revival.

Vitriolic condemnation of the traditional Brahmin monopoly of education and religious life and their hypnotic control over general mass was the characteristic of socio-religious reform movements.

The conditions of a fragmented and disunited Hindu society were distressing. The decadent ideas which hastened social degeneration, were highlighted by most of the social reformers of the period. "It is against a social edifice, resting upon traditional instinct and reinforced by religious conviction, that the Indian social reformer had to fight."[107]

Caste

Rigid caste system was prevalent. The old 'Varnavyavastha' or caste system prescribed by the scriptures had completely broken down. Hinduism witnessed an ever growing number of castes and sub-castes. Speaking on the evils of social institutions, one of the prominent social reformers G. Subramania Iyer said, "There is no other country in the world where caste and custom have greater influence than India, and where every incentive to action and every ideal are judged with reference to the dictates of these two worst tyrants. The Hindu has not lost the subtlety of his mind, but he can no longer boast of originality, enterprise or self-reliance."[108]

Despite his erudition, there was absolutely no chance for a low-caste person to become a Brahman.[109] Caste system had caused a great loss to the society. "It had made all the members of caste utterly helpless puppets, like so many sheep blindly following the example of the folk, with its thousand interdicts about food and drink, about sanctity and pollution, about social intermingling, and social intercourse."[110] "It had deprived the large number of Shudras of social justice. It had made the Brahmins arrogant and ignorant and had shut the door of competition and had given rise to class jealousness and animosities."[111]

Rigid caste system was attacked vehemently by all socio-religious reformers in the 19th century. Dayanand rejected caste system but held on to the Vedic "Varnashram Vyavastha according to one's action and conduct."[112] The caste distinction according to Dayanand was no religious or natural distinction but a socio-economic institution. Castes[113] were not created by God and salvation did not depend upon its observance. These were simply social orders established for better discharge of different functions.[114]

Untouchability

Segregation of lower castes as untouchables was a social evil associated with caste system. These 'low-caste' people were denied such elementary rights as entry to public temples and the use of public well and tanks. Referring to the reduction of religion to social regulations, Swami Vivekananda rightly observed, "Our religion is in the kitchen, our God is in the cooking pot, and our religion is 'Don't touch me, I am holy.' If this goes on for another century, everyone of us will be in a lunatic asylum".[115] Social reformer's crusade against untouchability led to a diminishing state of caste vanity. They condemned the atrocious treatment meted out to the lower classes and publicly declared that all men were equal. Reformers like Rammohan Roy had criticized caste system and untouchability as these evils bred undemocratic inhuman and anti-national feelings, while staunch revivalists like Swami Dayanand Saraswati referred to Vedas in condemning untouchability. According to Dayanand, the Varna of a person was to be determined by his character, good acts, and the Sanskars.[116] Truth, self-sacrifice, knowledge of God and Vedas, would lead a Sudra to enter into higher Varna.[117] The reverse will degrade a higher Varna member to a Sudra Varna.[118] Social reform endeavours to raise the status and conditions of outcastes in Hindu Society have achieved remarkable success.[119] In a real sense the Depressed Classes Mission of India was a forerunner of the Gandhian programs for the "Harijans".[120]

Status of Women

Much damage to the Indian social fabric was done by the deplorable conditions of women in Hindu society. Several social evils such as, polygamy, infanticide of the female child, enforced widowhood, child marriage had taken roots in the soil and the Hindu woman had to suffer from misery and humiliation.

Except perhaps in the early periods of Vedic times, woman was never assigned a position of equality with man. Law and religion did not recognise the equality and equal rights of man and woman. "Society permitted man to have rights and freedoms from which woman was excluded. Different standards were adopted to judge the individual and social conduct of man and woman."[121] Women of upper classes were left to rot in their generally inferior status. Their enforced seclusion, their early marriage and lack of education increased their miseries.[122] So far as the labouring classes were concerned, there was not much difference in the status and privileges of men and women.[123]

The system of child marriage was prevalent with its adverse effects. Young boys and girls, even children of one year age were married, which resulted in the procreation of feeble progenies. Girls whose husbands died in their infancy were to become helpless and lived a wretched life. A pamphlet entitled, "An Essay on the Promotion of Female Education in India", by Hari Keshwaji, the earliest champion of widow remarriage in Bombay gave a moving description of the misery of Hindu widows. He wrote in 1839 : "She who was originally intended to be the inseparable companion of man and to render him her assistance according to the divine laws, is doomed to spend her days unprofitably in the state of widowhood; disgusted with her gloomy life, with her shaved head, and the continual mournful dress and her exclusion from the company of married females on the occasion of marriage and such other rejoicings."[124]

The degraded and deprived social state of Hindu widows gave a stirring jolt to the sensitive perception of enlightened social reformers. For rebuilding Hindu society and creating social renaissance, they contemplated on reform movements aiming at the liberation and education of Indian Women. The crusade for emancipation of Indian women became the first tenet of the social reform every where in India.

In Bengal Rammohan Roy and Brahmo Samaj Movement, as a whole, took to the cause of social freedom and cultural advancement of Hindu Women. Rammohan pleaded for the removal of the legal and social disabilities which Hindu women had to suffer. The baneful custom of 'Sati' was abolished because of his vigorous campaign against it.

Reforms of marriage customs were advocated on the following lines : "Option of marriage to be allowed to women in the same way as to men. No girl to be married before 18 or at the earliest 16. No man to be married till he is able to maintain himself and his family. Abolition of customs which brings about unnecessary expenditure on occasions of marriage. Removal of the religious and social prohibition against the remarriage of a widow and the recognition of her claim to be socially treated in the same way as any other married woman of her caste."[125]

Thus India in the 18th and 19th centuries presented a very dark and dismal picture of social and cultural degeneration with many retrograde and abhorrent practices. Religious bigotry and ritualism had eclipsed the spiritual endeavour of man and social life was tormented by priestly tyrannies and by casteism and class conflicts.

There was undue emphasis on rituals and ceremonies.[126] Corruption and priestly tyranny ruined social cohesion. These evil practices divided the Hindus among themselves. Numerous local and village deities were worshipped with fanatical zeal and this was responsible for schism among the Hindus. 'Devadasis' and nautch girls were maintained by temples, which spread debauchery and sexual immorality.[127]

Indian Renaissance and Western Impact

The deep rooted priestly tyrannies and social maladies were used by the British Government under East India Company for their own benefit. A policy of passive non-interference in social and religious affairs was followed. For a considerable period of time, it refrained from taking any reformative measure to remove social and cultural despondence of the Indians. The British masters remained satisfied with the patronage of art, literature, and even religion without, interfering with the established customs of the land.[128]

The radicals, utilitarians, and liberals triumphed over the conservatives at a later stage of imperialist domination in influencing the government to accept concrete proposals for reform. Lord William Bentinck, the Governor General (1828 to 1835), implemented the policy of reforms in India.[129] With the abolition of Company's monopoly of trade and opening of the country to Missionary activities, started a new era of change in India. The sanction of an annual sum of Rs. 100,000 for the promotion of learning among the people in India was another remarkable step.

Anglicists Vs. Orientalists

The last provision led to significant and far-reaching changes in the history of India. The Committee of Public Instruction was formed for the purpose of spreading education. It was greatly divided between the Anglicists and the Orientalists. The Committee was presided over by Macaulay, a prominent Anglicist, and his famous Minute on Education brought triumph for the Anglicists by recommending "instruction in European language and science through the medium of English". It has been aptly observed by Tarachand that, "The Orientalists who urged the use of Sanskrit and Arabic were, unfortunately advocating a lost cause, for these languages, however rich in literature and philosophy and however revered for their sacred contents, were practically ruled out. They were not spoken languages of any considerable group of Indians, their knowledge was confined to a very small number, and they required prolonged labour for attaining proficiency in them, for which neither the rulers nor the ruled were prepared."[130]

Macaulay, through the introduction of English language and promotion of Western education wanted to create a class of persons "Indian in blood and colour, but English in taste, in opinion, words and intellect." He sincerely desired, as expressed in a letter to his father, a largescale conversion to Christianity to be affected, without any efforts to proselytize, without the smallest interference with religious liberty, merely by the natural operation of knowledge and reflection through English education.[131]

But irrespective of such motives to establish an alien culture by introducing a European system of education, English education supplied a potent stimulus for the development and promotion of a spirit of all India nationalism. Raja Rammohan Roy played a pioneering role in the introduction and spread of English education in India. It is English education that introduced India to modern science and western rationalism, which in the first half of the 19th century laid the foundations of a renaissant India. At a later stage, cultural and political leaders of India such as Tagore and Nehru welcomed science and western education with the realisation that these were essential for solving the problems of hunger and poverty as also of illiteracy, superstition, evil custom and tradition.[132] English education and learning helped in inculcating a new spirit of intellectual quest with the use of reason as the standard of judgement over various social, religious, and political problems.[133]

This task was performed by the great cultural leaders of modern, India, such as Rammohan, Dayananda and Vivekananda, who in their own different ways dealt with the cultural domination of the West. Brahmo Samaj and Western rationalism, the Arya Samaj and Hindu rivival, the Theosophical Society and Indian spiritualism and the Ramakrishna Mission Movement—all made their own contributions for the development of renaissant India. These socio-religious movements, whether reformistic or revivalistic, aimed at spiritual and social regeneration of India by eradicating the prevalent religious and social maladies that had for a long period of time crippled the moral and intellectual stature of the Indians. Most of these movements were national in the sense that they were organised and led by the people of the country and were grounded in the ancient culture of the land.[134]

Rammohan represented the new spirit of India bringing up unique rapproachment of two alien countries, India and Britain, where the Eastern and Western cultures have become intermingled. "He was the first Indian reformer who assimilated the liberal and humanitarian tradition of Europe and who yet sought to recapture and restate the true principles of Hinduism."[135] Rammohan's rationalistic interpretations of the Hindu scriptures helped to stem the tide of conversion of Hindus to Christianity. He found in Upanishadic monotheism, an answer to the most persistent criticism by Christian Missionaries that the worship of idols and images was the essence of Hinduism.

Nineteenth century Indian intellectuals like Rammohan Roy and Bhandarkar were guided by the conviction that the Indian society had to meet the standards of "social efficiency" in order to be fit for survival.[136] They reposed faith in Spencer's idea of evolution and change of human society which stated that change in social institutions was "a natural process, that it could be guided by men,... that ultimate progress was a certainty.[137] This explains that early 19th century leaders were reformers not revolutionaries. They wanted the degraded Indian society and culture to meet the 'standards of social efficiency' through the growth of liberal religious thought and development of social reform movements. Various superstitions and irrational social conventions, which rested on traditional instinct and were reinforced by religious conviction, were fought with the principles of reason, humanitarianism. This modern spirit of enquiry into ethics, however, has never reached the bulk of the Indian population.[138] Nevertheless, the new freedom to evaluate the foundations of social institutions, marked the beginning of India's modern development. Traditional Hindu thought on the origin and nature of ethics and human relations, in which a Hindu "is satisfied with tracing the origin of rules to some text of scripture or some authoritative tradition... and does not believe that mere unfettered intellectual reasoning can furnish guidance in matters of morality",[139] was opening up to the influences of intellectual discussions of ethics and comparative religion.

English education in India freed the minds of the educated men from the bondage of superstition and taught them the spirit of inquiry. They refused to accept things as sacrosanct, because they were so declared by people in authoritative positions. Some of the British teachers and professors who taught in the schools and colleges consciously and unconsciously inspired their pupils with idea of freedom as well as nationalism.[140] The new system of education discredited the functioning of many social institutions and superstitious customs connected with religion, which were often in conflict with the principles of reason, equality and liberalism.

Caste was one of such social institutions of the Hindus which went against the spirit of democracy and social equality. As one of the social reformers said: "Not only is caste the express badge of Hinduism, its stronghold and the perpetrator of status and function both by inheritance and endogamy, but at the root of that loss of catholic sympathy and originality in action, which are not painfully noticeable in Hindu society.[141] Many Indian political leaders realised that caste was a hindrance to the achievement of national unity by Indians and agitated for its removal.

Rammohan Roy's social reform crusade, against the evil of 'Sati' based on Hindu shastras as well as on appeals to humanitarian and natural rights doctrines ultimately led to the abolition of this gruesome practice of burning the widows.

Prominent social reformers of Bengal like Rammohan Roy and Iswar Chandra Vidyasagar, condemned the treatment of widows by the Hindus and advocated for the remarriage of widows on the grounds of humanitarianism, and equality of rights of individuals, and shastric sanctions of such marriages. After cataloguing the miseries of widows, Vidyasagar appealed to the Indians to follow the dictates of Sastras, to give the widows in marriage again, and thus relieve them from their intolerable sufferings, and themselves from miseries, crimes and vices.[142] The widow remarriage movement, despite its meagre showing in terms of general public acceptance, retained a surprising vigour well into the 20th century.[143] These reforms were directed to achieve a major objective of all Indian social reform movements and the social freedom and moral and cultural advancement of Hindu women.

The remarriage movement, became the first reform cause to be taken up throughout the country by social reformers. Many Indians, reformers like Karsandas Mulji, Narmada Shankar (1833-1886) of Gujarat and Vishnu Shastri Pundit (1827-76), M. G. Ranade, Gopal Hari Deshmukh of Bombay Presidency led the movement which in its aims and public recognition far outreached the social reform efforts in Bengal. In Northern India Dayananda Saraswati and the newly founded Arya Samaj advocated the remarriage of child widows.

The concept of social democracy in terms of removal of social and religious evils and superstitions and the enjoyment of equal rights by all, irrespective of the differences of class, caste, or creed dawned in India, much prior to political consciousness. It was the view of the social reformers that, social evils had to be destroyed for preparing the society to imbibe the principles of democracy, liberty and secularism.

For social reformation and for promoting the material prosperity of the subjects no agitation or debates on political issues were ever thought necessary. M. G. Ranade, the leading reformer of the Social Conference emphasized this point with particular significance. This could only be achieved with the sympathy and support of the British. Many of them emphasized the priority of social reform over political reform. Malabari's voice, heard through the Indian Spectator, was especially strong in arguing that if Indians wanted to acquire the political institutions of the West, they would first have to assimilate, to some extent at least, Western "moral and social usages."[144]

R. G. Bhandarkar was of the opinion that, "Without a reform of our social institutions, real political advance is impossible."[145] The work of building a modern nation was represented by the efforts of nationalist leaders who also put great emphasis on socio-religious reforms.

The dominant nationalist group, which was responsible for founding the Indian National Congress felt more concerned with the creation of conditions of mass education, economic advancement, social reform and a unity of a kind that Western nations enjoyed, before India's National identity could be felt. The anti-traditional, liberal democratic, secular and politically oriented concept of the nation, which began with Rammohan Roy, characterised the nationalism of the early Congress leaders.[146] Opposed to the moderate nationalism of early Congress leaders there was the emerging trend of militant or religious nationalism of the Extremists.

Thus there were two predominant groups. One group of leaders under the leadership of Rammohan Roy tried to emulate the Western model and assimilate the good aspects of other religions and cultures in order to reform the Indian society. Intellectual efforts were made for discovering the latent humanitarian tradition and ethical monotheism of Hindu shastras which had been obscured by "thoughtless beliefs and meaningless riturals." A remarkable combination of receptivity and self-respect was maintained.

The other group of people aimed at the revival of the great Indian culture and heritage and the spirit of nationalism came to be identified with the religious community of the Hindus. It was a response to the challenge of haphazard and superficial Westernisation of Indian life, thought and politics, which seemed to upset the balanced synthesis of Rammohan Roy.[147]

The Hindu revivalistic movement was spearheaded by the Arya Samaj and its leader Dayananda Saraswati to counter the threat to traditional Hindu religion, ethics and social values posed by Christianity and Brahmoic and Brahmanical influences. Out of the clash between the new mechanical civilization of the occident and the old pietistic and religious cultures of India, we find the emergence of a new India.[148]

The social reform movement was not a passing phase in India's history. It had farreaching consequences—social, cultural as well as political. It was also not a temporary phase of development due to alien influences. It can neither be interpreted as "mere revolt of the early nineteenth century against the evil social practices and gross religious beliefs; nor a simple attraction of the virtues of Western learning and adaptation of liberal, legal and social institutions and Western social ethics. The assessment of the benefits of British rule, according to Rammohan Roy and those who agreed with and followed him, rested on the conception of a renovated Indian society. It is now recognised that it was impossible, at that time, to envisage a reformed Indian religion unless it carried the message of social advancement, and both religious and social reforms were prerequisites to any enhancement of India's political status."[149]

Thus the Nineteenth century, under the impact of the new awakening, gave birth to movements of great vitality, such as the Brahmo Samaj, the Arya Samaj, the Ramakrishna Mission, and the Theosophical Society. While basically aiming at the eradication of the evil influences of religious tradition and superstition, these movements also tried to promote intensive social reform and uplift. Raja Rammohan Roy played a significant role in launching a bold struggle for "social purity, educational progress and journalistic freedom which together formed the basis of the demand for political liberty."[150]

Indian Renaissance embraced an extensively broad spectrum of life and had several dimensions. The following observation gives a pen-picture of the various aspects of Indian Renaissance:

"From the time of Rammohan Roy the Renaissance in Modern India may be said to have commenced, when the morning light travelled from the West to the East. Therefore, modern Indian Renaissance was essentially a product of Western civilization. The mantle on social and educational sides fell upon Pandit Iswar Chandra Vidyasagar, Prosonno Coomar Tagore, Sasipada Banerji, Mohmed Moshin, Sir Syed Ahmed, Roychand Premchand, Bal Gangadhar Sastri, Gopal Row, who were peculiarly sensitive to the impact of new ideas from the West. Educational Renaissance was firmly established in the country with the creation of the Universities (in Bombay, Madras, and Calcutta) in 1857-58. These Universities, besides imparting Western knowledge, were largely instrumental, in addition to what had been achieved by the Christian missionaries and other English protagonists, in reviving the vernacular languages and 'stimulating literary activities of remarkable vitality and fecundity.' The economic or industrial Renaissance was contemporary to the American Civil War (1861-65). A first important attempt was made (in the economic or industrial renaissance), when during that period, Bombay turned the cotton crisis of the world to her advantage. This was followed by Madras, Bengal and the Punjab, each in her own way strove to revive her trade and industry with fresh life and activity."[151]

Footnotes

1. Karan Singh : *Prophet of Indian Nationalism — A Study of the Political Thought of Sri Aurobindo Ghosh, 1893-1910*, George Allen & Unwin Ltd., (London, 1963) p. 17.
2. R. H. Tawney, *Religion and the Rise of Capitalism*, (London, 1937), p. 25.
3. Haridas Mukherjee and Uma Mukherjee, *The Origin of the National Education Movement (1905-1910)*, Calcutta, 1957, p. 65.
4. Charles H. Heimsath, *Indian Nationalism and Hindu Social Reform*, Princeton University Press, Princeton, 1964, p. 5.
5. N. G. Chandavarkar, *Speeches and Writings*, Bombay, 1911, p. 54.
6. Charles H. Heimsath, *op. cit.* p. 5.
7. R. P. Dua, *Social Factors in the Birth and Growth of the Indian National Congress Movement*, S. Chand & Co., Delhi, 1967, p. 4.
8. *Ibid., op. cit.* p. 4.
9. *Ibid.*, p. 5.
10. Shridharan in '*Warning to the West*' (Bombay, January 1944, pp. 34-37) calls the Missionaries 'the strange allies of Imperialism. They taught the Western way of life along with the Gospel'.
11. Charles H. Heimsath, *op. cit.*, p. 9.
12. Hari Hara Das, *Subhas Chandra Bose and the Indian National Movement*, Sterling Publishers Pvt. Ltd., New Delhi, 1983, p. 2.
13. *Ibid.*
14. H. H. Dodwell, ed., *The Cambridge History of India*, Vol. 1, London, 1932, p. 540.
15. Dr. S. Gopal, *Homage to Rammohan*, The Statesman, May 24, 1988, p. 3.
16. *Ibid.*
17. A. C. Mazumdar, *Indian National Evolution*, Madras, 1917, p. 3.
18. Hari Hara Das, *Subhash Chandra Bose and the Indian National Movement*, p. 3.
19. H. C. E. Zacharias, *Renascent India*, London, 1933, p. 15.
20. Charles H. Heimsath, *op. cit.*, p. 8.
21. K. P. Karunakaran, *Religion and Political Awakening in India*, Meenakshi Prakashan, Meerut, 1965, p. 15.
22. Jawaharlal Nehru, *Autobiography*, London, 1942, p. 24.
23. K. P. Karunakaran, *op. cit.*, pp. 15-16.
24. R. Palme Dutt, *India To-day*, Bombay, 1949, p. 303.
25. *Ibid.*
26. Hari Hara Das, *op. cit.*, p. 3.
27. K. P. Karunakaran, *op. cit.*, p. 4.
28. K. M. Panikkar, *A Survey of Indian History*, Bombay, 1947, p. 273.
29. Jawaharlal Nehru, *The Discovery of India*, Bombay, 1961, p. 361.
30. K. P. Karunakaran, *op. cit.*, p. 4.

31. Charles H. Heimsath, *op. cit.*, p. 8.
32. *Ibid.*
33. K. P. Karunakaran, *op. cit.*, p. 6.
34. Charles H. Heimsath, *op. cit.*, p. 49.
35. K. P. Karunakaran, *op. cit.*, p. 13.
36. K. P. Karunakaran, *op. cit.*, pp. 13-14.
37. Quoted by Romain Rolland, *Prophets of New India*, London, 1930, pp. 79-80.
38. F. Max Muller, *Rammohan to Ramakrishna*, Calcutta, 1952, p. 77.
39. K. P. Karunakaran, *op. cit.*, p. 19.
40. Quoted by W. N. Bell, Rammohan Roy, Cal., 1933, p. 197.
41. Quoted by M. V. Krishna Rao, *The Growth of Indian Liberalism in the Nineteenth Century*, Mysore, 1951, pp. 205-206.
42. Surendra Nath Banerji, *A Nation in Making*, London, 1925, p. 396.
43. Swami Vivekananda, *Selections from Swami Vivekananda*, Almora, 1944, pp. 198-99.
44. K. Narendra, *Hundred Years of the Arya Samaj, Illustrated Weekly of India*, 13 April, 1975.
45. T. V. Parvate, *Bal Gangadhar Tilak*.
46. Bankim Chandra Chatterji, *Bengal : Past and Present* (Calcutta, April-June, 1914), pp. 273-74.
47. R. C. Majumdar, *Three Phases of India's Struggle for Freedom*, Bombay, 1961, p. 7.
48. Bipin Chandra Pal, *Swadeshi and Swaraj*, Calcutta, 1954, p. 18.
49. Quoted by C. Y. Chintamani, *Indian Social Reform*, Madras, 1892, Part-II, p. 30.
50. William Theodore de Bary and others, *Sources of Indian Traditions*, New York, 1958, p. 610.
51. K. P. Karunakaran, *op. cit.*, p. 47.
52. *Ibid.*, p. 50.
53. Sankar Ghose, *The Renaissance to Militant Nationalism in India*, Allied Publishers, Bombay, 1969, p. 79.
54. R. P. Dua, *op. cit.*, p. 6.
55. Rabindranath Tagore, Gora (Bengali Novel) quoted by Sankar Ghose in *The Renaissance to Militant Nationalism in India*, p. 81.
56. Quoted by Sankar Ghose in *Ibid.*, p. 82.
57. K. P. Karunakaran, *op. cit.*, p. 59.
58. Sankar Ghose, *op. cit.*, p. 84.
59. *Ibid.*, p. 67.
60. Sankar Ghose, *op. cit.*, p. 85.
61. *Ibid.*, p. 82.
62. K. P. Karunakaran, *op. cit.*, p. 58.
63. A. R. Desai, *Social Background of Indian Nationalism*, Bombay, 1959, 3rd ed., p. 221.

64. K. P. Karunakaran, *op. cit.*, p. 26.
65. Dayananda Saraswati, *Satyartha Prakash*, (Allahabad, undated), p. 548.
66. It was founded by Helena Blavatsky and H. S. Olcott, in New York City on November 17, 1875. Its head-quarters were later transferred to Madras.
67. K. P. Karunakaran, *op. cit.*, p. 68.
68. Annie Besant, *Birth of New India*, Madras, 1917, pp. 353-55.
69. *Complete Works of Swami Vivekananda*, Vol. IV, Almora, 1932, pp. 263-65.
70. D. P. Mukherji, *Modern Indian Culture*, Bombay, 1948, pp. 27-28.
71. *The Complete Works of Swami Vivekananda, Vol. III*, p. 219.
72. *Ibid.*, p. 272.
73. Romain Rolland, *Prophets of the New India*, London, 1930, p. 462.
74. D. P. Mukherji, *Diversities*, New Delhi, 1958, p. 165.
75. Ram Gopal, *How India Struggled for Freedom*, The Book Centre Pvt. Ltd., Bombay, 1967, p. 9.
76. Dr. Tarachand, *History of the Freedom Movement in India, Vol. 1*, New Delhi, Ministry of I & B, 1961, pp. 338-392. Also see R. C. Mazumdar, *The Sepoy Mutiny and the Revolt of 1857*, Firma K. L. Mukhopadhyay, Calcutta, 1957, pp. 1-19.
77. For details of the economic consequences of British rule over India, see, D. D. Basu, *Ruin of Indian Trade and Industries*, Calcutta, 1935, pp. 38-51.
78. Jadunath Sarkar, *Economics of British India*, Calcutta, 1916, pp. 175-176.
79. Quoted in *The National Movement in India*, by Hari Hara Das and Sasmita Das, Renaissance Publishing House, Delhi, 1988, p. 4.
80. Sri Prashanto K. Chatterji, *The Making of India Policy*, 1853-65, University of Burdwan Publication, 1975, f. n. 1.4.13, p. 241.
81. L. C. A. Knowles, *Economic Development in the Nineteenth Century*, 1924, p. 307.
82. *Elgin's Journal*, 21 August 1857, quoted in John Morley, Life of Cobden, Vol. II, p. 190.
83. Sankar Ghose, *The Renaissance to Militant Nationalism in India*, Allied Publishers, New Delhi, 1969, p. 146.
84. *Ibid.*, pp. 146-147.
85. G. C. Trevelyan, *The Competition Wallah*, London, 1866, p. 242.
86. Quoted by Sankar Ghose : *The Renaissance to Militant Nationalism in India*, p. 147.
87. *The Times, 1 March 1883*, The Evolution of India and Pakistan, 1885-1947, Select Documents, (ed.) C. H. Philips, 1965, E. L. B. S. edition, pp. 56-60.

88. Quoted by Sankar Ghose, *The Renaissance to Militant Nationalism in India*, p. 151.
89. *Ibid.*, p. 157.
90. *Ibid.*, p. 157.
91. Ramsay Muir, *National Self-Government* (London, 1919), p. 34.
92. K. M. Panikkar, *A Survey of Indian History*, Asia Publishing House, 2nd edition, Bombay, 1944, pp. 204-5.
93. R. G. Bhandarkar, *Social History of India in Indian Social Reform* (edited by L. Y. Chaintamani), Part I, pp. 25-26.
94. Viswanath Prasad Varma, *Modern Indian Political Thought*, p. 2.
95. Quoted by R. P. Dua, *Social Factors in the Birth and Growth of the Indian National Congress Movement*, f. n. 1., p. 20.
96. R. S. Pareek, *The Contribution of Arya Samaj in the Making of Modern India*, p. 23.
97. Lajpat Rai, *A History of the Arya Samaj* (Ed. by Shri Ram Sharma), pp. 50-51.
98. Quoted by Lala Lajpat Rai, *op. cit.*, pp. 51-52.
99. R. G. Bhandarkar, Social History of India, in *Indian Social Reform* (ed.) C. Y. Chintamani, Part I, pp. 25-26.
100. R. S. Pareek, *Contribution of Arya Samaj in the Making of Modern India*, (1875-1947), p. 99.
101. Dayanand Saraswati, *Satyartha Prakash*, p. 261.
102. G. P. Upadhyaya, Dayanand's contribution to Hindu Solidarity, Ch. IX, p. 65.
103. Rammohan Roy in a letter to Digby, English Works, (ed.) J. C. Ghose, p. 929.
104. From "An Appeal to the Christian Public in Defence of The Precepts of Jesus", *Ibid.*, p. 559.
105. K. K. Dutta, *Survey of India's Social Life*, (1961), pp. 8-9.
106. C. H. Heimsath, *Indian Nationalism and Hindu Social Reform*, p. 25.
107. Surendranath Banerji, *A Nation in Making* (London, 1925), p. 396.
108. C. Y. Chintamani, (ed.) *Indian Social Reforms*, Part I (Madras, 1892), pp. 114-15.
109. V. Chirol, *Indian Unrest*, London, 1910, Ch. III, p. 32.
110. Ram Gopal, *Dayanand — The Man and His Mission* (an article) Dayanand Commemoration Volume, p. 116.
111. G. P. Upadhyaya, *Dayananda's Contribution to Hindu Solidarity*, 1939, p. 86.
112. H. B. Sarda, *Life of Dayanand Saraswati*, p. 90.
113. In the Vedas there is no mention of caste but the word 'Varna' is used. The word 'Varna' comes from the Sanskrit root 'Vri' which means, to 'choose' profession or occupation. The concept became corrupt and perverted during the post Vedic age— G. P. Upadhyaya,

Vedic Culture, Kala Press, Allahabad, 1962, p. 167.
114. Lala Lajpat Rai, *The Arya Samaj*, p. 46.
115. Vivekananda, *India and Her Problems*, p. 23.
116. Sanskara means good acts. There are 16 Sanskaras which are observed at different times by men on different occasions from birth to death.
117. Swamy Dayanand Saraswati, *Satyartha Prakash*, p. 106.
118. *Ibid.*
119. It was founded by Vithal Ramji Shinde in 1906, with the help of Bombay Presidency Social Reform Association under the leadership of Chandavarkar.
120. S. Natarajan cites view of the veteran social worker, V. A. Sovani, that even without efforts of Gandhi and the pressure from Dr. Ambedkar the depressed classes would have progressed equally, under the auspices of Depressed Classes Mission— *A Century of Social Reform*, p. 156.
121. A. R. Desai, *Social Background of Indian Nationalism*, n. 5, 210.
122. C. H. Heimsath, *op. cit.*, p. 14.
123. Bimanbehari Mazumdar, *History of Indian Social and Political Ideas: From Rammohan to Dayananda* (Calcutta, 1967), p. 148.
124. Quoted by B. Mazumdar, *op. cit.*, p. 149.
125. C. Y. Chintamani, (ed), *Indian Social Reforms*, n. 6, Part I, p. 171.
126. R. G. Bhandarkar, *Social History of India — in Indian Social Reform* (ed) C. Y. Chintamani, Part-I, pp. 25-26.
127. K. K. Dutta, *Survey of India's Social Life*, (1961), pp. 8-9.
128. H. Sharp (ed.), *Selections from Educational Records*, (Part 1), p. 17.
129. R. C. Mazumdar, *Glimpses of Bengal in the Nineteenth Century*, Calcutta, 1960, p. 23.
130. Dr. Tarachand, *History of the Freedom Movement in India*, Vol. II, p. 194.
131. Sankar Ghose, *op. cit.*, p. 3.
132. Jawaharlal Nehru, *The Unity of India*, 1944, p. 176.
133. C. H. Heimsath, *Indian Nationalism and Hindu Social Reform*, p. 46.
134. R. P. Dua, *Social Factors in the Birth and Growth of the Indian National Congress Movement*, New Delhi, 1967, f. n., p. 8.
135. Sankar Ghose, *op. cit.*, p. 15.
136. R. G. Bhandarkar in C. Y. Chintamani (ed) *Indian Social Reform*, Vol. III, pp. 188-89.
137. C. H. Heimsath, *Indian Nationalism and Hindu Social Reform*, Bombay, 1964, p. 49.
138. C. H. Heimsath, *Ibid.*, p. 49.
139. P. S. Sivaswamy Aiyer, *Evolution of Hindu Moral Ideas*, pp. 7-8.
140. Lajpat Rai, *Young India* (New York, 1916), p. 114.

141. C. Y. Chintamani, n. 6, Part I, p. 149.
142. Iswar Chandra Vidyasagar, *Marriage of Hindu Widows*, p. 93.
143. C. H. Heimsath, *op. cit.*, pp. 87-88.
144. Gidumal, *The Life and Lifework of Behramji M. Malabari*, p. 144.
145. Bhandarkar, *Collected Works*, I, p. 453.
146. C. H. Heimsath, *op. cit.*, p. 139.
147. *The Extremist Challenge*, India Between 1890 and 1910, Amales Tripathi (Delhi, 1967), p. 1.
148. J. N. Farquhar, *Modern Religious Movement in India*, pp. 430-444.
149. R. P. Dua, *op. cit.*, pp. 20-21.
150. *Ibid.*, p. 8.
151. *Ibid.*, *op. cit.*, pp. 9-10.

2
Raja Rammohan Roy and the Brahmo Samaj Movement

The making of modern India largely synchronized with the thought and contributions of Raja Rammohan Roy, the "first Modern Indian". Rammohan Roy (1772-1833), the precocious child of Bengal and the first in a long series of great leaders[1] of thought and action, blazed a trail in setting up 19th century social, religious and political reform movements. He also took a leading role in pioneering the introduction of progressive ideas of Western education, and in dragging India into a closer approximation of modern society. Backed by a robust intellect and a high degree of rational thinking, the dynamic personality of Rammohan Roy as Tagore put it, "Vitalized our national being with the urgency of creative endeavour, and launched it into the arduous adventure of self-realization. He is the great path-maker of this country, who has removed ponderous obstacles that impeded our progress at every step".[2] Rammohan stands forth "as the tribune and prophet of new India."[3]

Rammohan Roy was born on the 22nd May, 1772 in an orthodox Brahmin family of Radhanagar, a prosperous village in the Hooghly district of Bengal. The Raja was a man of great erudition and uncommon intellectual ability. He was a profound scholar of Persian, Arabic and Islamic theology as well as a keen student of Sanskrit and the Hindu shastras and scriptures. He was much impressed by the democratic teachings of the Koran and by the development of logic in Arabic thought and the rationality of some of their schools of thought notably the Mutazilas[4] and the philosophy of the Sufis. Rammohan became a rationalist free thinker under the influence of the Mutazilas. Possessed with the qualities of critical intellectualism and social rationalism, Rammohan initiated an era of crusade for the supremacy of reason over passive asquiescence to authority of pseudo-religious Puranic cults and dogmas that had crept into

Hinduism in much later periods of its history. The critical tone of revolt was exhibited by Rammohan at a very tender age when he first differed with his father on the question of idol worship.

Rammohan was greatly influenced by the rationalism, intelligence and firmness of character of his mother Phulthakurani, rather than his father Ramakant Roy, who was an orthodox Hindu, strictly following the Hindu 'Sastras'. Nevertheless, the impact of the personality of his father on him cannot be denied. Rammohan could never become oblivious to the role played by customs and traditions in the society. Thus while advocating socio-religious reforms, he never thought of totally alienating himself and his followers from the Hindu society. Both father and mother played an important role in moulding and shaping the personality of Rammohan Roy.

After his school education he was sent to Patna for higher studies, where he took keen interest in the study of Persian and Arabic and acquired for himself the title of 'Zabardust Maulvie'. He became highly critical of some of the Hindu religious practices, due to his deep study of Islamic metaphysics and sociology.

He developed deep interest in studying various religious scriptures to know about religious truth. He went to Benaras and studied ancient Indian scriptures in original Sanskrit and acquired profound scholarship in the subject. He also studied the Lamaist Buddhism of Tibet. He inherited a rare intellect which helped him in becoming a religious encyclopaedist. He studied the science of Theology with a rational outlook. He started the first important intellectual movement, which spread the ideas of rationalism and enlightenment in modern India. He took a cosmopolitan and universal approach towards religious questions and facilitated the introduction of Western political doctrines and liberal socio-religious ideas into the country. He rejected dogmas and promoted the spirit of toleration. His attack on hereditary priesthood and translation of sacred books from Sanskrit into a popular language bridged the gulf between the learned few and the rest of the people. Rammohan, by championing the cause of the exploited people and by openly advocating the right to free thinking and the spirit of inquiry indirectly helped the growth of the democratic spirit. It has been rightly observed that

> "The organisations Rammohan founded and the discussions they organised introduced into the

> Indian public life the practice of forming associations and holding debates. In the political field, where they found their most concrete expression, this was a healthy development. It is not an accident that many of the early leaders of the Congress were members of the Brahmo Samaj. By inaugurating a new era in the religious field, the Samaj and its founder Raja Rammohan Roy, laid the foundations of a new political movement in India."[5]

Thus Rammohan Roy was destined to play a very prominent role in the socio-religious and political life of India. He was the precursor of most of the movements which were started in India for the modernization of the society and eradicating the socio-religious evils and superstitions.

Rammohan Roy went to Murshidabad in 1803, after the death of his father, where he renewed his Arabic studies. There he wrote 'Tuhfat-ul-Mawahhidin' (a gift to the monotheist) in Persian, with an introduction in Arabic. He emphasized the existence of the 'One Supreme Being' and tried to show the general unity of religious thought among the whole mankind.

He was recruited to the service of the East India Company in 1809 as 'Shristadar', but resigned from his post in 1814. He came to Calcutta in 1815 and organised the 'Amitya Sabha' — Spiritual Society in 1816. He became greatly engrossed in social issues and started his crusade against the evil social custom of 'Sati', which meant burning the bride on the funeral pyre of the dead husband.

He organised the British India Unitarian Association in 1827 and founded the Brahmo Sabha on August 20, 1828, which was later renamed as the Brahmo Samaj. Under the able leadership of Rammohan, the Brahmo Samaj played a pioneering role for ushering the Indian Renaissance. Though born of devout Brahmin parents, "Rammohan represented the new spirit of India with its thirst for science and love of rationalism, reform, and a broad humanism."[6] Despite his passionate love for reform, he had a critical regard for the past and was opposed to any revolt. The Brahmo Samaj founded by him was the first religious reform movement. It tried to meet with the Western challenge and the new Western ideas which made inroads into the Indian society. In this endeavour his knowledge of English and contact with

European thought were of immense help :

> "If he had never come into contact with European thought, he might have become a religious reformer in the manner of Nanak or Kabir. In 1796 Rammohan began learning English. Rammohan also studied the Upanishads and the Vedanta Sutras in Sanskrit and the Old and New Testament in the original Hebrew and Greek. He published some translations of the Upanishads and a book called the precepts of Jesus, The Guide to Peace and Happiness which contained not so much a message for his own countrymen as an answer to the Christian missionaries."[7]

It is striking to note that despite his appreciation of Christianity, Christian ethics and his admiration for Western rationalism, science and broad humanism, he rejected the doctrine of the divinity of Jesus, although he was impressed by his ethical teachings.[8] He convincingly argued against the doctrine of Trinity and converted the Scotch missionary to his philosophy of Unitarianism. He successfully resisted the attempts of his Christian friends who tried to convert him to Christianity.[9] Rammohan reinterpreted Hinduism and tried to reform it, but he was not interested to change his religion. Like the Christian missionaries, he condemned polytheism and idolatry and explained to ·the people that polytheism and idolatry were completely antagonistic to the monotheistic spirit of the Upanishads.[10] Through his rationalistic interpretation of the Hindu scriptures, he could prevent the conversion of large number of Hindus to Christianity. He asked the English-educated Hindus, who had become disgusted with the evil customs and superstitions, not to accept Christianity, but to go back to the ethical monotheism of the Upanishads. Thus he had to wage a war both against the Christain missionaries and the Orthodox Hindus. He tried to prove that Hinduism did not sanction either idol worship or barbarous customs.

Through his reinterpretation of the Hindu scriptures, Rammohan Roy pointed out that the essence of Hinduism was the faith in one supreme being. "Idol worship was not the foundation, but an excrescence of Hinduism." The contact between the modern science and rationalism of the West with the ancient civilization of the East, as had taken place in the Indian context was bound to produce conflicts and tensions. Rammohan successfully dealt with the rationalist and liberal challenge of the West.[11] But in this process of meeting the challenge, he neither rejected the spirit of modern Europe, nor succumbed to it. He rather derived the necessary stimulus for discovering the latent traditions of humanitarianism and ethical monotheism in Hinduism. Rammohan deserves the credit for the harmonious blending of the two civilizations of the East and West for the benefit of the people of India.

> "Rammohan's supreme genius lay in this that he was able to recognize what was good and assimilable in the message of the West without forsaking faith or belief in Hinduism and without also forgetting the urgent need for its reform and purification."[12]

The 19th century social revolt, which is identified with the thought of Rammohan Roy, established the tone and substance of the various reform movements of the century. He had no hesitation in recognising the virtues of Western learning, liberal legal and social institutions, and the Western social ethic. He, therefore, appealed to the Indians to purify their religion and reconstitute their social institutions. Throughout the 19th century these ideas were repeated by his followers, "acknowledged or not, whose ideas were affected in some way by this first modern Indian."[13] Roy was convinced that without social advancement it was not possible to think of a reformed Indian religion. He argued that both social and religious reforms were fundamentally essential for the enhancement of India's political stature. He made the following observation in a letter written in 1828 :

> "I regret to say, that the present system of religion adhered to by the Hindus is not well calculated to promote their political interest. The distinction of castes, introducing innumerable divisions and subdivisions among them has entirely deprived them of patriotic feeling, and the multitude of religious rites and ceremonies and the laws of purification have totally disqualified them from undertaking any difficult enterprise... It is, I think, necessary that some change should take

> place in their religion, at least for the sake of their political advantage and social comfort."[14]

Through his iconoclasm and intellectual evocations of the new era, Rammohan greatly contributed to the making of modern India. But he was not a mere theoretician and he also launched a programme of action, through the Brahmo Samaj, founded by him, to re-establish the "natural texture of society". He preached new religious tenets and forms of worship, which he thought was suitable to India's heritage and contemporary needs. For his vision and bold struggle for socio-religious reforms credit should be given to him.[15]

Roy began his campaign against 'Sati' in 1818 and succeeded in getting the support of a government Regulation, prohibiting the evil custom in 1829. He sought the support of the foreign rulers to check the evil social practices by means of progressive legislation and in this sphere, he was the forerunner of later social reformers such as Ranade and Gokhale.[16] Rammohan co-operated with the foreign rulers in forbidding the cruel practice of widow burning.[17] Rammohan sailed for England in November in order to thwart the possibility of nullification of the Regulation against 'Sati', due to the impact of orthodox Brahmin propaganda.

In England, he came in contact with Jeremy Bentham and was greatly influenced by his progressive ideas for the development of human society. Bentham's "Fragments on Government" and the "Introduction to Morals and Legislation", provided him with the necessary inspiration for charting out his programme of action for socio-religious reforms. However, Rammohan did not become a prophet of psychological egoistic hedonism in India, despite his intimate relationship with Bentham. In a letter to Rammohan, Bentham said :

> "Your works are made known to me by a book in which I read a style which but for the name of a Hindu, I should certainly have ascribed to the pen of a superiorly educated and instructed Englishman."[18]

While in England Rammohan Roy also developed contacts with Robert Owen, the father of British socialism. In the words of Miss Collet, "Owen did his best to convert Rammohan to socialism. As the Scot finally lost his temper, the Hindu was considered to have led the best of the argument."

During the period of his stay in England the British Parliament passed the first Reform Act of 1832, and this was acclaimed by Rammohan as the victory of liberty, justice and right over oppression, injustice and wrong.

Rammohan's insatiable thirst for knowledge, led him to learn several foreign languages in addition to English, as Hebrew and Greek and he himself became a prolific writer.[19] His ideas regarding the socio-religious issues and his reactions to the various contemporary problems of his time are vividly expressed in his following writings.

1. Petition against the Press Regulation to the Supreme Court and to the King-in-Council (1823).
2. A letter to Lord Amherst on English Education (1823).
3. A Tract on the Religious Toleration (1823).
4. Rights of Hindus over Ancestral Property according to law of Bengal (1830).
5. Remarks on Settlement in India by Europeans (1831).
6. Question and Answers on the Judicial and Revenue System in India.

In most of his writings, he tried to popularise the theistic movement which grew up in the decades to follow.[20] He was one of the most vocal supporters of English education as he thought that apart from opening the flood-gates for the ideas of rationalism, modernism and scientific truth, this would open the way to Indians to advance towards equality with Westerners. His contributions have been rightly analysed by Heimsath in the following words :

> "For Roy, English education was the portal opening the way to Indians to advance toward equality with Westerners, and he provided crucial support for private and governmental efforts to introduce higher education along European lines. He could not have been expected to inaugurate a political movement at a time when the government itself was hardly consolidated in the country. Nevertheless, his political writings on judicial reform, civil rights, the separation of administrative powers, freedom of the press, and other liberal doctrines, became standard works for the political reform movement one half century later."[21]

It is interesting to note that Rammohan was a distinguished administrator in the Bengal Civil Service but he prematuredly retired from service at the age of forty-two, in order to devote himself completely to spiritual, social and political matters. Rammohan dedicated his whole life for the purpose of spiritual and social regeneration of India. He continued his reformistic activities with utmost sincerity and devotion despite the angry clamour and opposition of the orthodox Hindus.

During the last years of his life Rammohan went to England to plead for the powerless Moghul Emperor of Delhi and in so doing he again deliberately defied one of the prevalent taboos of Hindu society against crossing the sea.

Rammohan was the product of his time and he imbibed the right influences, which enabled him to become the father of the Hindu Reformation of the 19th century :

> "Rammohan emerged at a time when the light of Holbach, Condorcet, Diderot, and other great Encyclopaedists had not died down and when the influence of Bentham and the Utilitarians of England who were to have such a great influence on nineteenth century thought was just beginning to be felt. Rammohan was one of the last Encyclopaedists and a friend of Bentham. Rammohan brought India into direct contact with the European liberalism and humanism of the eighteenth century and of the early nineteenth century."[22]

Inspite of his great appreciation for the Western liberal and humanitarian traditions, he was the first great Indian reformer who made sincere attempts to restate and recapture the true principles of Hinduism. His reinterpretation of Hinduism, as a religion based on ethical monotheism, as supported by the Upanishads, provided great solace and inspiration to the educated Indians, who had come under the impact of modern European science and rationalism. According to Rammohan popular polytheism and idolatry were completely antagonistic to the monotheistic spirit of the Upanishads.[23] In his arguments against idolatry, Rammohan also quoted the authority of the Vedas. Due to his profoundity of knowledge and commitment to the cause of India, everywhere in England, he was honoured as an unofficial Ambassador of India. He died at Bristol in 1833.

As Founder of the School of Comparative Religion

The Raja was well known all over the world as the founder of the School of Comparative Religion, as the great Vedantist who on the one hand, combated the influence of Christian missionaries and on the other, laid the foundation of monotheistic revival in India.[24] His first publication Tuhfat-ul-Muwahhidin (A Gift to Monotheist), which came out in 1803, contained the fundamental religious thoughts of the Raja on the foundation of a universal religion on the principle of 'Unity of Godhead' as opposed to idolatry and superstitions. Rammohan believed it to be a natural tendency, ingrained in every individual to turn towards the *'One Eternal Being'*, who is the source of creation and governor of it. He was of the opinion that the inclination of each sect to a particular God or Goddess, holding certain special attributes, and to some peculiar forms of worship or devotion is a result of habit and training.[25] Rammohan's attitude and approach to religion and religious experiences was based on his ability to discriminate between these conditions. These innovative ideas constituted the core-content of the Brahmo Samaj founded by him.[26]

Rammohan Roy stands prominent in the first generation of Indian leaders who pioneered the work of Indian Modernisation, in social and cultural fields. A man of great learning he strove for a synthesis between the values of Hinduism, Islam and Christianity. "And this presupposed a keen insight into comparative religion, a strong grounding in the contending thought systems and a manly combination of receptivity and self-respect."[27] He wrestled with the problems of Indian religion and society with the modern concepts of liberalism, progressive social-legislation, democracy, science and reason which were typical of Western historical-critical methods. Yet in re-learning the pristine truth of 'Sruti' and rediscovering the precise meaning of 'Smriti' through Western approach, Rammohan showed undiluted faith in the rich heritage of knowledge and Indian Philosophy. He wrote, in a letter to Bengal Harkaru, "If the Christian says we are indebted to the English, (by which) he means the introduction of useful mechanical arts, I am ready to express my assent and also my gratitude; but with respect to science, literature, or religion, I do not acknowldge that we are placed under any obligation. For by a reference to history it may be proved that the world was indebted to our ancestors for the first dawn of knowledge which sprung up in the East and thanks to the Goddess of Wisdom, we have still a philosophical and copious language of our own, which distinguishes us from other nations who cannot express scientific or abstract ideas without borrowing the language of foreigners."[28] With selective assimilation of Western thought, the original Hindu-Brahminical Advaitin mooring was put forth by Rammohan against the Christian challenge with remarkable insight and self-respect. His religious innovation was his distinct contribution to the Hindu Renaissance Movement.

The influence of Western culture was typified by the Brahmo Samaj led by Rammohan Roy. But Rammohan insisted in maintaining some basic elements of the Indian or the Hindu culture, while imbibing the good elements from the West. However, it cannot be denied that the Indian Social Reform movement was the direct outcome of Christian and Western influences. In the words of J. N. Farquhar, "the primal impulse was communicated by the Serampore missionaries to Raja Rammohan Roy and by him to the Hindu Community; and throughout the whole history Christian teaching effort and examples have done more than anything else to quicken the movements."[29]

Rammohan made a distinct contribution by his religious innovations and in fitness of things, it may be said that he was the pioneer in the sphere of religious reform movements.[30] Sophia D. Collet, the biographer of Rammohan, has made the following observation on his contribution, which is characteristic of its vividness and objectivity :

> "Rammohan stands in history as the living bridge over which India marches from her immeasured past to her incalculable future. He was the arch which spanned the gulf that yawned between ancient caste and modern humanity, between superstition and science, between despotism and democracy, between immobile custom and a conservative progress, between... polytheism and ... theism. He was the mediator of his people harmonising in his own person, often by means of his own solitary sufferings, the conflicting tendencies of immemorial tradition and an inevitable enlightenment... He embodies the new spirit which arises from the compulsory mixture

> of races and faith and civilization... He embodies its freedom of enquiry, its thirst for science, its large human sympathy, its pure and ethics, along with its reverent but not uncritical regard for the past, and prudent ... discrimination towards revolt."[31]

In propounding his theory of comparative religion, Rammohan was primarily influenced by the ideas of seventeenth and eighteenth centuries— the age of rationalism and enlightenment in the West. Thus Christian theology and philosophy and Western ideas and institutions had their impact on him, when he preached the religious doctrine of monotheistic spiritualism and universal humanism for the Hindus.

One may trace the origin of influence on Rammohan's religious philosophy to the characteristics of that period in history, which have been aptly described in the following lines :

> "The essential circumstance of the new age is the coming together of diverse peoples and cultures, the frequency, the intensity and the variety of their contacts being ever on the increase. The need that arises out of this situation is one of the synthesis, universalism and unity, to enable men to rise superior to the limitations of localised, parochial isolated life of the preceding ages. In the India of Rammohan's youth the past was making its exit, leaving on the stage unrealised ideals of Hindu-Muslim synthesis, and growth of the Indian renaissance and reformation, and a social and political fabric torn by reactionary conflicts... The synthesis of the Hindu and Muslim reformers of the 15th and 16th centuries had for various reasons ceased to be operative for more than five generations, being clogged with the mud of the return tide of medievalism in the 17th and 18th centuries. On the other hand, the future was drawing apart the curtains for entry on that wreck-strawn stage. Following upon growing Indo-European trade and commerce, a true and abiding Indo-European state had come to be formed, strangely combining Indian and European

> elements of law, polity and civilization, and this was steadily breaking the fragments of the past and absorbing them. The Sunni-Muslim Padshahi had become a haunting shade after suicide, the rival Hindu Padshahi had missed its purpose and ended in a fiasco; the Sachcha Padshahi of the Sikhs had by disunion and narrowness become untrue and limited to inaction; while the new Inglistani Padshahi was acquiring stability and form."[32]

The Founding of Brahmo Samaj

The life and career of Raja Rammohan Roy was extremely varied and interesting,[33] but the main act for which he is remembered was his founding in 1828 of the Brahmo Sabha, which eighteen years later was developed by Maharshi Debendranath Tagore into the Brahmo Samaj. This organization marked the first deliberate attempt in modern India to reform Hinduism and, shearing off its unessential and often undesirable growths, to restore it to its pristine glory. Raja's reformative and revivalistic doctrines were based on his own highly controversial interpretation of the Vedas and the Upanishads. Brahmo Samaj established a standard for social reform movements in Bombay, Madras, and the Punjab. Both the proposals of Rammohan, for a new Indian religious life and assessment of the benefits of British rule rested on his conception of a renovated Indian society.[34] For him the picture of a reformed Indian religion must always carry the message of social advancement, of purging Hindu society of the absurd aberrations.

Rammohan believed that both religious and social reform were prerequisites to any enhancement of India's political condition. The Raja and his followers of Brahmo Samaj sought to accomplish the task of reforming Indian religion and society under the British rule. Their emphasis on political independence was slight, as the Raja, in fact, once remarked, "India required many more years of British domination". Nineteenth century social revolt is marked by the development of Western-inspired religious and social reform movements. The method of reforming the society was by organizing and setting up schools and thereby educating the public and making them rational, active and responsible members of the society. Introduction of Western education, its liberal social and ethical ideas were championed by the 19th century social reformers for creating rationalistic outlook towards various problems of the society.

Rammohan Roy immensely contributed to the allround development in Bengal in the 19th century, which is usually described as 'Awakening', 'Regeneration', 'Renaissance' or 'New Age'. The admiring followers of Raja Rammohan Roy try to assert, that practically all that was good or great in the 19th century and made the Renaissance possible, must be traced to Rammohan. There is an element of truth in this statement, although it is not the whole truth. There were socio-religious movements other than the one that was started by the Raja, and those movements had more enduring effect than the Brahmo Samaj movement started by him.

It may be mentioned that English education and the Western ideas that flowed with it, made the greatest contribution to the Renaissance of Bengal in the 19th century. Other important factors like the growth of Bengali prose literature and Bengali journals, rise of national consciousness, socio-religious reforms patriotic feelings and organized efforts for having more political and administrative rights also contributed to the inauguration of the 'New Age' in Bengal. Rammohan was the pioneer of English education and Western ideas among the young generations of Bengal. He is also acclaimed as the Father of the Bengali prose literature in the field of Bengali magazines or journals. He spearheaded the movement for Indian nationalism and patriotism and paved the way for starting political organizations and agitation for the achievement of political rights and administrative reforms.

Rammohan directed his agitation against the meaningless habits and decadent traditions that stifled all creative efforts in the fields of art and culture, religion and politics. The vital essence of Hinduism based upon the eternal principles of the Vedas and the Upanishads, had lost its value due to the impact of perversions, religious bigotry and superstitions. People succumbed to unreasoned acceptance instead of making critical analysis of the social system and its highly normative order of arrangement. There was formal dogmatism and blind acceptance of the dictates of the privileged few at the higher strata of the society. At this time India needed the advent of a man who could destroy the evils of orthodoxy in the religion and could rekindle the spirit of the whole nation. Raja Rammohan Roy was destined to play this great role for the millions of the poor and the downtrodden people of India by fighting against the evils of social stratification and deprivation. It was ordained by history and providence that he should not only rekindle the spirit of the whole nation, but also rediscover India's imperishable thoughts and the higher values of life. Swami Vivekananda described him as "the first man of new, regenerate India".

Modern India is greatly indebted to Rammohan Roy for the progressive ideas of secularism, adoption of social democracy, abolition of the rigid caste structure, the spread of English education and Western ideas and above all the rational and the scientific approach to the various problems of life, ways of thinking and living. In true sense of the term Rammohan Roy, can be called as Father of Modern India.

During the 19th century social, religious and political reform movements represented the primary areas of creative intellectual endeavour for most educated Indians.[35] The early phase of social reform movements was characterised by the urge of individuals to reshape their personal lives, in large measure in accordance with standards adopted from Western thought.[36] The ideas and subsequent personal influence of Raja Rammohan Roy in Bengal established the tone and substance of this phase of individualist revolt against existing socio-religious maladies.

Rammohan Roy was greatly influenced by Western ideas and institutions. He was the first modern Indian to rise above the contemporary distressing and depressing social anarchy in India at the beginning of 19th century. The socio-religious reform movement started by him avowedly aimed at a re-examination of existing social usages and institutions, religious beliefs, on the basis of reason, enlightenment and liberalism of Europe. He was one of the first Indians to expound the idea of a rationally ordered society along lines suggested by Bentham and Mill.

It is through Brahmo Samaj, Rammohan sought to carry out his practical work of reestablishing the "natural texture of society" having its basis on his iconoclastic ideas and the intellectual evocations of new era. "His Brahmo Samaj established a standard for social reform movements in Bombay, Madras and the Punjab, the most important of which rested firmly on religious reform premises."[37] Rammohan attacked the so-called religious sanction for the practice of 'Sati'. He opposed child marriage, stood for remarriage of widows and for equal rights of men and women. He refuted these evil social practices on the ground that neither Hindu religion nor the ancient history of the country justified their continuation. He acknowledged without embarrassment the virtues of Western learning, liberal, legal and social institutions, and the Western social ethics.[38]

In the field of religion, the cult of Brahmoism propagated by Rammohan, marked a striking deviation from the traditional mode of Hindu worship. Brahmo Sabha, a monotheistic religious body was founded by Rammohan in 1828 "to teach and to practice the worship of one supreme, undivided eternal God". The Sabha was renamed as Brahmo Samaj a year later. Prior to it Rammohan Roy was making efforts to spread his religious idea of the supremacy of monotheism through Atmiya Sabha — a religious association founded by him in 1815.

Brahmoism as a Challenge to Hinduism

New ideas preached by these religious bodies challenged many aspects of orthodox Hinduism. Many of the teachings of the Samaj and particularly its ethical tenets resembled Christian doctrines. The Samaj rejected the Brahman priesthood's intermediation between man and God (although the leaders of the Samaj were mostly Brahmins themselves), repudiated idolatry and sacrifices for its public services; ignored caste distinctions (in theory not in practice) and adopted a congregational form of worship similar to that of unitarians.

Though Rammohan had a strong inclination towards Christian ethics, he however, did not embrace Christianity. He was "no more chained to orthodox Christianity than to orthodox Hinduism, although he believed that he had discovered its real meaning. He remained an independent theist, essentially a rationalist and moralist. He extracted from Christianity its ethical system, but he rejected the divinity of Christ just as he rejected Hindu incarnation. As a passionate unitarian he attacked the Trinity no less than polytheism."[39] He believed that all fundamental religious truths could be found in Hindu scriptures, particularly in Upanishads.

Rammohan Roy worked devotedly to restore the Hindu faith to its orginal purity of Upanishadic era. He sought to reform Hinduism on the basis of his own interpretation of the Vedas and

Upanishads. According to him, the scriptures were not the ultimate authority. Man's highest realisation was built on neither supernatural nor metaphysical foundations, but rested on man's own consciousness. The senses, the mind and the intellect— all are the means of realising the supreme soul — the Brahma. The Vedanta, too, enunciates that. From the evidence of birth, life and destruction, the concept of Absolute may be established.

In Search of Popular Support for his Ideas

In order to make his religious views known to common man, Rammohan undertook the task of translating the sacred books of Hindus into vernacular languages. He called his countrymen, through his writings to discard idolatry and to worship one true God. He wrote : "My constant reflections on the inconvenient, or rather, injurious rites introduced by the peculiar practice of Hindu idolatry, which, more than any other pagan-worship destroys the texture of society, together with compassion for my countrymen, have compelled me to use every possible effort to awaken them from their dream of error; and by making them acquainted with their scriptures, enable them to contemplate, with true devotion, the unity and omnipresence of Nature's God."[40] The Vedanta Sutra, with Shankara's commentary, was translated and published by him into Bengali in 1815, followed by its abridged edition in Bengali and English in 1816. All those works preached the religious ideas of Rammohan on Monotheism, omnipresence of God, and the futility of observing numerous, meaningless religious rituals.

Rationalistic Non-idolatrous Monotheism :

Brahmo Samaj for its nontraditional religious views of non-idolatrous monotheistic religion earned the enmity of Dharma Sabha - a religious body of orthodox Hindus, organised by Raja Radhakanta Deb. After the death of Raja Rammohan in 1933, the weak and unpopular Samaj would have died out but for the new spiritual leadership given to it by Debendranath Tagore (1817-1901), a worthy disciple of Rammohan Roy and a staunch believer of monotheistic religion.

Debendranath Tagore before embracing Brahmoism in 1842 had established in 1839 the Tattvabodhini Sabha – a society of youthful intellectuals, in search of spiritual Truth. It tried to disseminate the truth about the 'Supreme Existent and Immutable

Reality'. Its informal but close association and its ultimate union with Brahmo Samaj in 1859, gave the latter new strength and dynamism.

The propagation of Brahmo Dharma was undertaken under his leadership more vigorously, what he stated to be the essence of Brahmo Dharma was the realization of God in the form of worshipper and worshipped relationship.

Debendranath and the Brahmo Creed :

For Debendranath, the religious truth was in essence the religion of 'bhakti', or as he expressed it, "The pure, unsophisticated heart was the seat of Brahmoism". As a devotee, and one who asserted the objective existence of the mundane world, Debendranath's compassion towards men was a real force in his life.[41]

He recognised the need for changes in Hindu social life, particularly in the matters regarding the treatment of women. His intense devotionalism, however, had little impact on the Brahmos on social reform matters, much less on Hindu society in general. The Samaj under him did not desire a separation from Hindu society and wished to steer a middle course between popular religion and total reform.[42] He was rather indifferent to the views of a group within the Samaj which urged for more radical measures for the Samaj in particular and Hinduism in general. Akshay Kumar Dutt (1820-1886), leader of the radical group, argued in favour of marriage reforms, which should include widow remarriage, intercaste marriage etc. Dutt viewed marriage of girls before puberty and practice of polygamy with abhorrence and advocated divorce under certain circumstances.[43]

Debendranath Tagore was a moderate and he did not support extremely radical views as sponsored by some of his colleagues. He was conscious that such radical ideas were likely to create resentment and opposition from the main body of the Hindu society. He, therefore, tries not to divorce his Brahmoism from Hindu society and wished to steer a middle course between total reform and the popularly accepted tenets of Hinduism.

His stand was clear, when giving a precise formulation of the Brahmo creed, Debendranath said, that the Brahmos were part of the great Hindu community, that though they did not believe in image-worship, they recognised that those who could not yet grasp the highest truth, may treat the religious path through image worship.[44] N. S. Bose rightly indicated that Debendranath's views on social reform presented somewhat a confusing picture.

Thus Debendranath Tagore was more concerned with the concepts of pantheistic immanence and exalted spiritual illumination, than social action leading to social reforms. He believed that spiritual elevation of the people would solve most of their problems. What was prohibited for the Brahmos according to him, was "The worship of any created being or thing as the creator."[45]

According to Debendranath Tagore this, "distinguishes us from all who are addicted to the worship of avatars or incarnations or who believe in the necessity of mediators, symbols or idols of any description. We base our faith on the fundamental truth of religion, attested by reason and conscience and refuse to permit men, book or image to stand in the way of the direct communion of our soul with the Supreme Spirit. This message of the Brahmo Samaj in the abstract does not materially differ from the doctrines of the pure theistic bodies all the world over."[46] A Brahmo had to realize the supreme spirit within himself. By applying his conscience he should not adore an image but at the same time he should not needlessly desecrate the image worshipped with reverence by others.

Keshab Chandra Sen and the Emergence of Radical Brahmoism

The enthusiasm among the radical Brahmos for various social reforms received a boost with the addition to their ranks of Keshab Chandra Sen, a brilliant young man and the third great theistic reformer of Bengal. In 1862, Debendranath appointed Sen as the leading minister and later the Secretary of the Samaj.

During 1850 and 1859 the Samaj was experiencing some rapid changes. The radical members of the Samaj tried to broaden the basis of Brahmoism by advocating new social ideals and attempted to critically examine even the fundamental articles of religious faith. Keshab Chandra Sen epitomized the new trends in the Samaj.

While Debendranath Tagore was a moderate in matters of social reform, Keshab Chandra Sen's views on social reform were radical and advanced. His radical social reform doctrines included opposition to any form of idolatry, even in domestic worship services; denial of significance of caste, and an appeal to illiterate adult wives to attend schools and receive education. He also argued in favour of inter-caste marriage and widow remarriage. Keshab Chandra Sen was very much inclined towards Christianity.

He pointed out that he was a lover of Christ.[47] He derived inspiration for social reform only from the Western values and philosophy. This led him to start an "advanced type of Hinduism", which he called as the "New Dispensation".[48]

The Split in the Brahmo Samaj

The quick tempo of change led to a schism between the conservative wing of the Brahmo Samaj led by Debendranath Tagore and the radical group led by Sen. Finally, the Brahmo unity was broken with the split of the Samaj into two separate bodies — the conservative Adi (original) Brahmo Samaj and Brahmo Samaj of India led by Keshab Chandra Sen.

The new organisation under Sen's influence worked to further spread the ideas of toleration and catholicity. Keshab Chandra Sen was a preacher of universal faith. But unlike the religious faith of Raja Rammohan Roy, that faith was based on devotion, not on rational thinking.

As a prophet of religious universalism, Keshab Chandra Sen in 1880, proclaimed the doctrine of Navavidhana or the New Dispensation. It signified the concept of harmony among all of religions. This doctrine brought forth the concept of harmony among all religions. But unlike the religious faith of Raja Rammohan Roy, it was based on devotion and extreme eclectic faith of Keshab Chandra Sen and not on rational thinking. Thus "the Brahmoism of Keshab Chandra Sen moved away from the original Hindu-Brahminical-Advaitin mooring of Rammohan, to be cast adrift in a sea of eclecticism which was assailed every day by the tempest of scepticism. It swung from the apothesis of Christ which was viewed with suspicion, to the apothesis of Keshab, which was viewed with sarcasm."[49] Thus the religious propagation of Brahmo Samaj, which was primarily a religious reform movement at the beginning, became a suspect in the eyes of the Hindus due to its proneness towards Christianity.

Keshab Chandra and the Indian Reform Association

The new organisation of Brahmo Samaj of India under Sen's

influence provided an active leadership to the causes of social services and reforms in India. He founded the Indian Reform Association in 1870 to vigorously carry on the task of social services and reforms. The Association sponsored new educational endeavours for women and working people, founded an Industrial School, worked for charity and temperance movements, and started inexpensive journals. It was on marriage reform issue that Keshab Chandra Sen tried vigorously for practical results, through the reform associations. The progressive Brahmos under his leadership inspite of the violent opposition of older Brahmos, succeeded in getting the Legislative Council pass a new Marriage Act legalising Brahmo Civil Marriages.

Decline of Keshab Chandra Sen's Leadership

For quite some time, K. C. Sen was regarded as the most vigorous religious and social reformer in the land. However, his influence over his followers began to wane subsequently. A gap could be seen between his pronounced religious and social reform precepts and practices. He himself became irrational seeking truth from intuitive and mystical sources, showing indifference towards rational and practical needs of the people. This was styled by him as the "New Dispensation".[50] According to Sivanath Sastri, the concentration of K. C. Sen on devotional practices turned his attention and that of the Samaj away from social welfare and reform.[51] His alleged neglect of his own daughter's welfare eliminated him from any future leadership. His fervent assertion of newly found spiritual revelation made him uncompromising with the religious ideas of others. His attitude gave rise to discontentment among his followers and signs of rebellion against his leadership were visible. The final breach occurred with the majority of Brahmos breaking away from the Samaj in 1878, to form the Sadharan Brahmo Samaj. The immediate cause of this split was the marriage of Sen's daughter a girl of 13 with the Maharaja of Cooch Behar, a boy below 16 years of age, in accordance with orthodox Hindu rites. After this second split, Bengal the homeland of Brahmo movement, had lost its claim to propagate social reform measures in the whole country.

The Brahmo Samaj movement and its leaders placed heavy reliance on the inspiration of Western model of development and alien ideologies in their advocacy of ethical and social reformative doctrines for India. They regarded India's contact with Christian civilization as the surest means of its moral regeneration. Like Raja Rammohan Roy, Keshab Chandra Sen referred to the English contact as a 'providential dispensation'.[52] Their influence on English educated Bengalis was great. This student of the Hindu College at Calcutta adopted an aggressive attitude to everything Hindu and openly defied the canons of his inherited religion. Some of his followers even offended public opinion by youthful exuberance,[53] while others embraced Christianity.[54] Many Western educated people detached themselves from the mainstream of national ethos.[55] It became the fashion even in the smaller things of life to imitate the West.[56]

The Brahmo Samaj had attempted to 'carry through certain social and educational reforms on purely Western lines.' Its leaders questioned the numerous religious absurdities and the sanctions these provided to superstitious and irrational social conventions, on the basis of reason, enlightenment and liberalism. They raised their voices vociferously against the practices of idolatry, casteism, hereditary priesthood and above all tried to elevate the degraded and depraved social positions of Indian women.

The Samaj and its ideals, however failed to strike roots in Hindu society. Its message of electicism, monotheistic devotion, abolition of caste, equal rights for women, its hostile denunciation of Hindu polytheism and above al its leaning towards Christian ethics, made the Brahmo movement repulsive to the sentiments of the common people. These ideas found intellectual appreciation and acceptance among a minority group of English educated people. The search for personal truth or for a new mode of life among a limited number of enlightened men had no effect at all on the ideas and customs of multitude, who had their socio-religious convictions placed firmly on sentiments rather than reason. All the Brahmo reformers faced what finally subdued Keshab Chandra Sen, against whom "were the three hundred million gods of India and three hundred million living beings in whom they were incarnate— the whole vast jungle of human dreams wherein his western outlook made him miss the track and scent. He invited them to lose themselves in his Indian Christ, but his invitation remained unanswered. They did not even seem to hear it."[57] The Brahmo acceptance of European culture and social forms proved a tactical error cutting them off from the 'confidence of the public.'[58]

Keshab Chandra's extreme radicalism and his ruthless behaviour led to the split in the Brahmo Samaj and he failed to maintain his supremacy over all the members of the Samaj. He became a despot and autocrat and spread the doctrine of the 'avatar' (incarnation of God). His followers were encouraged to roll down at his feet and dance in ecstacy around him.[59] During this period, the revivalist and other movements had been started to counteract the extremely Western and Christian leaning of the Brahmo Samaj and its impact on the people. As a result of this, Keshab Chandra Sen, who was an ardent supporter of radical reforms, freedom and rationalism, followed reactionary and retrograde measures. This change in the precepts and practices of Keshab Chandra alienated the radical section of his followers and they started a rebellion against him in 1871. The final breach took place in 1878, at the time of the marriage of Sen's daughter, which violated the principles of Brahmoism. As a protest against Keshab Chandra's autocratic and erratic behaviour, the dissidents organised the Sadharan Brahmo Samaj. They expressed their views against the hypocricy and double-standards of some of the Brahmo leaders in Brahmo Public Opinion, as follows :

> "Are there indeed they who in 1866 fought for a constitution, but who in 1878 baffled every honest effort to bring about a constitution? Are there indeed they who in 1866 eloquently cried down despotism in the Calcutta Samaj but in 1878 support that despotism? Are there indeed they who, while members of the Calcutta Samaj, objected to persons who, notwithstanding that they wore holy thread, a symbol of idolatry, were Brahmos in their conviction to officiate at the marriage cermony of Baboo Debendranath Tagore's daughter but who in 1878 as minister and missionaries of the Brahmo Samaj of India, permitted persons wearing the very symbol of idolatry, and who were orthodox Hindus by profession and practice, to officiate at the mariage cermony of the minister's daughter? Are there indeed they who in 1866 fought for the liberty of

> conscience, but who call in the aid of police that they may successfully do so? If indeed they are those identical persons, we feel disposed to exclaim with Milton, 'Oh ! how altered ! how fallen !'"[60]

The gap between theory and practice of the Brahmo Samaj, not only exposed it to redicule by others, but also led to dissension among its members and followers. From the practical side, it was not possible to implement socio-religious reforms of a very radical nature in India of the nineteenth century. The stronghold of traditions on the people created obstacles in the application of European ideas. The commitment of the Brahmo Samajists to Western and Christian way of life and social ethics also led to a genuine apprehension in the minds of the people that the Brahmo Samaj was acting as a collaborator with the Christian Missionaries in their highly organized and state-aided proselytising efforts. The Brahmo Samajists were also blissfully ignorant of the fact that it was not possible to introduce radical reforms in the absence of rapid economic changes, which are highly essential for changing social patterns. The Brahmo Samaj also lost its credibility as some of the members deviated from the pronounced principles of Brahmoism, when it came to their own private lives. Those members of the Samaj who were bold and radical in their views were rejected by the society and they failed miserably to persuade people to follow them. Thus the Brahmo Samaj was forced to reconcile itself with some of the Hindu social norms. It did not move away completely from Indian traditions.

The Impact of Indian Tradition on the Brahmo Samaj

Although thc Brahmo Samaj and most of its leaders, in their general approach and activities, were inspired by alien ideologies, they did not remain totally blind to some of the predominant Hindu traditions and their impacts on the Hindu society. However, due to its Western and Christian leanings, it could not take deep roots in the country. "The history of the Brahmo Samaj was symbolic of the ideological advance and organizational weakness of a few devoted people who were called upon to popularise ideas which were much ahead of the times."[61]

Raja Rammohan Roy, the chief architect of the Brahmo Samaj movement was criticized both by the Christian missionaries and the orthodox Hindu Pundits. The missionaries attacked him for the 'heathen' interpretation of, and meddling with the Christian religion. His unorthodox interpretation of Hinduism, provoked the attack of the Hindu Pandits.

Rammohan appreciated only the moral precepts of the New Testament and expressed grave doubts regarding the historical aspects and miraculous relations, mentioned therein :

> "I feel persuaded that by separating from the other matters contained in the New Testament, the moral precepts found in that book, they will be more likely to produce the desirable effect of improving the hearts and minds of men of different persuasions and degrees of understanding. For historical and some other passages are liable to the doubts and disputes of free-thinkers and anti-Christians, especially miraculous relations, which are not much less wonderful than the fabricated tales handed down to the natives of Asia, and consequently would be apt, at least, to carry little weight with them. On the contrary, moral doctrines, tending evidently to the maintenance of the peace and harmony of mankind at large, are beyond the reach of metaphysical perversions, and intelligible alike to the learned and the unlearned."[62]

Rammohan made several efforts to prevent the conversion of Hindus to Christianity. He tried to counteract the attack of the Christian missionaries, which continued unabated :

"If by the 'ray of intelligence' for which the Christian says, we are indebted to the English, he means the introduction of useful mechanical arts, I am ready to express my assent and also my gratitude, but with respect to science, literature or religion, I do not think that we are placed under any obligation. For by a reference to History it may be proved that the world was indebted to our ancestors for the first dawn of knowledge... Before the 'Christian' indulged in a tirade about persons being degraded by Asiatic inefficiency, he should have recollected that almost all the ancient prophets and patriarchs venerated by Christians, nay even Jesus Christ himself, a divine incarnation and the founder of the Christian faith, were Asiatics."[63]

Despite many shortcomings and weaknesses in their socio-religious system, the educated Hindus, under the leadership of

Brahmo Samaj, did not embrace Christianity, but tried to introduce reforms to purify Hinduism by getting rid of its crudities and reviving the pure stream of Hindu monotheism. This has been analysed as follows :

> "Men of the type of Rammohan Roy could not, and did not, shut their eyes to the superiority of Christianity from the ethical point of view. They despised in their hearts the idols, as worshipped by the vulgar; they saw through the pretensions of their priests and had long learnt to doubt the efficacies of their sacrifices. But their social institutions were so intimately interwoven with their religion that it required no small amount of moral courage openly to break with it, and to lose caste, that is, to become estranged from all relations, friends and acquaintances. But while they clearly perceived that their religion was behind the time, and, as a social institution, could not stand long against Christianity, they were by no means inclined to admit that from a philosophical point of view it was inferior to Christianity."[64]

During this period of India's history, there was assertion of strong national sentiment in the country and many Indian leaders had started pointing out the proud achievement of their ancestors. The Brahmo Samajists must have been aware, that they did not have any future in India, if they completely antagonised Indian traditions and preached the blind acceptance of alien socio-religious ideologies.

Debendranath Tagore (1817-1905), who succeeded Rammohan, as the leader of the Brahmo Samaj and introduced a high note of piety and spirituality in the life of the Samaj, had greater regards for the Hindu traditions and culture than his predecessor. He and his friend Akshay Kumar Datta, the editor of the Tatvabodhini Patrika, checked several cases of conversion of Hindus to Christianity.[65] When Debendranath heard that the graduates of the Mission School were being converted to Christianity, he started a free school for children, by collecting funds from the Hindus and due to this "the tide of Christian conversion was slimmed and the designs of the missionaries were knocked on the head."[66] In addition to this, the Tatvabodhini Patrika had proclaimed the Vedas as the basis of the faith of the Brahmo Samaj "as a set-off against the Bible of the Christians".[67] Debendranath sent four students to Banaras, with the avowed purpose of learning the four Vedas.

Debendranath asked the Brahmos to proceed with circumspection and not to be guided by too much enthusiasm for implementation and application of alien ideologies. He said it emphatically that the Brahmos were part of the great Hindu community. Though the Brahmos did not believe in image-worship they recognised, according to Debendranath, that those who could not yet grasp higher truth may tread the religious path through image-worship. He said :

> "We are worshippers of Brahma, the supreme Being. In this we are at one with Orthodox Hinduism, for all our Shastras declare with one voice the supremacy of the worship of Brahma, in joining image worship for the help of those who are incapable of grasping the highest Truth."[68]

Debendranath knew it better than Rammohan, that a revolutionary zeal for social or religious reform would defeat itself as it would produce severe form of counter reaction. He, therefore, advocated the path of gradualism :

> "We are in and of the great Hindu community and it devolves upon us by example and precept to hold up as a beacon the highest truth of the Hindu Shastras ... Why should we needlessly wound the feelings of our parents and elders by desecrating an image which they regard with the highest reverence, when all that our conscience can demand of us is to refrain from its adoration... The steering of this course is by no means an easy task ... Nevertheless, great as are the claims of our land and our people, we must never forget that we are Brahmos first, and Indians or Hindus afterwards. We must on no account depart from our vow of renouncing the worship of images and incarnations, which is of the essence of our religions ... Our Motherland is dear to us, but Religion is dearer, Brahman is dearest of all, dearer than

> son, dearer than riches, supreme over everything else."[69]

Debendranath was a very righteous person who gave great importance to self-respect. He did not seek any help or assistance from the foreign rulers, as he did not agree with most of their views regarding Indian affairs and by getting help from them, he would have been forced to compromise his own ideas and principles. Rajnarayan Bose writes : "Debendra Babu is usually unwilling to be acquainted with the Europeans because he cannot agree with them on.... Indian affairs. It is easy to get recognition in England and India by endorsing their views, but Debendra Babu is not anxious to get recognition from the British." Referring to Debendranath, the Principal of the Krishnanagar College, Mr. Lobb, once wrote : "The proud old man does not condescend to accept the praise of Europeans."

Keshab Chandra Sen (1838-84) was the next important leader of the Brahmo Samaj after Debendranath Tagore. The devotion of Keshab to Jesus was much more intense than that of Rammohan and he considered that in her fallen condition, India was destined to sit at the feet of England for many long years to learn Western art and science. He said :

> "England sits at the feet of hoary-headed India to study the ancient literature of this country. All Europe seems to be turning her attention in these days towards Indian antiquities, to gather the priceless treasures which lie buried in the literature of Vedism and Buddhism. Thus while we learn modern science from England, England learns ancient wisdom from India."[70]

Keshab Chandra Sen was one of the first leaders of modern India who felt that when the West could teach India science and practical arts, it must learn from India religion and spirituality. He pleaded for the harmonious blending of the ideas of the East and West for the "salvation of the world". Great Indian leaders like Vivekananda, Aurobindo, Rabindranath and many others supported this view of Keshab Chandra in later years. Like Keshab, in subsequent years Vivekananda gave the call to young Indians to act as missionaries of practical Vedanta and to conquer the world with Indian spirituality.

Although Keshab Chandra was a great admirer of Western

culture, science, practical arts and the ethical principles of Christianity and referred to the establishment of British rule in India as part of the design of providence, he was proud of his Indianness. He had great admiration for India's sages and rishis and the venerable devotees of ancient India who taught the eternal principles of "meditation, asceticism and loving communication with God." He made great impression on young minds in India. Referring to this B. C. Pal writes :

"By his victories over the Christian missionaries, Keshab's countrymen even outside his Church and community, felt a genuine pride, which powerfully fed their national conceit. Keshab's English visit and the way he was lionised by the British public and the British press, also reacted very powerfully upon the mind of his people in India. The old paralysing sense of superiority of their new political masters over them was visibly replaced by a new self confidence in our educated countrymen."[71]

Ideological Impact of the Brahmo Samaj

Organizationally the Brahmo Samaj was never strong and particularly its third schism proved disastrous for the organization. At the time of the formation of the Indian National Congress (1885), the Brahmo Samaj was not a big force at the institutional level. However, it made significant contributions in the realm of innovative ideas. Credit should be given to it for spreading the ideas of rationalism and enlightenment in modern India. Its cosmopolitan and universal appraoch towards religious questions, helped the growth and development of Western political doctrines in India. Arya Samaj, rejected dogmas and encouraged the spirit of toleration. It bridged the gulf between the learned few and rest of the people by attacking the despotic control of hereditary priesthood and access to Vedic knowledge only by the people of higher castes. The translation of the sacred books of the Hindus by Raja Rammohan Roy from Sanskrit to popular language, destroyed class-monopoly and caste-hierarchy in terms of scriptural learning and indirectly helped the growth of the democratic spirit. Through his multifarious organisations and emphasis on free-thinking and discussion, Rammohan had introduced into the Indian public life the practice of forming associations and holding debates. These ideas were clearly manifested in the political life of the country and it is noteworthy that many of the early leaders of the Congress were members of the Brahmo Samaj. It would not be an exaggeration to say, that Raja Rammohan Roy and the Brahmo Samaj founded by him, laid the foundation of a new political movement in the country. The Brahmo Samaj provided the inspiration for the formation of the Prarthana Samaj of Bombay Presidency in 1867. It was founded by Mahadev Govind Ranade, who was also an important leader of the Social Reform Conference in Bombay. The Prarthana Samaj advocated similar ideologies like the Brahmo Samaj and took great interest in the introduction of widow-remarriage, abolition of caste hierarchy, the encouragement of female education and the abolition of child marriage. It was also opposed to idolatry and advocated theistic spiritualism. It, however, did not insist on abandonment of caste and exclusion of idolatry as conditions of its membership. From this stand point the Prarthana Samaj was closer to Hinduism and the Hindu community than the Brahmo Samaj.

But despite its tremendous influence, the Brahmo Samaj could not take deep roots in the Indian soil because many ideas propounded by it were ahead of the times in India. In addition to this, it became a suspect in the eyes of the people due to its too much inclination towards Western ideas and ideologies. The Brahmo Samaj could not become successful like the Arya Samaj or the Ramakrishna Mission, which were revivalistic in approach and gave greater concessions to Indian traditions. But the new awareness created by the Brahmo Samaj regarding rationalism and humanism, remained the most predominant aspect of all later reform movements. Vivekananda was the true representative of this synthesis. He said : "Personally I take as much of the Vedas as agrees with reason. Part of the Vedas are apparently contradictory."[72]

Vivekananda's philosophy of humanism as opposed to religious formalism and ritualism is immensely manifested in the following lines :

> "If you seek your own salvation, you will go to hell. It is the salvation of others that you must seek and even if you have to go to hell in working for others, that is worth more than to gain heaven by seeking your own salvation... So long as the millions die in hunger and ignorance, I hold every man a traitor who, having been educated at their expense, pay not the least heed to them ... so long as even

> a single dog in my country is without food, my whole religion will be to feed it... Where should you go to seek for God? Are not all the poor, the miserable, the weak gods? Why not worship them first? Why go to dig a well on the shores of the Ganges? Let these people be your God— think of them, work for them, pray for them incessantly— the Lord will show you the way."[73]

Thus the Brahmo Samaj in its attempt to refashion religion and society on new lines based on humanism and rationalism, produced farreaching impacts on Indian socio-political and religious life which continue unabated even till to-day. Reformism or revivalism are no longer the subjects of debate. Rationalism and humanism have symbolised the spirit of the modern age and have become the hallmarks of socio-religious and political movements.

Footnotes

1. Other great leaders were Devendranath Thakur, Ishwar Chandra Gupta, Madhusudan Datta, Ishwar Chandra Vidyasagar (1820-1891), Ramkrishan Paramhansa, Vivekananda, Bankim Chandra Chatterjee (1833-1894), Rabindranath Tagore, and Aurobindo.
2. Quoted from M. A. Buch, Rise and Growth of Indian Liberalism, Vol. I, pp. 80-81.
3. Sophia Dobson Collet, *Life and Letters of Raja Rammohan Roy,* Calcutta (A. C. Sarkar & Co., 1913), p. 155.
4. The rationalistic school of Mutazila was founded by Wasil b. Ata and Amr. b. Ubaid in the 8th century A. D. at Basra. It believed in the strictest form of Monotheism, denied any resemblance between God and his creatures, and rejected avatarvad.
5. K. P. Karunakaran, *op. cit.,* p. 51.
6. Sankar Ghose, *op. cit.,* p. 14.
7. Ibid., *op. cit.,* pp. 14-15.
8. *The English Works of Raja Rammohan Roy* (ed.) J. C. Ghose, Vol. II, pp. 4-5.
9. Max Muller, *Biographical Essays,* London, 1884, p. 24.
10. The *English Works of Raja Rammohan Roy,* Vol. 1, pp. 115-'18.
11. C. H. Heimsath, *op. cit.,* pp. 10-11.
12. Sankar Ghose, *op. cit.,* p. 16.

13. C. H. Heimsath, *op. cit.*, p. 11.
14. Rammohan Roy, *English Works* (ed.) J. C. Ghose, pp. 929-'30.
15. R. P. Dua, *op. cit.*, p. 8.
16. Sankar Ghose, *op. cit.*, p. 18.
17. See the anti-Sati petition to the House of Commons, *The English Works of Raja Rammohan Roy*, Vol. 1., pp. 487-'88.
18. Quoted by Sankar Ghose, *op. cit.*, p. 15.
19. His important works are : (i) Tulifat-ul-Mawahhidin (1803), (ii) Vedantagrantha (1815), (iii) Vedantasara (1815, in Bengali), (iv) Kenopanishads (1816, in Bengali), (v) Isopanishads (1816, in Bengali), (vi) Kathopanishads (1817), (vii) Mandukyopanishad (1817, in Bengali), (viii) The Precepts of Jesus— The Guide to Peace and Happiness.
20. C. H. Heimsath, *op. cit.*, p. 12.
21. *Ibid.*
22. *Ibid., op. cit.*, p. 14.
23. *The English Works of Raja Rammohan Roy* (ed.), J. C. Ghose, Vol. 1, pp. 105-'18.
24. Biman Bihari Mazumdar *History of Indian Social and Political Ideas,* 1967, p. 22.
25. Saumyendra Nath Tagore, *Ram Mohan Roy — His Role in Indian Renaissance,* 1975, p. 9.
26. For details about Roy and Brahmo Samaj, see K. C. Vyas, *The Social Renaissance in India* (Vora & Co., Bombay, 1957), pp. 9-45; D. S. Sarma, *Hinduism Through the Ages,* (Bharatiya Vidya Bhavan, Bombay, 1956), pp. 65-83; K. M. Panikkar, *A Survey of Indian History* (Asia Publishing House, Bombay, 1954), p. 213 and Biman Bihari Mazumdar, *History of Indian Social and Political Ideas* (Bookland Pvt. Ltd., Calcutta, 1967), pp. 22-49 and 75-94.
27. Amales Tripathi, *The Extremist Challenge — India between 1890 and 1910* (Calcutta, 1967), p. vii.
28. *The English Works of Raja Rammohan Roy,* Vol. III, Part II, p. 148.
29. Quoted by R. P. Dua, *op. cit.* f. n. 1, p. 14.
30. K. P. Karunakaran, *op. cit.*, p. 89.
31. Quoted by the Rammohan Roy Centenary Committee in, "*The Father of Modern India*", Rammohan Roy Commemoration Volume, Calcutta, 1935, p. 89.
32. *Ibid.*, p. 353.
33. It was well summed up by de Reincourt as follows : "Rammohan Roy's fantastic knowledge and amazing life symbolized this very synthesis for which he laboured all his life; steeped in both Hindu & Muslim cultures, fluent in Arabic, Persian, Sanskrit, English, Hebrew, Greek expelled for a time by caste and family having lived for years thereafter in Benaras and Tibet, he finally returned home in 1796

and set about his life's work. Campaigning tirelessly against the monstrous distortions which centuries of sloth, corruption and inertia had inflicted on Hinduism, he tackled every social, political and cultural problem of his time."

34. Charles H. Heimsath, *op. cit.,* p. 11.
35. C. H. Heimsath, *op. cit.,* p. 6.
36. *Ibid.,* pp. 6-7.
37. C. H. Heimsath, *op. cit.,* p. 7.
38. *Ibid.,* pp. 10-11.
39. Romain Rolland, *Prophets of New India,* (London, 1930) p. 70.
40. William Theodore de Bury and Others, *Sources of Indian Tradition,* New York, 1958, p. 575.
41. He wrote with a firmness comparable to Dayananda Saraswati, in denying the doctrine of Maya, or illusion. "This universe is not dream-stuff, neither is it a mental illusion, but it exists in reality". Autobiography, pp. 175-176.
42. C. H. Heimsath, *op. cit.,* p. 78.
43. B. Majumdar, *op. cit.,* pp. 137-139.
44. Sankar Ghose, *op. cit.,* pp. 22-23.
45. The Autobiography of Debendranath Tagore, 1909, p. 152.
46. *Ibid.*
47. Keshab Chandra always favoured those who regarded him as the divinely commissioned leader of the movement. J. N. Farquhar, *Modern Religious Movements in India*, MacMillan & Co., New York, p. 50.
48. See Keshab's letter of 16 May 1881 to Max Muller, F. Max Muller, *Biographical Essays*, London, 1884, p. 117.
49. Amales Tripathi, *The Extremist Challenge,* p. ix.
50. According to Keshab any one who accepted the 'New Dispensation' should say : "The Lord Jesus is my will, Socrates my head, Chaitanya my heart, the Hindu Rishi is my soul, and the Philanthropic Howard my right hand." — Lecture in Jan. 1881, Keshab Chandra Sen's Lectures in India, London, 1901, p. 491.
51. As cited by Farquhar in *Modern Religious Movements in India,* p. 52. Sastri, it should be noted, led the criticism at the time of Sen's declining interest in social reform. P. C. Mazoomdar, Sen's chief disciple and successor, denied Sen's loss of interest in social reform in his 'Faith and Progress of Brahmo Samaj', pp. 325-326.
52. V. P. Varma, *Modern Indian Political Thought,* p. 29.
53. M. M. Ahluwalia : *Swamy Dayananda Saraswati,* p. 6.
54. Quoted by C. H. Heimsath, *Indian Nationalism and Hindu Social Reform,* p. 13.
55. Girija K. Mookerjee, *History of Indian National Congress* (1832-1947), p. 13.

56. *Ibid.*
57. R. Rolland, *Life of Ramkrishna,* p. 139.
58. Kenneth W. Jones, *Arya Dharm-Hindu Consciousness in 19th Century Punjab,* p. 43.
59. K. P. Karunakaran, *op. cit.,* p. 46.
60. Editorial in Brahmo Public Opinion (Calcutta), Vol. 1, No. 10, 23rd May, 1878.
61. K. P. Karunakaran, *op. cit.,* p. 50.
62. Raja Rammohan Roy, His Life and Teachings, p. 15.
63. Wm. Theodore de Bary and Others, *Sources of Indian Tradition* (New York, 1958), n. 5, p. 518.
64. Max Muller, *Rammohan to Ramakrishna,* (Calcutta, 1952), p. 59.
65. Autobiography of Maharshi Debendranath Tagore (tr. from the original Bengali by S. Tagore and Indira Devi, London, 1914), pp. 98-99.
66. *Ibid.,* pp. 3-9.
67. Pandit S. N. Sastri, *The Brahmo Samaj, A Statement of its Religious Principles and Brief History,* p. 33.
68. The Autobiography of Debendranath Tagore, 1909, p. 152.
69. *Ibid.,* p. 153.
70. Quoted by Wm. Theodore de Bary and Others, Sources of Indian Tradition, p. 619.
71. Bipin Chandra Pal, *Story of my Life and Times,* (Calcutta, 1932), p. 229.
72. The Complete Works of Swami Vivekananda, Vol. IV, n. 16, p. 3.
73. Swami Pavitrananda, *A Short Life of Swami Vivekananda* (Almora, 1943), p. 113.

3

Raja Rammohan : A Study of his Socio-Religious Concepts

Social revolt against established traditions and customs of India became markedly prominent with the emergence of Rammohan Roy in the early 19th century. His thought and writings influenced the younger generation of his time.[1] He was the first modern man to rise above current beliefs and prejudices and extend his vision to a distant horizon, far beyond the general conception of time.[2]

Rammohan Roy found "Hindus in general more superstitious and miserable, both in performance of their religious rites, and in their domestic concerns, than the rest of the known nations on the earth".[3] They were "with few exceptions, immersed in gross idolatry, and in belief of the most extravagant descriptions respecting futurity, antiquity and the miracles of their deities and saints."[4]

He found that the great majority of Hindus accepted the literal teachings of idolatrous Brahmins, and "therefore, continue, under the form of religious devotion, to practice a system which destroys, to the utmost degree, the natural texture of society and prescribes crimes of the most heinous nature".[5] Social advancement, Rammohan believed, depended upon reformation of religious beliefs and practices.[6]

He held a vision of an Indian society ultimately renovated by centuries of exposure to Western science and Christian morality.[7] The Raja rested his social reform doctrines on the premises of humanitarianism and spiritual equality of people. Western ideas of individualism, natural rights, the ethical duties of an individual to society at large, the possibility of human progress, "social efficiency", and the religious doctrine of acquiring merit through good work[8] — all constituted the doctrinal bases of modern social reform movements as initiated by Raja Rammohan Roy. The very core of Rammohan's social philosophy was "Lokasreya" or the good of people.

Campaign against Sati :

The campaign against 'Sati' became the major preoccupation with the Raja in his social reform crusade. The practice of 'Sati' meant the custom of widow burning. Often a woman was forced to commit the act of self-immolation on the funeral pyre of her dead husband, in order to become a 'Sati'. Before Rammohan Roy took up the campaign against 'Sati' publicly in 1818, the government had been under pressure for years from Christian Missionaries, to use its authority to stop the evil practice. Little was however, done by the government till 1813 beyond expressing horror at the gruesome practice. The government refrained from stopping the practice by legislation in pursuance of its adopted policy of non-interference with Indian religious practices. Only laws were passed in 1812, 1815 and 1817 with a view to checking the evil of 'Sati'.

Roy's vigorous and active condemnation of the rite based on Hindu Shastras as well as on appeals to humanitarian and natural right doctrines, began to appear in 1818, with his public opposition to the petition of orthodox Hindus which urged the removal of restrictions on the practice of 'Sati' under the regulations. In a counter petition Rammohan after describing the evils of the practice vividly stated that, "All these instances.... are murder according to every Shastra, as well as to the common sense of all nations, as well as to your Lordship's Government."

Rammohan published his first tract in 1818 refuting the sanction of Shastras behind this practice. He pointed out that though 'Sati' had been permitted by some of the ancient Smritis and Puranas, Manu, the greatest law-giver of Hindus, had recommended an ascetic life for the widows in preference to self-immolation.[9] Through his tracts, Rammohan tried to educate the opinion of the people of Bengal against the practice of 'Sati'. The root of this pernicious practice lay in the fear that a widow would become immoral if she were allowed to survive her husband. Rammohan viewed such a fear as unreal and imaginary. He argued that such a fear might be removed by educating women and by instilling in their hearts the fear of God.[10] Similar views were expressed by Mritinjay Vidyalankar against the practice of 'Sati' before Rammohan. But it was Rammohan who launched for the first time an organized movement of resistance against this ghastly practice.

It was with Rammohan taking up vigorously the cause of abolishing completely the heinous practice through his journal, 'Samvada Kaumudi', that the Government of Lord Hastings was compelled to recognise its importance. Finally, Lord William Bentinck, determined to ban the practice, thought of suppressing it through legislation. When Rammohan was consulted with on this matter, his suggestion was to abolish the practice "quietly and unobservedly".

Rammohan's cautious policy had been mistaken by some scholars as his denial of the right of a foreign government to interfere in the social reform of the Hindus.[11]

Dr. R. C. Mazumdar compares his attitude with that of Tilak with regard to the Age of Consent Bill.[12] Dr. Mazumdar observes, "People who blamed him (Tilak) hardly realised that Tilak merely continued his traditions of Rammohan Roy, the pioneer of Social Reforms, followed by many Hindu leaders through out the century."[13] This comparison is, however, a half truth. It was Rammohan who played a crucial part in contending the opposition of orthodox Hindus to the legislation of 1829. He extended full support to the government. "Tilak carried on a vigorous propaganda against the Age of Consent Bill even after its enactment, whereas submitted to the House of Lords a petition in favour of the regulation in July, 1931."[14] Rammohan's strong stand against the Orthodox Hindus provided moral support and courage to Lord William Bentinck to come up with a legislation to stop the practice of 'Sati'.

Advocacy of the Rights of Women

He was the earliest champion of the rights of women.[15] He wrote a book entitled, "Brief Remarks Regarding Modern Encroachments on the Ancient Rights of Females According to the Hindu Law of Inheritance." He pleaded for the older and more liberal views of ancient lawgivers which gave daughters the right to possess one-fourth part of the portion which a son could inherit. The Hindu Code framed in Independent India is the logical fulfilment of the work commenced by Rammohan.[16]

He was opposed to polygamy, kulinism and the practice of selling girls in the garb of marriage.

The question of widow-marriage, which in the following years received much attention from the social reformers like Iswara Chandra Vidyasagar did not get support from Rammohan Roy.

The Saiva[17] form of marriage advocated by him, however, aimed at facilitating widow-remarriage, inter-caste and inter-racial marriages. But his plan was not acceptable to the people.

Rammohan was convinced that women constituted a substantial part of the society both numerically and qualitatively and any discrimination against them would be harmful to the social interest. Apart from being a religious reform movement, the Brahmo Samaj, under the stewardship of Raja Rammohan Roy, accepted the objective of social reform, in which elevation of the status of the Hindu women got top most priority. Under Rammohan's leadership the Samaj launched a vigorous attack against the evils of Hindu society relating to discrimination against women, which were practised in the name of religion and social custom. Such programmes of the Samaj for the elevation of the status of the women, were highly acclaimed by a large number of educated people in Bengal and other parts of India.

Rammohan Roy identified some evil social practices among the Hindus like burning of widows, selling of female children, female infanticide, polygamy and such other evils, which were responsible for the suffering of women and their inferior status in the society. He wanted to root out these evil practices from the Hindu society, which were practised in the name of religious sanctions. In 1811, his brother Jagmohan Roy died and the widow was forcibly burnt alive. This was a rude shock to Rammohan and he took a vow not to rest till this obnoxious custom was totally banned.

He started a vigorous campaign in support of the rights of women and cited examples from the Vedas, Upanishads and the Bhagavadgita. He pointed out that Hindu Shastras only prescribed pure and pious life for the widow and no Dharma Shastra has ever given the sanction for burning of the widows. Despite stiff opposition from the 'Dharmasabha' he succeeded in mobilising public opinion against the heinous practice of 'Sati' and other discriminatory practices against women.

Rammohan was convinced that the most important cause for the miserable condition of Hindu women, was the practice of polygamy, particularly among the rich people.[18] The victims of polygamy were left only with three alternatives, namely, to burn themselves to death, or to lead an immoral life, or to suffer the misery and insult in the home of the deceased husband. Most of the victims of polygamy opted for the first alternative. Rammohan condemned polygamy and categorically stated that there was no scriptural sanction for this practice. As a humanist and a great feminist, he argued emphatically, that the human race cannot march forward if the women were forced to remain in a degraded condition. He abhorred the false religious sanctity attached to social evils and attributed these to the evil designs of opportunist self-seekers. He pointed out that all social problems pertaining to inequality of women owed their origin to selfish and inhuman practices by men and humane solutions must be provided for these problems. If this was not done, the Hindu society would ultimately disintegrate. Rammohan was the first Indian, who noticed the disintegrating elements in the evil social practices of the Hindu society and he tried his best to fight against these evil practices.

As child-marriage was detrimental to the interest of women, Rammohan was opposed to child-marriage. He questioned the religious sanction for the practice of Sati, and advocated for the remarriage of the widows. He vigorously fought for equal rights of man and woman. While championing the rights of women, he maintained that neither Hindu religion nor the ancient history of the country justified the continuation of these social evils.

Referring to the evil consequences of child marriage C. Y. Chintamani makes the following observation :

"Thus throughout the whole society the spectacle is presented of boys of 17 and 18 and girls of 13 and 14 entering upon married life and subjected to all its responsibilities. Little children of 14 becoming mothers is a very common sight... The general deterioration in physique universally noticeable is justly attributed to this baneful custom, the greatest sufferers being the poor girls who enter upon maternity before their bodies are properly developed. The progeny of such parents cannot be otherwise than weak and sickly. Equally harmful to the individuals concerned and to the country generally, is the interference with education and the crushing out of all spirit of enterprise."[19]

Under the banner of the Brahmo Samaj agitation was launched to raise the marriage of girls to higher age and to make the conducting of any marriage below that age a legal offence. This agitation constituted an important phase and the Indian social reformers had to organise a continuous movement for the achievement of this objective.

Rammohan Roy and the other social reformers advocated reforms in this field mainly on the following lines :

"Option of marriage to be allowed to women in the same way as the men. No girl to be married before 18 or at the earliest 16. No man to be married till he is at least 20, and in no case till he is able to maintain himself and his family. Abolition of customs which bring about unnecessary expenditure on occasions of marriage. Removal of the religious and social prohibition against the marriage of a widow and the recognition of her claim to be socially treated in the same was as any other married woman of her caste."[20]

The movement started by Raja Rammohan for the enancipation of women was given great support by Iswara Chandra Vidyasagar (1820-1891). He was the most outstanding reformer who raised his voice against the evil customs like child-marriage and the prohibition of the marriage of widows. Realising the importance of education of women, he organised a total of thirty-four girls' schools and twenty model schools in four districts of Bengal. Professor D. K. Karve was another important figure, who tried to spread education among the girls and promote widow remarriage. The Indian Women's University founded in 1916, was the culmination of his successful work in this field.

The social reformers who championed the cause of women had to face stiff resistance from many quarters. This has been described by A. R. Desai as follows :

"In the pre-British Indian society, except perhaps in the early periods of the Vedic times, woman was assigned a position subordinate to man. Law and religion did not recognise the equality and equal rights of man and woman. Society permitted to have rights and freedom from which woman was excluded. Different standards were adopted to judge the individual and social conduct of man and woman."[21]

Rammohan Roy and the other reformers, rendered a great service to the social reforms movement, at least in the realm of ideas, by challenging the assumptions on which the society was then based. By their vigorous and continuous efforts, they created an atmosphere conducive for the emancipation of women and the raising of their status.[22] It has been rightly observed that :

"The Brahmo Samaj movement as a whole, beginning with

Rammohan Roy, can be credited with establishing a major objective of all Indian social reform movements, the social freedom and cultural advancement of Hindu women."[23]

Rammohan's Views Against Caste System

Social reform in India, did not ordinarily mean, a reorganization of the structure of society, as was the case in the West. In India the social structure has been maintained in tact, although there has been infusion of new ideas and new ways of life, with a view to preserve the society, while its members are being transformed. Rammohan was the first Indian social reformer who tried to change the social structure for the purpose of giving benefits to the under-priviledged social classes. "By the beginning of the 20th century some reformers, stimulated by the ideas of a truly national awakening, were advocating the uplift of lower castes and outcasts and were repudiating the caste structure of society itself. The introduction of these ideas into the programme of the Hindu social reformers was a significant shift away from the earlier pre-occupation with the advancement of individuals or restricted groups. The ideas of uplift and rehabilitation, when translated into practical action, often produced programs of a social service nature, and among Indians it was the social reformers who were chiefly responsible for inaugurating the social-service movement."[24]

However, it may be admitted that although Rammohan Roy and many of his followers criticized the caste system and caste hierarchy among the Hindus, they did not result in any direct action comparable to the crusades for widow remarriage or even inter-caste dining. No doubt, they regarded the caste system as the main cause of India's social ills, but they failed to suggest practical ways for eliminating this evil practice from the Hindu society.

The Indian caste system provided for a highly stratified society, which went against the spirit of democracy and social equality. In the opinion of one of the 19th century reformers : "Not only is caste the express badge of Hinduism, its stronghold and the perpetuator of status and functions both by inheritance and endogamy, but at the root of that loss of catholic sympathy and originality in action which are not painfully noticeable in Hindu society."[25] The caste system created hatred and illwill and played a disintegrating role in the Hindu society. It has also many other undesirable elements :

"The caste system was undemocratic and authoritarian in the extreme. The castes constituting the series were hierarchically graded, each caste being considered inferior to those below it. The status of a man born in a particular caste was determined by the rank of that caste in this hierarchy. Once born in that caste, his status was predetermined and immutable. Thus birth decided his status which could not be altered by any talent he might show or wealth he might accumulate."[26]

Raja Rammohan Roy attacked the arbitrary and anti-democratic character of the Indian caste system and exposed its various defects. He pointed out that the caste system not only perpetuated inequality, but also made inheritance the basis of that inequality. Rammohan expressed in clear-cut terms that caste system was a hindrance to the achievement of national unity and progress of the Hindu community

The most dangerous aspect of the Hindu Caste system was the segregation of the lower castes as untouchables. These untouchables were denied the elementary rights of entering into Hindu public temples and using public wells and tanks and in some cases even public roads. It was the common belief of some sections of people that the physical touch of these low-caste people, would contaminate the high-caste Hindu. The untouchables were required not to come within a particular distance of the high-caste people lest their shadows may fall upon the latter and contaminate them. This practice was most inhuman and the human beings were treated in a manner worse than the beasts. Rammohan Roy fought boldly and vigorously for the abolition of the caste system.

Rammohan was highly critical of the predominance of the priestly class over all social norms and codes of conduct. He alleged that this was possible only due to the impact of false religion. Caste system was one of the predominant reasons for hastening the decline of the Hindu society during the past three thousand years or so. Referring to this aspect of decline of the Hindu society, Ranade said :

"These ideas may be briefly setforth as isolation, submission to outward force or power more than to the voice of inward conscience, perception of fictitious differences between men and men due to heredity and birth, passive acquiescence in civil wrong-doing and a general indifference to secular well-being, almost bordering on fatalism."[27]

Ramakrishna Gopal Bhandarkar (1837-1925) and Narayan Ganesh Chandavarkar (1855-1923) and Mahadev Govind Ranade (1842-1901) followed the footsteps of Rammohan Roy and joined the mainstream of national social reform movement in Bombay. All of them were also highly critical of the Indian caste system like Raja Rammohan Roy. Bhandarkar pointed out that the caste system was the root of all India's ills. Chandavarkar went a step ahead and observed that caste even in its Vedic form was a formula for social disruption, weakness and immorality. "Thorough and reasoned denunciations of the caste system and appeals for the uplift of low castes and outcasts were added to the enumerations of India's social ills by most reformers towards the end of the century."

Rammohan questioned the exclusive right of the Brahmins to scriptural knowledge. The study of the Vedas was considered to be the monopoly of the Brahmins or the priestly class. The Vedanta, written by Vyas, about two thousand years ago, was a complete and compendious abstract of the whole system of Vedic knowledge. An attempt was made to reconcile all the texts, some of which were conflicting with each other. It continued to be the most revered book of the Hindus which was always referred to as of equal authority. Rammohan was critical of the Brahmins who did not allow others to touch this book. He pointed out that although the Brahmins frequently quoted this book and exercised the monopoly of interpreting it, "the practice of few Hindus indeed bears the least accordance with its precepts."[28]

Protest against other Social Evils

Social reformers during the early part of the 19th century criticized the joint family system as it hindered individual initiative and freedom. They argued that the Joint-family system by imposing heavy burden on the most capable member of family, denied him the full scope for the elevation and expansion of his personality.[29]

Rammohan who was the champion of individual liberty and freedom was also critical of the despotic stranglehold of the Joint-family system over the individual.

Another social custom against which Rammohan raised his voice, was the prohibition of foreign travel by high-caste Hindus. The people who were guilty of violating this custom were often bycotted by other members of their community. They were excomunicated from the religion by the priests and were forced to lead an isolated and miserable life. Rammohan Roy realised that the prohibitions against the crossing of the seas has serious repercussions on other aspects of social life. He himself violated this custom and went to England. In crossing "the black waters" to go to England, Rammohan defied one of the prevalent taboos of Hindu society against crossing the seas. In fighting against this social custom, Rammohan tried to "remove all hindrances to individual initiative and widen the horizon of Indian people in the realm of ideas and actions."[30] Later on Swami Vivekananda took up this cause and advocated the removal of obstacles in the way of travel by Indians to other countries.

It may be pointed out that most of the ideas of social reform advocated by Raja Rammohan Roy, were vigorously championed by the Social Reform Conference, which covered the following subjects of social reform :

"(1) The reduction of birth, marriage, death and other expenses according to means;
(2) The gradual raising of the marriageable age;
(3) The remarriage of child-widows;
(4) The removal of social disabilities attending sea voyages to foreign countries;
(5) The prevention of the disfigurement of child-widows prevailing in certain parts of India;
(6) Inter-marriage between members of the sub-castes;
(7) The discouragement of unequal marriages;
(8) The disapproval of the custom of exacting money in consideration of the gift of girls in marriage;
(9) The discouragement of polygamy;
(10) The appointment of Panchayats to settle religious disputes between Hindus and Muslims and advising the Panchayats to promote friendly feeling;
(11) The promotion of higher female education;
(12) The education and amelioration of the pariahs and other outcasts;
(13) Widow remarriage, protection of widows and the training of

widows in useful work;

(14) The abolition of castes;

(15) The recommendation of inter-caste marriage".[31]

Rammohan's Religious Reform Movement

Rammohan was the first modern Indian to raise the voice of protest against the prevalent Hindu religious practices and doctrines, which were injurious both to the social living of the people as well as to their growth of individuality. His greatest religious reform crusade was directed against the Hindu belief in a multiplicity of Gods and the worship of their images. He preached the concept of monotheistic spiritualism.

Rammohan was the first consmopolitan religious thinker of modern India. He accepted eternal principles from all religions and wanted to fuse them into one integrated whole for the welfare of the humanity. He "perceived that the universal truth was stressed in different ways, and different accents in its different historic utterances. The Vedantas, which had restored him to faith, he always considered as strongest in Jnana, the knowledge of the unity of all souls and of the world in Brahma; Islam, which had given him his early iconoclastic zeal, he considered as strongest in the sense of divine government, and a militant of man with man; and Christianity, which gave him the Divine Exemplar, he considered as strongest in the ethical and social guidance to peace and happiness in the path of life."[32]

Rammohan made extensive study on theology and religion, but he did not start a new religion. He developed a cosmopolitan and universal outlook towards religion. His Brahmo Samaj made direct attacks against the evils of Hinduism.

The Trust Deed of the Brahmo Samaj embodied the following important provisions : (a) the Samaj would be a place of public meeting for all persons without any distinction of caste and creed for the worship of Brahmo — the Supreme Immortal Soul from whom all human souls originated and rejoined after death; (b) no sacrifice or religious rituals to be permitted on the Samaj or the Samaj buildings; (c) no form of idol, image, status, painting or portrait was to be admitted within the Samaj buildings.[33] He deplored the futility of Brahmanical rites and opposed the unquestionable authority of prietsts and Hindu sastras. He was of opinion that religion and divine worship were personal matters of an individual unjustly controlled by priests. Idolatry was against shastras, ethics and social wellbeing. He asserted that God was omnipresent and are Supreme Being."[34]

Rammohan was particularly influenced by the ethics of Christianity. He found the doctrines of Christ more conducive to moral principles and better adapted for the use of rational beings than any other religion.[35]

Rammohan gave the concept of a universal religion based on monotheism. His announced purpose was to restore the Hindu faith to its original purity.[36] He launched a formidable onslaught against the prevalent religious bigotry and perversions and wanted to rejoin Hinduism with its original classical concepts of monotheism of Upanishadic teachings.

While preaching these new doctrines based on reason and the principles of scientific test, Rammohan tried to inaugurate the Indian Renaissance in the true sense of the term. Some scholars draw a comparison between the European Renaissance and the Indian Renaissance inaugurated by Raja Rammohan Roy and point out that since all the features of the European Renaissance were not present in the movement started by Rammohan, it could not be properly called as the Indian Renaissance. This argument is not convincing enough as there is no historical logic according to which movements in different countries could be based on identical principles or motive factors. The resurgent movement that took place in India under the leadership of Rammohan Roy, in order to be considered by the historians as a Renaissance, need not be an exact copy of the European Renaissance. The attitude of the scholars and writers who refuse credit to Rammohan for initiating the Indian Renaissance, is not only unhistorical but also extremely illogical.

It may be pointed out that the Renaissance was started in Europe in the 15th century, whereas the Indian movement was started in the 19th century, as many new forces and factors had come into play during these centuries. In this context one should also take into account the differences in the historical developments in Europe and India. But inspite of these differences, there were striking similarities between the European Renaissance and its Indian counterpart.

The Renaissance, initiated by Rammohan was a many sided movement and like its European counterpart, it was a revolt against medievalism in every aspect of our life. It was a crusade for the supremacy of reason over dogmatic worship of authority, but it did not mean the total rejection of the Hindu Shastras. Rammoahn insisted on the fresh evaluation of the Hindu Shastras in the right of human reason and basic principles of truth and enlightenment. He was vehemently opposed to the pseudo-religious Puranic cults and dogmas, which had crept into Hinduism in much later periods of its history. He also rendered a great service to Hinduism by translating the original Sanskrit work into Bengali and English and making them available for the Indians who did not know Sanskrit to have access to the sacred texts and scriptures. He gave prime importance to feelings and emotions of the individual and tried to make him free from the tyranny of rigid socio-religious regulations mostly based upon obscurantist and outdated ideas. He rejected asceticism as the only means of realizing God and emphasized the need for fundamental human virtues. Man's intellectual freedom was uppermost in his mind. The Renaissance of Rammohan was aimed at raising a revolt against social oppression and tyranny. Rammohan was convinced that social oppression and tyranny were more dangerous and debasing than political tyranny of a dictatorial regime.

Rammohan tried to make a synthesis of the fundamental principles of the three world religions— Hinduism, Islam and Christianity with a view to avoid most of the ill-feelings among the people based on diversity of religion. He also extended unqualified support to democratic struggles, for freedom of the oppressed people all over the world. It was not possible on the part of the leaders of the European Renaissance in the 15th century to think in terms of such innovative and liberal principles. It may thus be emphasized that, the Indian Renaissance of Rammohan Roy, truly served the historical need of the epoch.

Rammohan had great confidence on the innate faculty exisiting in the nature of mankind, which makes an enquiry into the nature of the principles of religious doctrines with a sense of impartiality and justice, before accepting such religious principles. Further, he is also confident that man will be able to distinguish the truth from the untruth, and would ultimately turn to 'One Supreme Being', who is the foundation of the harmonious organisation of the universe.

Rammohan was against blind belief and inability to enquire

into the cause and effect of a particular phenomenon. He emphatically argued that worshipping a tree, bathing in a river or purchasing forgiveness from the high priest could not lead to purification from sins and ultimate salvation. The incapacity of the man to enquire into the sequence between the cause and effect, according to him, was the result of such blind belief. He was of the opinion that such beliefs had come to be held by the people through the influence of habit and custom. He argued that these imaginary things had no real effect and had there been any truth in these things, then they must have been common to all nations of different persuasions and should not have been confined to one particular nation's belief and habit.

He also rejected the dogma of supernatural powers and miracles. He argued that in this world, the existence of everything depended upon certain causes and conditions. Things were mutually related to one another by a sequent relation of cause and effect. If the remote causes are taken into consideration, we might see that in the existence of any one thing in nature, the whole universe was connected.

Rammohan insisted upon the cultivation of inductive reasoning with the help of which, people can safeguard themselves against being deceived by supernatural activities. In every such case of supernatural activity, the man should depend on his own intention and question whether it was compatible with reason to be convinced of one's own inability to understand, the cause or attribute it to some impossible agency, inconsistent with the law of nature.

Rammohan refuted the argument that the Omnipotent Creator, who had brought the whole universe into existence from absolute non-entity, could unite life with the body of the dead a second time or could give the earthly bodies the property of light. According to Rammohan this did not prove anything beyond the fact that there was a probability of occurrence of such things but it did not prove the power of miracle of ancient religious leaders or the doctors of religion. In his own words : "It is an admitted fact that the creator has no power to create impossible things; for instance, co-partnership with God or non-existence of God or existence of two contradictories."

He was of the opinion that the traditions which produced positive belief must be distinguished from the traditions blindly followed by adherants of a particular religion. As contradictions are noticed in the affirmation and negation of prophecy and other good attributes of the leaders of different religions, while the truth of the traditions are taken for granted, it would also amount to admission of the contradictions.

He rejected the necessity of the instrumentality of the prophets. He argued that prophecy had nothing to do with God and was created by an intermediate agency for the purpose of its own benefit. The advent of prophets and revelations like other things in nature depended upon external causes without reference to God. He rejected the commonly accepted belief that God's guidance would be made known through the medium of prophecy. The same people who argued that the prophets are sent by God to give guidance to mortal beings, they also believed that the existence of all things in God's creation, whether good or bad, was directly connected with the great creator without any intermediary agency. He argued that the people should try to find out revelation to them from God were immediately from God or through intermediate agency.

Rammohan was opposed to sectarian dogmatism in religion. He defined a sectarian dogmatist as one who was ready to refute the creeds of others owing to disagreement with them regarding the true meaning of the sayings of their predecessors, who like other men were liable to commit mistakes. He states his views in the following words :

"Happy is the state of those persons who are able to discriminate between the conditions which are found in individuals owing to habit and frequent association, and those intrinsic qualities which are the results of the cravings of nature in species and individuals, and try their utmost to make an enquiry to the truth and falsehoood of the different principles of religion held by different people, unbiased in favour of anyone, and scrutinize even those propositions which are admitted by all without looking into the position of those persons by whom they have been asserted."

In order to project the inner meaning of classical Hinduism and to make it free from the evil impacts of ritualistic idolatrous Brahminism, Rammohan prescribed the methodology of Mimangsa School of Philosophy. According to this School for arriving at truth one should start with a particular sloka of a Shastra, challenge its validity, re-examine it, and then arrive at a conclusion. According to Rammohan, ultimate authority in the sphere of religion should not be attributed to the scriptures. Man's own consciousness alone can bring him the highest realization, it cannot be based upon supernatural or metaphysical foundations.

According to the Upanishads the Brahma can be realized by means of the senses, the mind and the intellect. There is no reference to supernatural character of Brahmatattwa and that it can be realized by the authority of the Shastras. The Vedanta also gives a highly realistic interpretation of the realisation of the Absolute which is inseparably connected with human experiences of birth, life and destruction. To establish the truth of his statement on the basis of scriptural sanction Rammohan always quoted the famous sloka of Brihaspati :

"Kevalam Sastramashritya Na
Kartavyo Arthamirnaya
Buddhineena Vicharena
Dharmahamih Prajayate".[37]

Rammohan accepted the Brahma Sutra as the Vedanta. The Upanishads are in reality the real Vedanta. The validity of the teachings of the Upanishads was also corroborated by the Gita. The great Vedavyasa discussed all the mantras of the Upanishads, and wrote 555 Sutras based on the mantras, and upheld their validity by rational explanations. This collection of Sutras is known as the Brahma Sutra and is also known as the Naya Prasthava of the Vedanta. The Commentary that Shankara wrote on the Brahma Sutra is generally known as the Vedanta. Rammohan had also accepted the Brahma Sutra as the Vedanta. Rammohan translated all the Hindu classical scriptures into Bengali and English with the object of convincing the Indians about the true meaning of these sacred books and thereby enable them "to contemplate with true devotion the unity and omnipresence of God."

The spirit of reform in the first half of the 19th century was grounded in the consciousness of Rammohan and his followers who had come in contact with the Western civilization and desired to leave the society from the abyss of superstition, obscurantism and stagnation. This was thought to be necessary to make their society and people enjoy the benefits of social advancement similar to the Western model. For this purpose the early social reformers, like Rammohan Roy and others, were eager to draw upon the sources of Western ideas and thoughts. They used the pattern of Western education as a convenient tool to broaden the individual's social outlook and to sow the seeds of rationalism.

Rammohan was vehemently opposed to every form of social inequality and oppression in the Bengali society of his time. As described by Dr. Brajendranath Seal, Rammohan held that "individual progress is the touchstone and the measuring rod of social progress, but the individual progress could be secured only by organising and establishing the condition of social progress." Rammohan believed that all law and social regulations should aim at promoting the welfare of the people. Thus the humanistic concept of 'Lokasreya' was the guiding principle which governed all efforts of Rammohan Roy for reform — social, political and economic.

It is stated against Rammohan that before his agitation against the practice of Sati, steps had already been taken in this direction by the British and hence undue credit in this respect should not be given to him. Raja Rammohan had been conducting his tearing campaign against this evil practice, before Lord William Bentinck assumed this office. Bentinck consulted the Raja in this matter as he knew his (Raja's) endeavours in this direction. In the words of Bentinck, "It must be acknowledged that a similar opinion as to the probable excitation of deep distrust of our future intention was mentioned to me in conversation by the enlightened Native, Rammohan Roy, a warm advocate for the abolition of Sati and of all other superstitions and corruptions engulfing the Hindu religion...". Rammohan's opposition to stringent regulations to stop the practice of Sati was based on his belief that this should come directly from the people through a process of enlightenment and not through coersion by the government. This attitude was fundamentally in consonance with the concept of 'Lokasreya', the welfare of the people.

It would be a travesty of truth to say that there existed a movement against the practice of Sati before Rammohan started his campaign in 1818. When the orthodox party tried to appeal Bentinck for the abolition of the Regulation, preventing the practice of Sati, Rammohan started a vigorous campaign in favour of the Regulation. He himself led a deputation to Bentinck and presented him with a congratulatory message, written by him which was read out by Munshi Kalinath Roy.

The leaders of the 'Dharma Sabha' decided to carry the appeal to England and for that purpose engaged an attorney of the Calcutta Supreme Court for a fee of Rs. 50,000. Rammohan went to England and filed a counter petition against the move of the orthodox party to get the anti-Sati Regulation cancelled. On his arrival at London Rammohan presented his petition to the House of Lords. In July, 1832, the hearing of the appeal of the 'Dharma Sabha' took place before the Privy Council and after due hearing the appeal was rejected. This incident also reveals the commitment of the Raja to the cause of social reform in general and the abolition of the practice of Sati in particular.

The Bengal Harkara, trying to assess the role of Rammohan Roy in the agitation against the practice of Sati, in an editorial stated :

"Let us not, therefore, offer our exclusive praise and gratitude either to Rammohan Roy or Lord Wiliam Bentinck. The former would never have succeeded in his patriotic and enlightened labours without the co-operation of the latter, nor would Lord Bentinck have ventured on so desirable a measure, if the minds of the Natives had not been prepared to abandon the worst of superstitions by the unwearied labours of their distinguished countrymen."

This was a reasonable and a fair assessment of the contributions of Raja Rammohan Roy to the socio-religious reform movement of the 19th century in India.

Footnotes

1. Charles H. Heimsath, *Indian Nationalism and Hindu Social Reform*, pp. 10-11.
2. Ramesh Chandra Mazumdar, On Rammohan Roy, The Asiatic Society, 1972, p. 19.
3. As quoted by C. H. Heimsath, *op. cit.*, p. 11.
4. From "An Appeal to the Christian Public" in Defence of 'The Precepts of Jesus' English Works, p. 559.
5. Preface to the "Katha upanishad", *ibid.*, p. 45.
6. C. H. Heimsath, *op. cit.*, p. 76.
7. *Ibid.*, p. 73.
8. *Ibid.*, p. 46.

9. K. Nag and D. Burman, as quoted by V. A. Narain, in his book, *Social History of Modern India,* p. 62.
10. B. N. Banerjee and S. K. Das, (ed.) *Rammohan Granthavali* (in Bengali), Vol. III, pp. 1-12.
11. Biman Bihari Mazumdar, *History of Indian Social and Political Ideas*, Calcutta, 1967, p. 8.
12. *Ibid.*
13. Dr. R. C. Mazumdar, *Glimpses of Bengal in the Nineteenth Century*, p. 69.
14. Biman Bihari Mazumdar, *op. cit.,* p. 8.
15. *Ibid.*, p. 47.
16. *Ibid.*
17. In Mahanirvana Tantra the Saiva form of marriage is thus described : "There is no discrimination in age or caste or race in Saiva marriage. As enjoined by Siva, one should marry a woman who has no husband and who is not 'Sapinda', i.e., who is not within the prohibited degree of marriage."
18. Raja Rammohan Roy, His Life, Writings and Speeches, p. 35.
19. C. Y. Chintamani, (ed.), *Indian Social Reforms, op. cit.*, n. 6, pp. 168-169.
20. *Ibid.*, p. 171.
21. A. R. Desai, *Social Background of Indian Nationalism*, n. 5, p. 210.
22. K. P. Karunakaran, *op. cit.*, pp. 32-33.
23. Charles H. Heimsath, *op. cit.*, p. 91.
24. *Ibid., op. cit.,* pp. 5-6.
25. C. H. Chintamani, *op. cit.,* n. 6, p. 149.
26. A. R. Desai, *op. cit.,* n. 5, p. 213.
27. Ranade, Miscellaneous Writings, *op. cit.,* p. 192.
28. The English Works of Raja Rammohan Roy, pp. 3-4.
29. C. Y. Chintamani, n. 6, p. 131.
30. K. P. Karunakaran, *op. cit.,* p. 34.
31. K. C. Vyas, *The Social Renaissance in India* (Bombay, 1957), pp. 152-154.
32. B. N. Seal, *The Universal Man in The Father of Modern India,* (Calcutta, 1935), Part II, p. 101.
33. *Tattvabodhini Patrika,* Magh 1772, Saka.
34. Rammohan Roy, *In Defence of Hindu Theism*, pp. 3-9, 13.
35. Letter to John Digby : Roy, *English Works*, (J. C. Ghose, ed.), pp. 928-29.
36. C. H. Heimsath, *op. cit.*, p. 74.
37. It is not correct to find out the meaning of any text depending only on the Shastras. The Dharma suffers if one has recourse to a method of analysis which has dispensed with rationalism.

4

Rammohan's Ideas on Education and Politics

Raja Rammohan Roy was well-known as a protagonist of Western civilization. He wanted incorporation of Western ideas and institutions for the purpose of social reconstruction in India on modern lines. For him English education was the portal for the Indians to have access to Western ideas and civilization and to advance towards equality of status with Westerners.[1]

English education supplied a potent stimulus for allround awakening in India during the nineteenth century. English education, which, Chandavarkar once noted was "accomplishing silently what no law could have accomplished— unsettling people's minds, raising controversies... and thus forwarding the cause of social progress."[2] The single most important contributory factor to the Renaissance of Bengal in the 19th century was the introduction of English education and the Western ideas that followed along with it.[3] Introduction of English education in India was made possible largely through the efforts of a small but discerning section of intelligent Indians who were formally or informally exposed to the Western system of education. Raja Rammohan Roy was the first and foremost representative of this group of supporters of English education.

The British government under the East India Company followed a very slow and discreet policy of non-interference in social, religious and educational matters of Indians. In pursuance of its policy, the Company refrained from developing an educational system upto 1781 when the Calcutta Madrasa was established by Warren Hastings to promote the study of the Arabic and the Persian languages and of Muslim Law. The ultimate objective was to produce qualified men for the existing courts of law.[4]

Establishment of Benaras Sanskrit College in 1792 by Jonathan-Dunkan, a resident of Benaras, marked another effort in the direction of spreading education. The Company also recognised all educational endowments and land grants to educational institutions.[5] But oriental learning as such did not receive any appreciable patronage until 1811, when Lord Minto recommended for the establishment of Sanskrit College at Tirhut and Nuddes.

Before any action could be taken on Minto's recommendation the Charter Act of 1813 was passed. The Charter provided that "a sum of not less than one Lac of rupees in each year shall be set apart and applied to the revival and improvement of literature and the encouragement of the learned natives of India and for the introduction and promotion of a knowledge of the science among the inhabitants of the British territories in India."[6] The second part of this clause, however, did not find the support of the Court of Directors who rejected the plan of founding public colleges on English lines. The Committee of Public Instruction which was created under the provision of the Charter Act of 1813, served as a forum for the deliberation on relative merits and demerits of Western and Oriental learning. Demand for the introduction of English education, particularly in Bengal, began to gain ground. The Hindu College came into existence in 1817 mainly through the efforts of progressive men of Bengal like Baidyanath Mukherjee, Radhakant Deb, Ram Kamal Sen, Rammohan Roy and others.

As regards the spread of English education, "the Hindu College may be regarded as the premier institution which was mainly instrumental in spreading English education and Western ideas among the young generation of Bengal in the first half of the 19th century, whose pesonalities, activities and achievements mainly contributed to the gradual development of the New Age."[7] The Raja, undoubtedly, played a prominent role in appealing to the British government for the introduction of English education in India.

His approach towards the nature of educational system was clearly stated in his famous letter of December 11, 1823, to Lord Amherst : "If it had been intended to keep the British nation in ignorance of real knowledge, the Baconian philosophy, would not have been allowed to displace the system of the schoolmen, which was best calculated to perpetuate ignorance. In the same manner the Sanskrit system of education would be best calculated to keep this country in darkness, if such has been the policy of the British legislature. But as the improvement of the native population is the object of the Government, it will consequently promote a more liberal and enlightened system of instruction, embracing Mathematics, Natural Philosophy, Chemistry, Anatomy with other useful sciences."[8] Rammohan Roy wrote this letter objecting the decision of the Government to set up "The Sanskrit College which he considered was designed only to develop and sustain a type of education and a species of literature which would be utterly worthless."[9]

Rammohan thus strongly pleaded for the introduction of Science and scientific teaching. English education according to him, could help greater diffusion of knowledge among the Indians. Hindu College worked in the direction of speedy emission of English education and learning, fulfilling the purposes as was envisaged by Raja Rammohan Roy. But conflicting opinion prevail among historians as to who was or were the prime movers of the idea for foundation of the Hindu College. Eminent historians gave the credit to David Hare and Rammohan Roy. But as Dr. R. C. Mazumdar comments, it is only a Rammohan Myth that guides "the opinions of a later date giving credit, first to David Hare, then jointly to David Hare and Rammohan and finally to Rammohan alone for being the prime mover of Hindu College". Dr. Mazumdar puts his own view thus, "The only legitimate conclusion from the facts so far known is that no individual has any claim to be the founder of the Hindu College or originators of the idea. It was really speaking, conceived by the orthodox Hindus and established by the orthodox Hindus, for the orthodox Hindus."[10] Dr. Mazumdar has, very cogently, put his arguments saying that neither Rammohan Roy nor David Hare could be regarded as the prime mover of the idea for the establishment of Hindoo College. He cites several inconsistencies, on almost every essential point, between the later accounts giving credit to David Hare and Rammohan Roy and the letter of Sir Hyde East dated 18 May, 1816. "Hyde East in his letter says that he called the meeting at the request of the Hindus who were very eager to establish a college for English education, a fact which struck him as unusual, and the general plan of the College was settled at the very first meeting. According to the accounts of Pearychand Mitra, Hare makes the plan which is accepted by Hyde East with slight alterations; after this, inquiry is made whether the Hindus were agreeable to the proposal of such a College, and even then several meetings were held before it was resolved to establish a college. But according to Hyde East he hesitated even to call a meeting at his house without the sanction of government".[11] According to Dr. Mazumdar, the truth of the later account would depend upon the ultimate proof that East's letter was a forged document.

Similarly, according to Dr. Mazumdar it would be in defiance of historical fact to give Rammohan the credit for the foundation of the college or any active part in it, in view of many obvious points against such a stand. It is now conclusively established that the 'Brahmin' who approached Hyde East with the proposal of founding a College, could not be Rammohan Roy. It is clear from the statement of Hyde East himself "I do not know what Rammohan's religion is, not being acquainted or having had any communication with him."[12] The facts, that Rammohan Roy's name was not associated with the foundation of the Hindoo College before 1862, i.e., nearly half a century after the inaugural meeting to establish it was held, that neither he nor David Hare were present at that meeting which was attended by "50 and upwards of the most respectable Hindu inhabitants of rank and wealth, including also principal pandits". The fact that Rammohan was not a member of the Committee, originally appointed to organise the college, does not lend support to the view that "Rammohan's hands and brain were behind the whole proposal".[13]

The idea of founding a college for imparting education on Western lines was the fruition of a great desire entertained for a long time by the leading Hindus of Calcutta. But Rammohan Roy, though he was not the founder of the Hindoo college, was a staunch advocate of, and founded schools for, spreading English education.

His vigorous advocacy for liberal scientific education struck at the very root of orientalism, and produced the memorable controversy between the orientalists and the occidentalists. Lord Macaulay, put forward arguments in favour of introducing European science and literature fully endorsing the views of Rammohan on the matter. With the triumph of occidentalists over orientalists, active governmental decision was taken during the period of Bentinck in favour of the promotion of European literature and science. Indian reformers, mainly Rammohan Roy, David Hare and missionaries such as Alexander Duff significantly contributed to influence the decision of the Government to introduce English system of education.

Rammohan's enthusiasm for the cause of English education should not be taken to mean an expression of disdain on his part, for oriental learning. His efforts for the promotion and development of oriental learning were no less important. The Veda Vidyalaya founded by him aimed at the teaching of Hindu Shastras or Hindu literature and philosophy. The basis of Rammohan's educational policy was to help India break away from the chains of medieval scholasticism by introducing the study of modern sciences and literatures.[14]

Political Ideas of Rammohan Roy

The Raja's political thought and his contribution to this field should be viewed in the context of a time when the emergence of nationalism had not taken place in an organized form. Political reform movements occupied a less important position in the public and private lives of educated Indians than religious social reform movements.[15] A limited group of partly westernized and progressive Indians were more intensely concerned with the idea of elevating the society from the deplorable conditions and the restrictions which traditions and customs imposed upon it. Thoughts about India's inferior political status provided much less inducement to action in comparison to ideas about social and religious bondage.[16] The social and religious reform movements were considered as a necessary prelude to the political awakening in the country.

"Rammohan Roy fought vigorously against the corrupt practices in the Hindu religion; against the superstitions and inhuman customs of the Hindu society and against the narrow parochial outlook of Indian mind".[17] He considered the prevalent social and religious aberrations as causes responsible for India's falling prey to foreign conquest and obstructing any social regeneration. According to Rammohan Roy, India's political advancement and that in turn depended upon reformation of religious beliefs and practices.[18] He stated his convictions on India's political advancement thus "I regret to say that the present system of religion adhered to by the Hindus is not well calculated to promote their political interest. The distinction of castes, introducing innumerable divisions and sub-divisions among them, has entirely deprived them of political feeling, and the multitude of religious rites and ceremonies and laws of purification have totally disqualified them from undertaking any difficult enterprise. It is I think, necessary that changes should take place in their religion at least for the sake of political advantage and social comfort.[19] His political programme was intimately and indissolubly connected with the social uplift of the nation.[20]

His conception of a renovated Indian society was based on his overt acknowledgement of the superiority of western civilization and on his desire to incorporate western liberal legal and social institutions, western learning and western ethics within Indian social system.

For the introduction of changes in his own country on western lines he considered the Western rule as conducive. He believed that political progress could be achieved by operating within the British system.[21] Rammohan's ultimate object was clearly stated by Adam when he said, "He (Rammohan) said, a man of his acute mind and local knowledge could not but see, the selfish, cruel, almost insane errors of the English in governing India, but he also said that their system of government and policy had redeeming qualities not to be found in native governments. Without seeking to destroy, therefore, his object was to reform and improve the system of foreign government to which his native country had become subject; and, without stimulating his countrymen to discontent or disaffection, his endeavour was, by teaching them a pure religion and promoting among them an enlightened education, to qualify them for enjoyment of more extensive civil and political franchise.[22] Rammohan Roy thus appreciated the liberal aspects of British rule and his political thought was marked by his pleas to incorporate those elements into his own country. He made a careful study of the English constitution.[23] He was anxious to secure for his countrymen the same guarantee of individual liberty as were enjoyed by Englishmen.[24] The most outstanding element in Rammohan's political ideas was his abstract love of liberty which was universal and cosmopolitan.[25] He passionately advocated the freedom of thought. The Raja, however, never advocated political liberty for his countrymen, who, in his view, were ignorant and superstitious and 'betrayed a deplorable lack of public spirit in their conduct'.[26] He was not concerned with the autonomy for India but with the bare recognition of the principles of justice and security of life and property for the citizens.[27]

Rammohan was enamoured of the colonization of India by the British and glorified the role played by them for civilizing the Indians.[28] At the same time, he was quite aware of the political transformation along nationalist lines then taking place in Europe and even expressed his jubilation at the liberation of Spanish colonies of South America. It appears thus Rammohan attached a greater value to cosmopolitanism or internationalism than to nationalism. He believed that Indian nationalism would gain ground only when the nations of the Western world would become free. The free nations of the world then would find a bond of union in the same principle of government.[29]

Rammohan Roy while he was appreciative of the British rule, was also equally vigorous in condemning measures he considered as wrong or unjust. This is well illustrated by his protest and vigorous campaign against the Press Ordinance of 1823 and the Jury Act of 1827. These acts of Rammohan Roy paved the way for the constitutional agitation as a regular weapon in political struggle for reforms within the frame-work of British administration throughout the 19th century.[30]

One of the many objectives in undertaking his trip to England in 1833 was his desire to present India's case before the Home authorities.[31] He submitted before the Select Committee of the House of Commons his considered views in the form of "Communications to the Board of Control". In these, Rammohan suggested appointment of Indian judicial accessories; joint judges, i.e., Indian judges to try cases along with European judges, well defined codes of civil and criminal laws; Separation of the executive from judiciary, reduction of government expenditure and abolition of standing army and its replacement by people's militia.[32]

Rammohan's concern for the freedom of the Press was another remarkable idea of his programme of political reform. His Memorial to the Supreme Court and Appeal to the King-in-Council regarding the freedom of the Press were regarded as "The Areopagitica of Indian History". Rammohan suggested that the free press was the first and foremost condition necessary to secure good laws for India. In this regard he adduced four different arguments.

Firstly, freedom of the press would make laws correspond to public opinion.[33]

Secondly, the Free Press would obviate the danger of revolution that might be caused due to unrepresented and unredressed grievances of people.[34]

Thirdly, freedom of press would enable the people of India to appeal to the honour and justice of the British nation against any possible oppressive and tyrannical act of Indian Government.[35]

Fourthly, the Court of Directors would be enabled by a free press, to ascertain correctly 'whether the systems introduced in their possession prove so beneficial to the natives of the country, as their authors might fondly suppose or would have others believe and whether rules and regulations, which may appear excellent in their eyes are strictly put into practice.'[36]

Rammohan Roy failed, inspite of all his arguments and eloquence in favour of freedom of press, to get the Press Ordinance Act repealed. But he continued his relentless crusade against irrationalism and suppression of freedom by being associated with several periodicals of the time. His demand for the freedom of press in India was identified with a demand for the establishment of Rule of Law in place of Rule of Persons.

Rammohan played a distinguished part in the political field in many ways. His political doctrines set the standards of liberalism and individualism in the 19th century.[37] His devotion to the principles of British constitutional government and his confidence in the possibilities for advancement within the framework of British rule, constituted his most significant political legacy to the generations of leaders following him. The lines of political agitation that Rammohan laid down in the forms of reliance on the British parliament for arbitration of political conflict, redress of popular grievances and guidance in constitutional advancement, were more conspicuously incorporated fifty years later by the liberal leaders of Indian National Congress in their political programme.

Rammohan Roy held ideas about Indian national unity that were embryonic and had little effect on his political thought.[38] He was sensitive to the forces of nationalism then emerging in Europe and even celebrated the victory of Spanish nationalist forces over colonial power. But Rammohan practically reconciled his love of freedom in the abstract sense with India's subservience to the British rule.[39] With reference to India Rammohan expounded his ideas on national freedom, to Victor Jacquemont, in the following words : "Conquest is very rarely an evil when the conquering people were more civilized than the conquered, because the former bring to later the benefits of civilization. India requires many more years of English domination so that she may not have many things to lose while she is reclaiming her political independence.[40] The Raja thus looked at the continuance of British rule as a blessing and beneficial in literary, social and political fields, to the Indians. In view of such a mentality and practical attitude displayed by Rammohan Roy to British rule, it was certain that his political ideas "could not serve as an inspiration and far less contributed in any way to, the dawning of the New Age or National Resurgence in Bengal in the 19th century based on the glory of the past and hope for the future, and marked by a sturdy spirit of Hindu nationalism."[41]

Rammohan Roy did take much pains to bring home to the British government the Indian's reactions to British rule, as expressed through the newspapers and direct petitions. It was also expressed through evidence before commissions, and the advice rendered on pending legislation before parliament. But his ideas and protests were in the form of disorganized, individual statements which "never took the form of, or directly led to anything like political organisation.[42] However they formed in later years the most distinctive characteristic of the regeneration of political life in India in the 19th century ending in the formation of the All India National Congress.

Rammohan Roy was a patriot who felt concerned at the subordinate and degrading position of Indians in different spheres and desired their upliftment through various reforms pertaining to social and religious matters. For him national political advancement was dependent on prior social advancement of the people. But his patriotism, in the sense, in which it was only an expression of national consciousness, failed to inspire the posterity with patriotic fervour. And for this expression of patriotism and national consciousness in Rammohan's days, credit must be given to Derozio. He inculcated patriotic and anti-English national ideas among the younger generations of Bengalis through his students of the Hindoo College.[43]

Footnotes

1. C. H. Heimsath, *Indian Nationalism and Hindu Social Reform*, p. 12.
2. N. G. Chandavarkar, *Speeches and Writings,* p. 47.
3. Dr. R. C. Mazumdar, *op. cit.*
4. S. Tagore, *Rammohan Roy, His Role in Indian Renaissance,* p. 15.
5. S. N. Mukerjee, *The Educational Policy, The Comprehensive History of India,* Vol. XI.
6. H. Sharp (ed.), Selections from Educational Records, Part I, p. 22.
7. Dr. R. C. Mazumdar, *On Rammohan Roy,* p. 20.
8. The English Works of Rammohan Roy, Vol. III, p. 327.
9. S. Tagore, *Rammohan Roy, His Role in Indian Renaissance*, p. 22.
10. Dr. R. C. Mazumdar, *op. cit.*, p. 39.
11. Dr. R. C. Mazumdar, *On Rammohan Roy*, p. 34.
12. *Ibid.*, p. 37.
13. *Ibid.*
14. S. Tagore, *Rammohan Roy, His Role in Indian Renaissance,* The Asiatic Society, 1975, p. 25
15. A partial enumeration of public organisations in 19th century Bengal by N.S. Bose shows their overwhelming concern with social reform, cultural life and education.
16. Writing about the 1870's, B.C. Pal recalled that "......in those early days consciousness of sacerodotal and social bondage was far keener than the consciousness of political bondage". Pal, *Memoires of My Life & Times*, p. 252.
17. Bimanbehari Mazumdar, *History of Indian Social and Political Ideas,* Calcutta, 1967, p. 24.
18. C.H. Heimsath, *Indian Nationalism and Hindu Social Reform,* p. 76.
19. Rammohan Roy, *English Works* (J. C. Ghose, ed.), pp. 929-30.
20. B. Mazumdar, *op. cit.*, p. 24.
21. C. H. Heimsath, *op. cit.*, p. 58.
22. Quoted by S. Tagore, *Rammohan Roy*, p. 58.
23. B. Mazumdar, *op. cit.*, p. 27.
24. *Ibid.*
25. Dr. R. C. Mazumdar, *On Rammohan Roy*, The Asiatic Society, 1972, p. 47.
26. B. Mazumdar, *op. cit.*, p. 28.
27. B. Mazumdar, *op. cit.*, p. 28.
28. R. C. Mazumdar, *op. cit.*, p. 47.
29. Works of Rammohan Roy, pp. 316-17.
30. R. C. Mazumdar, *op. cit.*, p. 48.
31. S. Tagore, *Rammohan Roy, His Role in Indian Renaissance,* p. 59.
32. *Ibid.*, pp. 59-60.

33. Works of Rammohan, Appeal to the King-in-Council, para 29, p. 456.
34. *Ibid.*, p. 457, para 31.
35. Ibid., p. 458, para 33.
36. Ibid., p. 464, para 46.
37. C. H. Heimsath, *Indian Nationalism and Hindu Social Reform*, p. 58.
38. *Ibid.*, p. 59.
39. Dr. R. C. Mazumdar, On Rammohan Roy, p. 47.
40. Arabinda Poddar, Renaissance in Bengal - Quests and Confrontations, 1800-1860 (Indian Institute of Advanced Study, Simla, 1970), pp. 61-62.
41. Dr. R. C. Mazumdar, *op. cit.*, p. 48.
42. *Ibid.*
43. Dr. R. C. Mazumdar, *op. cit.*, pp. 48-49.

5
Rammohan's Ideas on Economic and Judicial Reforms

The progressiveness of the ideas of Rammohan noticed in the field of socio-religious reforms are not found in relation to the political ideas. He practically reconciled his abstract love of freedom with India's subjugation to the British rule.[1] This was evident from his discourse with Victor Jacquemont, whom he asked : "Is not this fiery love of national independence a chimera ?" He had justified imperialism of a superior power over the less developed countries and directly provided support to the imperial theory of the 'White Man's responsibility to civilize the coloured people'. In his own words : "Conquest is very rarely an evil when the conquering people are more civilized than the conquered, because the former bring to latter the benefits of civilization. India requires many more years of English domination so that she may not have many things to lose while she is reclaiming her political independence."[2] Many prominent leaders of the Brahmo Samaj had unqualified praises for the British way of thinking and living, their system of the law and morality, their judicial system and the dispensation of justice and their socio-political system. They accepted the myth of the "providential role of the British" and insisted on the never ending rule of Great Britain over India. Many prominent leaders of the Brahmo Samaj, expressed the view that the Indians must have the proper training before they could demand political democracy. They also believed in the essential goodness of the British and their sincere intentions for promoting the good of the Indians. Keshab Chandra Sen one of the most prominent and respected leaders of the Brahmo Samaj said:

> "We look upon Victoria as our Queen Mother and we are politically her children. She sits upon the throne as India's mother protecting the lives and property of her children, promoting their material and moral prosperity and helping them to attain

> political and social manhood. She represents law, order and justice and is appointed by providence to rule over us."[3]

The Brahmo Samajist's approach greatly influenced the Congress and its leaders during its formative period. The Congress did not have any political aspiration and the question of fighting for India's political independence did not arise. The Congress consisted of a small minority, greatly influenced by Western education and culture, loyal to the rule with its zeal for social uplift and was never considered as a hostile organisation by the British government. The Rule and the Congress were friendly to each other and had mutual appreciation and co-operation. Referring to the Congress aspirations in the formative period, Dr. Pattabhi Sitaramayya has rightly observed that :

> "The Congress at that time honestly believed that the English constitution was the bulwork of popular liberties everywhere and the English parliament was the mother of democracy all over, the British constitution was the best of all constitutions. That the Press and the forest laws should be relaxed, the police should become friendly to the people, that the taxes should be moderate, that the military expenditure should be curtailed."[4]

The Brahmo Samaj movement of the 19th century had created a social awareness for improving the socio-economic conditions of the people and eradicating the evil effects of religious superstitions and blind belief. It did not talk in terms of political freedom. The early Congress shared all the views of the Brahmo Samaj in religious and socio-political matters. The formation of the Indian National Congress was never viewed as the consummation of political forces in the country which might act as an effective political organisation for demanding political rights and liberties. Even in matters of the social, economic and religious reforms the Congress was only making humble prayers and petitions as it pinned all its hopes on the British sense of justice and goodness. Dadabhai Naoroji was representative of the Congress opinion and attitude and this is evident from his following words :

> "I, for one, have not the shadow of a doubt that in dealing with such justice-loving, fair minded

> people as the British, we may rest fully assured ... have always believed that the time will come when the sentiments of the British nation and our gracious Queen's Proclamation of 1858 will be realised".[5]

By the time of the formation of the Congress in 1885, the British government was so firmly entrenched in the Indian soil and so tremendous was its educational and cultural impact that the educated Indians had become the servile and loyal admirers of anything and everything that was either British or Western. It would not be out of place to mention here that the Brahmo Samaj created a cultural and psychological atmosphere in India which was out and out pro-British, pro-West and pro-Christian. Despite the various reform measures of the Brahmo Samaj, it created an atmosphere of utter servility and helpless dependence on the British and this attitude greatly hampered the cultural and political resurgence of India and the development of the right perspective to the concept of political independence. Congress had to take a very long time to make itself free from the iron grip of the psycho-cultural impact of the Brahmo Samaj, which had substantially influenced most of its members during its formative period. C. Sankaran Nair, the 13th President of the Indian National Congress (1897) was reiterating the attitude of the Brahmo Samaj to the British rule when he said :

> "Just look for a moment at the training we are receiving. From our earliest school days, the great English writers have been our classics, Englishmen had been our Professors in Colleges, English history is taught us in our schools. The books we generally read are English books which describe in details all the forms of English life, give us all the English types of character".[6]

Due to the impact of the Brahmo attitude and philosophy, the Congress was weak and tollering. Like the Brahmo Samaj it was also designed as an organisation meant to promote social uplift with the support and co-operation of the British. It was just a forum for the purpose of promoting friendly relations among the educated classes. A policy of breaking away from England or of intense political activities was alien to the Congress, during its formative period. Its demand for complete independence was never clearly enunciated or articulated till 1930.

Explaining the basic principles of the Congress movement, W.C. Bonnerjee, the first President had made the following observation :

> "Indeed the principle on which the Indian National Congress is based is that, British Rule should be permanent and abiding in India and that given this axiom, it is the duty of educated Indians to endeavour to the best of their power to help their rulers so to govern the country as to improve her material prosperity and make the people of all classes and communities happy and prosperous and contented as subjects of the British 'Empire'.[7]

But the Brahmo Samajists and people who shared their point of view forgot the hold of traditions on the people. They ignored the difficulties of introducing radical reforms when there were no rapid economic change, which created a change of social patterns. The Brahmo Samaj had no definite economic policy and although its leader Raja Rammohan Roy had some liberal economic ideas supporting the rights of the tenants as against the Zamindars, his support for European colonization in India made him a most misunderstood person. He was considered pro-British and anti-national in his economic policies due to his support for large-scale settlement of Englishmen in India. In supporting European colonization and their permanent settlement in India in large numbers, particularly, the British and the Europeans belonging to the higher strata in the society, Rammohan was again guided by the false notion of their superiority and the misconceived notion that the British would really help India to transform itself. Rammohan forgot to realize the simple principle that no imperial power would ever help with sincerity the social, economic and political development of the people of its colony as that would go against its imperial interest.

The East India Company was established according to an Act of the British Parliament, which granted monopolistic powers to the Company to trade with India. The Company thus got the right to prevent any European from coming to this country and settle for purposes of agriculture, trade and commerce.[8] The Company exploited India and its resources for procuring raw-materials for British industries and this was done ruthlessly with the help of the monopolistic privileges. The monopolistic control over trade gave the East India Company immense powers to exploit the Indian people and extract the maximum profit by excluding others from this highly profitable enterprise.

The East India Company came to India as a trading body, but was subsequently converted into a terriotorial power due to the dissensions and rivalries among the Indian Princes and Rulers. But the inherent weakness and the incapacity of the trading body to carry on the administration of a vast country like India, became evident soon after its assumption of power.[9] The salary of the Company's servants was ridiculously low, but this was not the index of their real income. They used their official position for extracting bribes, presents and levies from the poor Indians. Preposterous dividends were claimed by shareholders of the Company and the British tax-payers demanded relief at the cost of the Indian peasants. Due to these claims, the East India Company was speeding towards insolvency, but the servants of the Comapny in Bengal made more money than they knew what to do with. The administration that was practised by the British in those days lay in graft and extortion.

There was consistent exploitation of the Indian economy for the prosperity of Britain. Heavy duties were imposed on Indian goods imported into England, while British goods were forced on the Indians, without the payment of any duty.[10] This led to speedy impoverishment of India and there was no end to the miseries of the people. According to the Cambridge History of India :

> "There seemed a danger not only that misgovernment in India might tarnish the name of Great Britain as an Imperial State, but that the Indian interests in England, supported by huge revenues and corrupt parliamentary influence, might gain a preponderance and improper power in home affairs."

In 1858 when a debate was going on in the House of Commons, after the First War of Indian Independence, Cornwall Lewis, a member of the House said that "No civilized government existed on this earth, which was more corrupt, more perfidious than the Government of the East India Company from 1765 to 1784". The well planned economic exploitation of India by the East India Company and its illegal interference in the affairs of the Indian

States, created a bitter sense of resentment in the minds of the people. Lecky had rightly observed that : "Never before had the natives experienced a tyranny which was at once so skillful, so searching and so strong... Districts which had been populous and flourishing were at last utterly depopulated, and it was noticed that on the appearance of a party of English merchants, the villages were atonce deserted and shops shut and the roads thronged with panic-stricken fugutives." Despite its exploitative policy due to the Company's misrule and the rampant bribery, favouritism, corruption and inefficiency among its employees, it was in grave financial difficulties. By and large the Indian opinion was bitter against the East India Company's extremely exploitative and tyrannical rule.

The British Government wanted to share the political and military gains of the East India Company and cast its lustful eyes on the fabulous riches of India. The financial difficulties into which the Company had landed provided the required opportunity to the British Government to gradually extend its power of control which became absolute after the First War of Indian Independence in 1858.

It is strange to believe that Rammohan Roy was oblivious of all these facts while puttingforth his arguments in favour of European colonization in India and the indefinite sovereign control of the British over the Indian subjects. It is clear that towards the beginning of the 20th century a tussle had started in England between the protagonists of free trade and those of monopoly. The Company which was enjoying all the benefits exerted its influence in favour of its monopolist privileges and enjoyed monopoly rights of trade and commerce in Bengal till 1824.

In the same year Government decided to introduce cultivation of Coffee and allowed the Europeans to own land with some restriction, in order to develop coffee plantation. Coffee plantation started in India, with this concession to Free Trade. The Europeans were unhappy with the restrictions imposed by the Government on European settlement in India and organised a protest meeting at the Town Hall on November 7, 1827. Dwarkanath Tagore, a friend and ardent supporter of Rammohan was against the Indian opinion and the attitude of the company in the matter of concession to Free Trade to the Europeans. Dwarkanath supported

European colonization and in publishing his letter in Sambad Kaumudi on February 26, 1828, was only articulatiing the opinion of his friend, Rammohan Roy. In his letter Dwarkanath pointed out :

> "Both in their conversation and writings, they generally refer to the alleged disadvantages and injuries resulting from indigo plantations throughout the country by European gentlemen, and make attempts to give the public to understand, that Europeans having already occupied a great portion of land productive of paddy etc., for the plantation of indigo, the scarcity of rice, the principal food of the native population, is severely felt and consequently, the lower classes have been involved in great distress and trouble from the want of the necessaries of life."

In his letter Dwarkanath flayed all charges which were levelled against the Europeans and fervently appealed to the Government to allow the Europeans concession for Free Trade and other residential facilities. Referring to the zamindars and their exploitation he said :

> "They ultimately compel many of the cultivators through extortion to fly to other villages leaving their huts unoccupied and soils totally waste. The false excuse which they offer to their masters is that owing to the tyranny exercised by indigo planters, the revenue is reduced and cultivators diminished, and thereby they keep their masters in darkness."

Any attempt to defend the Zamindars as the champions of the cause of the cultivators and the promotion of national interest as their sole motive in opposing extensive indigo cultivation and European colonization, would be a distortion of history. But in doing so probably, they were certainly promoting the national interest though unconsciously. On the other hand Rammohan Roy, his friend Dwarkanath and others who supported extensive indigo cultivation, very often through compulsive methods, and European colonization were consciously doing a disservice to the nation irrespective of the immediate economic benefit to some peasants. In their support for European colonization and control over Indian economy by the Europeans with their advanced skill and technology, Rammohan Roy and his friends were guided more by their obsession for everything Western than by logic and reason. This is evident from the following emotional statement of Dwarkanath :

> "Under these circumstances, I hope I shall be justified when I say, that whoever is inclined to oppose the diffusion of knowledge among the natives by the British Government of India and by many private individuals among European, or whoever is disposed to oppose the unrestricted residence of Europeans in this country, provided certain changes shall at the same time be introduced into the system of administering justice, is an enemy of the natives and to their rising and future generations."

This is evident from the fact that Rammohan made a similar statement on European colonization in a meeting at Calcutta Town Hall on December 15, 1829. In the meeting he publicly expressed his "conviction that the greater our intercourse with European gentlemen, the greater will be our improvement in literary, social and political affairs". Subsequent developments in India belied the expectations of Rammohan Roy. The British economically bled India white through merciless and inhuman exploitation. Culturally India became degenerated and deprived and politically it was devastated. Large number of educated Indians who blindly imitated Western civilization and Western way of life, looked down upon their religion, culture and heritage. This promoted a servile attitude in the people and hindered the development of political consciousness. This sense of inferiority complex and diffidence helped the proselytization attempts of the Christian missionaries, with active help from the government. The British followed the policy of 'divide and rule' and set one community against the other through crude methods of diplomacy and hypocrisy. The British government actively collaborated with the Muslim League in sabotaging the early attainment of freedom by India as well as the creation of a separate homeland for the Muslims. By 1829, any layman could see the devastating effects of British rule in India and it was strange that a highly educated person having all the critical faculties of mind like Rammohan

Roy could not see what was writ large on the walls of contemporary times.

Rammohan's obsession with the British and the Europeans was so great that he was not prepared to see any evil in their administration or civilization. He gave a carte blanche to the British to do whatever they liked on the ground of their superior civilization, which again was an imperialist myth. It was extremely naive on the part of Rammohan to believe that if the conquering people were more civilized than the conquered, then the former would bring to latter, the benefits of civilization.

The British Indigo Planters who were notorious for their exploitation and inhuman treatment towards the poor peasants, were also highly praised by Rammohan. In his own words :

> "As to the Indigo Planters, there may be some partial injury done by the indigo planters; but on the whole they have performed more good to the generality of the natives of this country than any other class of Europeans whether in or out of the service."[11]

Thus Rammohan's defence of European colonization and his praises in support of the superior quality of the Western civilization in comparison to the Indian civilization made him a suspect in the eyes of millions of Indians who did not share either his universalism or his so-called cosmopolitanism. In this connection R. C. Majumdar has rightly observed that :

> "So far as India was concerned Rammohan had an unbounded faith in the sense of justice and goodness of the British Government, and accepted the British rule as an act of Divine Providence to deliver India from the the tyranny of its Muslim rulers. But, curiously enough, he was enamoured of the colonization of India by the British and glorified the role played by them for civilizing the Indians".[12]

Some people try to defend Rammohan's support for European colonization at the expense of India by saying that he would have only "Europeans of character and capital" to settle in India and was not in favour of thousands and thousands of Europeans being allowed to descend on India like locusts and spread all over the countryside. This was, however, a very weak defense as the power of determining the character and capital of the Europeans would have been left to the discretion of the British Government and it would have never taken the Indian opinion on the matter into consideration.

Rammohan was one, of the opinion that the European settlers would be instrumental in the spread of education and "the diffusion of a knowledge of European arts and sciences". He argued that they would broaden the channels of communication between India and the West. As a result both the public in Britain and the Government would be better informed, so that the latter would be "much better qualified to legislate on Indian matters than at present. For information on India, the British government would not have to rely solely on East India Company officials who, in any case, could hardly fail to regard the result of their own labours with a favourable eye".[13]

Praising the advantages of European colonization Rammohan observed that, "European settlers will introduce the knowledge they possess of superior modes of cultivating the soil and improving the products". It would also be beneficial to the Indians as it would bring "improvements in the technical arts, and in the agricultural and commercial systems". Rammohan also expressed the pious hope that the association with the Indians would make the Europeans free from their prejudices, which prompted them to subject "the great body of the Indian people to social and domestic inconvenience, and disqualified them from useful exertions".

Analysing the advantages of European colonization, Rammohan further argued that as a result of this the European settlers would be "aware of the rights belonging to the subjects of a liberal government and the proper mode of administering justice, and would obtain from the local government, or from the Legislature in England, the introduction of many necessary improvements in the law and judicial system, the benefit of which would, of course, extend to the inhabitants generally, whose condition would thus be raised". Further, he argued that the "presence, countenance and support of the European settlers would not only afford to the natives protection against the impositions and oppression of their landlords and other superiors, but also against any abuse of power on the part of those in authority".

In defence of Rammohan, however, it may be said that while pleading for colonization by the Europeans, he was conscious of the evil consequences that might be produced because of their kinship with the ruling race. They "may be apt to assume an ascendancy over the native inhabitants and aim at enjoying exclusive rights and privileges, to the depression of the larger and less favourable class". In their arrogance of power, they could wound the feelings of the Indians. To check the abuse of powers by the European settlers, he strongly suggested the "enactment of equal laws, placing all classes on the same footing as to civil rights and the establishment of trial by jury (the jury being composed impartially of both classes). This would place a curb on overbearing characters among Europeans."

Rammohan was of the view that the European settlers would be able to put life into the moribund Indian economy by starting a process of industrialization. He wanted that the Company's monopoly should be broken and he was convinced that this could only be done by the European settlers as being guided by the desire for profit, the settlers would set up industrial plants and set in train an industrial revolution. The Company only encouraged such agricultural produce as could be utilized in British factories at that time. He hoped that the settlers would diversify agricultural production and would give impetus on agriculture as a whole. Rammohan supported European colonization and Free Trade with a view to press into service European capital and technology for the economic development of India. Rammohan had little knowledge that the European settlers in due course of time would become worst monopolist exploiters.

Rammohan, however was very much concerned with the economic plight of the Indian people. His testimony before the parliamentary committee set up to review the Charter of the East India Company in 1833, gives sufficient evidence of his economic ideas. He had great love for the poor and the downtrodden and worked incessantly for the improvement of the economic condition of the Indian people. He was bitter against the economic ill effects of the Permanent Settlement. It did not help the cultivators in any way, while it greatly improved the economic condition of the proprietors. He insisted that the proprietors should be forced by law to impose a fixed rent on the cultivators to give relief to them and the loss of revenue thus incurred was to be compensated by imposing tax on luxury goods and the replacement of high-salaried English officials by Indians as Collectors. Rammohan suggested some judicial reforms to save the interest of the tenants from the exploitation of the Zamindars.

Rammohan made the following suggestion for the improvement in government revenue and providing protection to the people :

> "The regulations already in force are fully adequate to secure government revenue. But to secure the people against any unjust exactions on the part of the revenue officers, I would propose, first, that the Collectors should not by any means be armed with magisterial powers. Secondly, that any charge against the revenue officers should be at once investigated by the judicial courts to which they are subject, without reference to the number of cases on the file of the Court, (as has been the practice with regard to cases in which the Collectors are prosecutors) so that both parties may have an equal chance of legal redress. This under existing circumstances, seems to be the best remedy that presents itself but with the present system, I must repeat that redress will not always be attainable".

Rammohan protested against the colossal sums of money which were sent to England in the form of pension of the Europeans retiring from service in India. He also fought against the monopoly of salt trade by the servants of the East India Company.

Through this monopoly the Company used to increase the price of salt a thousand percent above its normal price. On the salt brought from England the Company imposed heavy import duty. The poor people were very much affected by this increased price. The agitation of Rammohan against the monopoly of salt was supported by the Parliamentary Select Committee and the Company was forced to do away with salt monopoly.

Judicial reform proposals of Rammohan :

The judicial system was not properly organised during the early days of the East India Company and it had no codes of law and uniform procedure for deciding cases. Rule of Law which formed the fundamental basis of the judicial and legal system in

England was conspicuous by its absence in India. Distinction were made between "His Majesty's Subjects" and the so-called 'natives' of India. 'Natives' professing different religions were also treated differently by the Courts of Law.

He was aware that due to lack of knowledge about the Indian languages and differences in manners the European judges could not acquire adequate information about the real nature of grievances of the persons seeking redress or of the real character and validity of the evidence by which the Indians putforth their respective claims. Rammohan therefore demanded that in order to eliminate these lapses, Indians with knowledge of the habits, languages and manners of their countrymen should be given direct and considerable share in the administration of justice.

Prior to the passage of the Indian Jury Bill on May 5, 1826, for which the initiative was taken by William Wynn, the then President of the Board of Control, the Indians were not allowed to sit on either the Petty Jury or the Grand Jury. This Act for the first time made the Indo-Britons and the Indians eligible to sit on juries in criminal cases, before the Supreme Courts. But it made an insidious distinction between the rights and privileges of the Indian 'natives' and the Indo-Britons. It allowed full rights and privileges to the Indo-Britons to sit on both grand and Petty Juries and try both the Christians and the 'natives'. The Indians, on the other hand were allowed only to sit on Petty Juries and were prevented to take part in trials of Christians.

Rammohan suspected that this unreasonable distinction between the Christians and the people of the other faiths was deliberately made by the Government to favour the spread of Christianity in the country. He protested against this insidious attempt and wrote in Sambad Kaumudi :

> "The consequences of this new Act is that in matters where a man's life is at stake or where banishment, imprisonment and severe punishment are awarded, we Hindoos and Mussulmans, must submit to the verdict of Christians whether they be natives of Britain or the off-springs of British father by Indian mother, whether they be the Portuguese Armenians or the 'rice Christians of Serampore'. These persons shall have the privilege of joining in cases where

> our lives are concerned; whereas we, although living in the same country or in the same hamlet with them and partaking in their virtues and vices, shall have no power of judging, respecting them. In like manner our descendants must also submit their lives to the decisions of the sons of Christians."[14]

Rammohan organised protest meetings and collected signatures of large number of Hindus and Muslims to submit a petition of remonstrance to the British Parliament, opposing the insidious move to establish the superiority of the Christians on the one hand and to introduce animosity among the different communities on the other. It was asserted in the petition that, "if these disabilities were not removed in time, no Hindoo or Mohammedan inhabitant will willingly serve as a juror in any capacity".[15] But when the petition was submitted to the Parliament, there was severe opposition to it from the Tory organisation John Bull and the Court of Directors and the British Parliament could not take any decision regarding the objectionable clause of the bill.

There were also protests against the Bill and two petitions were submitted by the inhabitants of Bombay almost on the lines of the one submitted earlier by Rammohan Roy. When these were taken up by the Parliament, Charles Grant, the new President of the Board of Control informed the formation of a Committee of Enquiry to discuss the complaints of Rammohan and others. He subsequently introduced a new Bill to repeal the last clause of Wynn's Jury Act, to which objection had been taken. Inspite of strong opposition from the Court of Directors and the Tory Press in India and England, the Bill was passed by the House of Commons on June 12, 1832. This was a great victory for Rammohan Roy. The European Tory Press in India was greatly exercised by the Indian Justices and Juries Act and viewed it as subversive of European ascendancy in India. One British editor of a newspaper wrote that Mr. Grant was, an inexperienced legislator, who had been "mystified by Rammohan Roy".

The virulent attacks made against Rammohan by the European Press in India, decisively prove that he played a prominent role in bringing about changes in the Jury system and was successful in removing the distinctions based on religious faith and beliefs.

Footnotes

1. Dr. R. C. Mazumdar, *On Rammohan Roy*, p. 47.
2. Arabinda Poddar, Renaissance in Bengal - Quests and Confrontations, 1800-1860, pp. 61-62.
3. Quoted by Daniel Argov in *Moderates and Extremists in the Indian National Movement*, 1967, p. 66.
4. Pattabhi Sitaramayya, *The History of the Indian National Congress, Vol. 1,* Bombay, Padma Publications, p. 34.
5. *Speeches and Writings of Dadabhai Naoroji,* Madras, G. Natesan & Co., pp. 66-67.
6. Congress Presidential Address, p. 363.
7. Extracts from Indian Politics.
8. S. Tagore, *op. cit.*, p. 36.
9. Sri Ram Sharma, *Constitutional History of India,* Orient Longmans Ltd., 3rd Edition, New Delhi, 1974, p. 1.
10. For details of the economic consequences of British rule over India see, D.D. Basu, *Ruin of Indian Trade and Industries,* Calcutta, 1935, pp. 38-51; and Dr. Tara Chand, *History of the Freedom Movement in India,* Vol. 1, New Delhi, Ministry of Information and Broadcasting, 1961, pp. 338-92.
11. *Royal Asiatic Journal,* Vol. II, New Series, May-August, 1830.
12. R. C. Mazumdar, *op. cit.,* p. 47.
13. As quoted by Saumyendranath Tagore, *op. cit.,* p. 53.
14. Quoted by Saumyendranath Tagore, *op. cit.,* p. 80.
15. *Ibid.,* p. 81.

6

Arya Samajist Revivalism : A Study of the Challenge to Brahmo Reformism

The Brahmo Samaj Movement and its leaders placed heavy reliance on the inspiration of Western model of development and alien ideologies in their advocacy of ethical and social reformative doctrines for India. They regarded India's contact with Christian civilization as the surest means of its moral regeneration. Like Rammohan Roy, Keshab Chandra Sen referred to the English contact as a 'providential dispensation'.[1]

Their influence on English educated Bengalis was great. This student of the Hindu College at Calcutta adopted an aggressive attitude to everything Hindu and openly defied the cannons of his inherited religion. Some of his followers even offended public opinion by youthful exuberance,[2] while others embraced Christianity.[3] Many Western educated people detached themselves from the mainstream of national ethos.[4] It became the fashion even in smaller things of life to imitate the West.[5] Spread of Western education led to the shrinking of Sanskritic studies with a headless surrender to alien thought by the Derozians.[6] Their intoxicating absorption and dogmatic dissemination of knowledge of nature, science and psychology greatly upset the basic Indian postulate of spirituality.

The Brahmo Samaj had attempted to 'carry through certain social and educational reforms on purely Western lines'. Its leaders questioned the numerous religious absurdities and the sanctions those provided to superstitious and irrational social conventions, on the basis of reason, enlightenment and liberalism. They raised their voices vociferously against the practices of idolatry, casteism, hereditary priesthood and above all tried to elevate the degraded and depraved social position of Indian women.

The Samaj and its ideals, however, failed to strike roots in Hindu society. Its message of electicism, monotheistic devotion, abolition of caste, equal rights for women, its hostile denunciation of Hindu polytheism and above all its leaning towards Christian ethics, for the purpose of evolving a universal and harmonious religion certainly depicted ideological advancements far ahead of the time. These made Brahmo movement repulsive to the sentiments of the common people who psychologically perceived its leaders and followers as a group of intellectual aliens. Their ideas found intellectual appreciation and acceptance among a minority group of English educated people. The search for personal truth or for a new mode of life among a limited number of enlightened men had no effect at all on the ideas and customs of the multitude, who had their socio-religious convictions placed firmly on sentiments rather than reason. All the Brahmo reformers were placed in the same unenviable and miserable position what finally subdued Sen, against whom "were the three hundred million gods of India and three hundred million living beings in whom they were incarnate–the whole vast jungle of human dreams wherein his Western outlook made him miss the track and scent. He invited them to lose themselves in his Indian Christ, but his invitation remained unanswered. They did not even seem to hear it."[7] The Brahmo acceptance of European culture and social reforms proved a tactical error cutting them off from the 'confidence of the public'.[8] Explaining the decline of the Brahmo Samaj and subsequent development, Bipin Chandra Pal, himself a Brahmo Samajist wrote :

> "Middle Nineteenth century rationalism and individualism of European culture were still the dominating ideas in the life and evolution of modern Bengal. But the conflict of political interests between the new generation of English educated Indians and the British officialdom in the country and the more fundamental cultural conflict between European modernism and Indian medievalism soon provoked a new revolt against this foreign domination in the wake of which followed a new national self-consciousness which, in the first flush of its newly found pride of race and culture, commenced to repudiate whatever was foreign, irrespective of the intrinsic reason and value of it and set up a new defence even of

> these social institutions and religious and spiritual tendencies that had previously been openly repudiated as false and harmful".[9]

Revivalist Trends

As the influence of Brahmo Samaj waned, the revolutionary zeal of ardent social reformers, who wanted to recast Indian social and religious life on the lines of Western model, softened. Even staunch reformers like Ranade, the founder of Prarthana Samaj, which was often referred to as the Brahmo Samaj of Bombay, considered it efficacious to maintain continuity while introducing reforms. He said :

> "The true reformer has not to write upon a clean slate. His work is more often to complete the half-written sentence. He has to produce the ideal out of the actual'...'we must accept as valid the acts which were noted, in the past, and on the principles of the past', 'and seek to turn the stream with a gentle bend here, and a gentle bend there, to fructify the land', we cannot afford to dam it up altogether, or force it into a new channel..." [10]

Thus at one stage, only the Brahmins who wore sacred threads were allowed to lead prayers in the Brahmo Samaj halls and the Prarthana Samajists rarely went against the prescription against intercaste marriage.[11] On the use of idols in worship also the Prarthana Samaj did not adopt as strict a prohibition as did the Brahmo Samaj of India. The Prarthana Samaj and its followers of the Bombay Presidency did not set themselves apart from Hindu society, as the Brahmos of Bengal did, by adopting a novel religious creed and assuming unconventional manners.[12] The socio-religious reformers of Western India, unlike the Brahmo reformers, did not base their works of reform primarily on religious tenets. The Western Indian reformers were "men paying allegiance to Hinduism and to Hindu society with a protest".[13] Their predominant attitude, was to introduce Western ideas and institutions as crucial amendments to the Indian traditions, but not as determinants of a wholly transformed way of life.[14]

While a cautious policy in matters of practical social reform was adopted by the social reformers and various reform organisations in the aftermath of 1850s, there was the development of a new attitude of self-confident militancy fortified by all that was heroic and splendid in India's past. It characterized the activities of eminent socio-cultural leaders of India. Unmistakable reactions against the West, Western way of life, Western civilization and Christianity, were expressed by the people.

Emergence of the Revivalist Movements

The impact of the Brahmo Samaj on Hindu society and religion was overshadowed by the development of a Hindu revivalist and extremely dynamic movement like the Arya Samaj movement. Arya Samaj and similar nationalistic movements of Theosophical Society and Ramkrishna Mission expressed the voice of protest against the Western impact which had become morally and intellectually all pervasive.

The young English educated successors of Derozians in Bengal were undergoing unhealthy impacts in the process of anglicization. They acquired new philosophies of materialism, realism and idealism and began denouncing their own civilization and culture, traditions and beliefs. "Even the good was rejected because it came from the past encumbered with effective traditions and practices.[15] People began to forget Kalidas and Bhavabhuti and studied Shakespeare and Milton. Six schools of Hindu Philosophy were abandoned for the sake of Barkley.[16] The more ardent their admiration for everything Western, the more vehement became their denunciation of everything Eastern.[17] They were empty imitators of the Western form and often indulged in exhibitionist hedonism or airy reformism.[18]

It was in such a state of intellectual perversion that the revivalist movement was started and the traditional leaders struck with a note of reaction. Even Rammohan, in order to defend his stand, had to take the support of the Upanishads, the ancient Hindu scriptures. Later Bankim Chandra appealed to Gita (as also to tradition, if it contributed to purity of mind) and Vivekananda to the 'Advaita' of Shankara (though its rigours were mellowed down by the teachings of Ramakrishna who reconciled Advaita and Dvaita as two modes of experiencing the Brahman), and Dayananda Saraswati, the great religious thinker, appealed to the Vedas.[19] The aim of these leaders was to make Indians proud of their own race, culture and civilization.

Dayananda Saraswati and Arya Samaj

The Arya Samaj founded by Swami Dayananda Saraswati in Bombay in 1875 was the most notable of revivalist movements in India. Swami Dayananda rejected Western values and relied solely on the Vedas as the chief source of knowledge and inspiration.

Dayananda, the prominent religious revivalist of Gujarat appeared on the scene when the Vedic Dharma and Aryan culture "were panting lying wrapped in darkness of ignorance which had swollen to enormousness in the course of thousands of years".[20] Hindu religion presented itself in vast congeries of faiths with heterogeneous elements during his time. It ranged all the way from the strict 'Advaita' doctrine of Shankara to the crudest and grossest superstitions embodied in 'Tantras', the whole being held together in a kind of external unity by the vast hierarchical organisation of caste.[21] Dayananda observed with dismay the noble teachings of the great Aryan Rishis being trampled under foot and the superstitions and dogma, the inventions of selfish priesthood, "held sway over the minds of the people".[22]

The Brahmo Samaj movement, led to the development of the Arya Samaj and other nationalist movements which expressed the voice of protest against the Western impact which had become morally and intellectually all pervasive. Regeneration of purified Hindu Society based on a spiritual revival was made the ultimate goal in the place of a evolutionary progress towards a new society based on "social efficiency" and alien foundations.[23] Unlike Brahmo Samaj with its leaning towards Christianity, the Arya Samaj founded by Swami Dayananda Saraswati, was a true Hindu protestant movement. Swami Dayananda rejected Western values and relied solely on the Vedas which he upheld as the "repository of knowledge".[24] He gave the call "back to the Vedas and to the pristine purity of Vedic Hinduism". The Aryan doctrine of Vedic scriptures may be summed up as follows : (1) The Vedas are a revelation from God, as is proved by their correspondence with nature. (2) They are the sole revelation from God, since no other books show this correspondence. (3) They are accordingly the fountain-head of the science and religion of all mankind.

The two great duties of the Arya Samaj were : (a) to recall India to the foreshaken Vedic paths, and (b) to preach the Vedic gospel throughout the whole world.[25] These are some of the sayings of Swami Dayananda Saraswati in regard to the infallibility of the Vedas :

> "All that confronts to the teachings of Vedas; nature, attributes and characteristics of God is right, the contrary is wrong ... We believed that the Vedas alone are the supreme authority in the ascertainment of true religion — the true conduct of life ... All men, especially the Aryans, should believe in the Vedas and thereby cultivate unity in religion".[26]

He called upon the people regardless of caste and creed to study Vedas.

Emphasis on Vedic Principles

In a bid to inculcate vigour, self-assertion and physical courage in Hindu culture, Arya Samaj started two programmes : 'Sudhi', meaning purification which aimed at reconversion of Hindus to Hinduism who had embraced other religions, and 'Sangathan', meaning union, i.e., promotion of solidarity among the Hindus. These were the programmes started by Dayananda Saraswati to stop proselytisation of Hindus into Christianity. He was uncompromising in his attitude towards other religions like Christianity and Islam. In his book 'Satyarth Prakash' he vehemently condemned Bible and Koran as pretentious and held the Vedas as 'timeless, revealed truth, divine in origin'. As one of the supporters of the Arya Samaj records, "It has met with considerable success in reclaiming Hindus converted to other faiths, and in stemming the tide of conversion of Hindus to other faiths. But its greater success lies in raising the social status of the depressed classes among the Hindus and preventing them from leaving Hinduism and joining other religious denominations".[27] The work of Arya Samaj in this field was very popular among Hindus of North and North-Western India. Arya Samaj richly deserves the credit for creating a consciousness of religious nationalism in India.

Denial of the Vedic revelation and reverence for Christianity by the Brahmo leaders made any identification of Dayananda's faith with them impossible. He referred to the influence of the Brahmo Samaj as 'denationalizing'.[28] He pointed out that instead of praising our ancient seers, membes of the Brahmo Samaj expressed cynicism towards, their teachings.

Arya Samaj and Spiritual Revivalism

While Brahmo Samaj and its leaders considered Western rule as beneficial for the purpose of social and religious reformation and for that matter wanted it to continue, Dayananda on the other hand, believed that foreign rule had been imposed upon the Indians due to their own failings. India's degradation, as he believed, was chiefly due to the Hindu pre-occupation with superfluous rituals sponsored by Brahmin priests.[29] He rightly observed that : "The causes of foreign rule in India are : mutual feud, child marriage, indulgence in carnal gratification, untruthfulness and other evil habits, the neglect of study of the Veda, and other malpractices. It is only when brothers fight among themselves that outsider poses as an arbiter".[30] And the forces of counteraction to these maladies, he could see, lie in the regeneration of Indian society on true 'Vedic Faith'.

Arya Samaj was primarily a revivalist religious organisation. It was, however, not completely devoid of modernist trends and in some aspects it continued the task of social reconstruction on modern lines as started by Brahmo Samaj. It condemned in unequivocal terms, idolatry, animal sacrifice, ancestor worship, priestcraft, offerings in temples, untouchability and child marriage. What differentiates Arya Samaj from Brahmo Samaj is that while Brahmo Samaj under Sen's influence annouced itself as a religious sect that was "nct Hinduism,[31] Arya Samaj was entirely a Hindu religious organisation". According to Sivanath Sastri the Brahmo Marriage Act supported by the progressive Brahmos under the leadership of Keshab Chandra Sen had been one of the principal causes that alienated the Brahmos from the sympathies of their orthodox countrymen.[32]

The success of Arya Samaj in appealing to common people lies in the fact that it established faith on the indigenous methods for the purpose of social and religious reformation. The programme of action adopted by Dayananda Saraswati was quite national and free from those aspects that made the Brahmo Samaj a suspect in the eyes of the Indian people.[33]

Under the influence of Brahmoism, the Congress followed a policy of extreme softness towards the British government.[34] The Extremists who were the products of spiritual revivalism in India dubbed it as the "policy of mendicancy". The way the followers of the Brahmo Samaj were following the Western ideas and institution and praising everything that was Western, it appeared that the dream of Macaulay had come true. While introducing English education he had expressed the view that it was his desire to create a class of people, "Indian in blood and colour, but English in taste, in opinion, words and intellect". The English educated Indians developed a romantic vision of the West though this did not last long. The Brahmo Samajists took the advantage of this Western inclination of the educated people and recruited them into their cadre. There was nothing wrong in English education itself or some of the liberal and democratic ideas of the West and the Indians in general would not have suspected the Indianness and integrity of the Brahmo Samaj, had it not acted as an instrument of the Rule and exhibited blind adherence to everything that was either British or Western.

Raja Rammohan Roy was one of the pioneers of introducing English education in India. It was good in one sense as it opened the doors to the wind of liberalism and democracy blowing from the West. But the actual intention of the British masters was sickening and was packed with dangerous consequences. Macaulay had expressed the pious hope that the introduction of English education would not only create a class of people who would be English in taste and opinion but also would ultimately result in the destruction of Hinduism by large-scale conversion to Christianity. He wrote to his father; "It is my firm belief that if our plans of education are followed up, there will not be a single idolator among the respectable classes of Bengal thirty years hence. And this will be effected without any efforts to proselytize, without the smallest interference with religious liberty, merely by natural operation of knowledge and reflection". Sir Charles Trevelyen, the President of the Committee of Public Instruction also expressed similar hopes and said that the introduction of English education in India would "shake Hinduism and Mohammedanism to their centre and firmly establish our language and learning and ultimately our religion in India."

The inclinations of the Brahmo Samaj towards Christianity, its pioneering efforts in the sphere of spreading English education, its blind adherence to everything Western and its criticism of Hinduism, the socio-cultural practices and the very basis of Indian way of living and thinking, made it appear like another foreign missionary organisation, though its members were of

Indian origin. Such an organisation which was not based on firm footings on its own soil and was a suspect in the eyes of majority of the Indians, was bound not only to collapse in not a very distant future, but was also bound to produce its reaction in the form of other organisations.

Rabindranath Tagore who also admired the West and pleaded for a synthesis of the ideas of East and West did not like the blind imitation of the West and a cynical attitude towards India's culture, customs and traditions. India had always kept its windows open to all civilizations and impacts. She has regulated and disciplined the different races who have come here and has accorded recognition to their distinctiveness. This could achieve cohesion in society which resulted in social and spiritual unity with one another. Tagore did not spare the orthodox Indian who became reactionary and conservative and refuted to accept that the real principle of life is to think and doubt, accept and reject, progress, change and evolve. This note of self-confidence and pride in India's past traditions and heritage counteracted against blind imitation of the West and promoted intense nationalism which was not prepared to compromise Indian interests at any cost.

The advocacy of the 'Providential role' of the British, the policy of extreme softness towards the British and the all out support for Westernism by the Brahmo Samajists, were bound to produce the reaction. Thus the Arya Samaj of Swami Dayananda Saraswati had emerged as a powerful rival organisation which challenged most of the ideas and precepts of the Brahmo Samaj and its pro-West and pro-British attitude.

Swami Dayananda Saraswati's Arya Samaj movement was a Hindu Protestant Reformation movement, which gave the call to the Indians, to return to the pristine purity of Vedic Hinduism. "The influence of Swami Dayananda, a remarkable human dynamo endowed with extraordinary power and energy, was immense. His Arya Samaj succeeded in shaking the whole structure of Hinduism in the Punjab and infusing into it new blood and vigour in a manner which the Brahmo Samajists never achieved."

The appeal of the Arya Samaj like the Brahmo Samaj was mainly intellectural, but the Arya Samaj movement had greater and more effective political impact than the Brahmo Samaj. In recognition of its political role, Reincourt rightly observed that "there is little doubt to-day that the great revolt in Bengal in 1905 was largely the indirect result of the Arya Samaj's religious nationalism, and that Dayananda's organisation was the first real concrete nucleus of political nationalism.

The practices of polytheism, idolatry, untouchability were regarded as essential features of Hindu religion by people who believed in superstitious practices. But none of them Dayananda found, could be justified by the Vedic standard.[35] For these corrupt practices, the Hindu India was greatly vilified and dishonoured by the Christians.

Emerging in a secular-nationalist period when political agitation for the freedom of India was slowly gaining ground, it was Dayananda who asserted that India's salvation lay in its moral and spiritual regeneration by inculcating in the Indian mind a sense of pride in their glorious past. He gave the call 'back to the Vedas and to the pristine purity of Vedic Hinduism', where it would be free from the "deadening weight of form and ritual, blind faith and superstition".[36] Dayananda sought vigorously to enliven the pulse of a sick nation by devoting his life to "the raising of moral timbre and in harnessing spirituality to the cultural rearmament of India."[37]

Dayananda's Concept of Religion and Vedic Dharma

Dayananda set out on his mission to carry out the pledge, given by him to his preceptor, His Holiness Swamy Virijanand Saraswati, to disseminate true knowledge of the Vedas, and condemn works which teach false doctrines and tenets in order to re-establish the Vedic religion.[38] His conception of religion was based on the substance of the Vedas. His revival of Hindu religion and his social reformistic works were based on unique and novel interpretation of Vedic religion. Dayananda Saraswati, a seeker after perpetual truth held that, "Equitable dealings, the acceptance of truth and the rejection of untruth, under all circumstances constitute the true conduct of the life, or religion, and the reverse of this is irreligion."[39] He asserted : "I believe in the religion based on universal and all-embracing principles which have always been accepted as true by mankind."[40] Admittedly Dayananda found the oldest book in the library of mankind, the Vedas, as the embodiment of perfect truth[41] and hence, the only repository of true religion. "It is a well-known fact that 5000 years ago in the whole world there existed no other religion but the Vedic."[42]

The revelationary character of the Vedas, Dayananda regarded as the sheet anchor of Hinduism. The test of revelation is that it is a communication of something which the person or persons to whom the thing is revealed did not know it before.[43] The Vedas, according to Dayananda, "were revealed in Sanskrit as Sanskrit belongs to no country, and is the mother of all other languages."[44] Holding the Vedas as eternal Dayananda argues that 'God, being eternal, His knowledge and attributes must necessarily be eternal, because the nature, attributes and character of an eternal substance are also eternal and vice-versa."[45] Vedas are books of knowledge revealed by God to the humanity. The linguistic, stylistic and etymological study of the Vedas also leads us to accept the 'super human creation' theory of the Vedas.[46] Dayananda followed the cannons laid down by Yaska, the author of Nirukta, the greatest authority on Vedic interpretation, to find out the right clues and correct meanings of the revealed words in the Vedas.[47] The most essential cannon for the interpretation of Vedic terms, Yaska held, is to treat all the Vedic terms as "Yangika", i.e., terms having derivative meaning. The terms are purely connotative and are to be judged by the context alone. But the only clue to the true signification of the term lies in the structural elements of which the word is compounded.[48] One such Vedic term 'devata', has popularly been misinterpreted by Sayana and Mahidhar (medieaval commentators) and many other European scholars, to mean the worship of innumerable mythological Gods and Goddesses called 'devatas' in the Vedas. But when used in the context of Vedic texts and understood following the clues given by ancient authorities, the true meaning of the word 'Devata', according to Pandit Gurudatta, refers to "all that can form the subject of human knowledge. All human knowledge is limited by two conditions, i.e., time and space. Our knowledge of causation is mainly that of succession of events. All succession is nothing but an order in time. Secondly, our knowledge must be a knowledge of something, and that something must be somewhere. It must have locality of its existence and occurrence, ... the most exhaustive division of human knowledge is between objective and subjective. Objective knowledge is the knowledge of the phenomena of the external universe... In speaking of subjective knowledge, there is firstly, the ego, the human spirit, the conscious entity; secondly, the internal phenomena of which the human spirit is conscious.

These latter are again divided into 'deliberate activities' and 'vital activities',... since our prior analysis of knowable leads to six things, time, locality, force, human spirit, deliberate activities and vital activities, these are fit to be called devatas; and if the account of the Nirukta concerning Vedic devatas be accepted as true, the Vedas should be understood to inculcate these six things as 'devatas' and no others".[49]

Dayananda basing his interpretation of Vedas on the light of ancient Vedic Grammar, discarded the practice of polytheism as perverted Hindu religion which was spread by selfish and ignorant priests with the help of puranas, which Dayananda held were full of false teachings. Swamy Dayananda reposed firm faith on Vedas, which he regarded as infallible, being the inspired word of God, and fount of all true knowledge--religious, spiritual as well as scientific. Dayananda took the Veda "for his guiding view of life, his rule of inner existence and his inspiration for external work, but he regarded it as even more, the word of eternal 'Truth' on which man's knowledge of God and his relations with the Divine Being and with his fellows can be rightly and securely founded".[50] His total dependance on the Vedas and only the four Vedas and their infallibility gave Dayananda's religious teachings an orthodox colouring in more than one sense. For infallibility meant that human reason was not to be the final deciding factor.[51] However, his approach has a rationalistic aspect in-as-much-as, he conceded the right to interpret the Vedas to others in accordance with the true canons of interpretation of Vedic terms. Thus individual reason was accorded its due place in the interpretation of the sacred Vedic scriptures. He believed that every person had the right to direct access to God.[52]

Prof. Amales Tripathy observes that, "This journey to the fountain head of Aryan Truth denoted a sort of denial of the validity of later religious evolutions in India".[53] In the process, Dayananda excludes even the Vedanta (the Upanishads and Vedanta Sutras) from the category of revealed scriptures. Dayananda's religious conviction put him in distinct opposition to the religious thought and teachings of many noted religious reformers of his time. "His refutation of 'Advaita' and 'Nirguna Brahman' distinguished him from Rammohan and Vivekananda as his refutation of 'Sankara' and 'avatara' distinguished him from Bankim and Ramakrishana".[54] Dayananda stood by what he thought to be the pure Vedic religion and tradition and differed from noted Brahmo leaders in many respects. Raja Rammohan Roy, a staunch believer in Upanishads wanted synthesis of Western and Eastern culture and though, belligerent against Trinitarian Christianity, he had gladly borrowed ideas from unitarianism and Islam. Debendranath denied the revelationary character of the Vedas of which Dayananda was the ardent supporter. Dayananda, however, like Debendranath, was a believer in dualist thought and asserted that the empirical world was no illusion and had an independent objective existence, that God created it and that 'Brahman' and 'Jiva' were distinct. But while the two were distinct and inseparable for Debendranath, they were absolutely separate as far as Dayananda was concerned.

Dayananda was not a believer of transcendental and pervading human soul as it was believed by the Neovedantists of his time. Accordingly he considered the worldly existence of good and evil as a reality and would not turn his back, against it as a mere illusion or 'maya'. He did not rely on special insights of a spiritual or mystic sort as was done by most Hindu religious leaders. "A careful reading of Dayananda's works and of his autobiography fails to reveal any great positive and illuminating experience of God... He nowhere speaks of any great illumination of his own spirit... though he sought long for some mystic experience, it was not forthcoming and... he threw himself into the way of strenuous activity".[55]

A man of energetic and active habits, Dayananda speaking assertively of man's involvement in this world wrote :

> "It is the soul that thinks, knows, remembers, and feels its individuality through organs of thought, discernment, memory and individuality... It is, therefore, the soul that enjoys or suffers,... it is the soul that... does acts— good or evil— and consequently it is the soul alone that reaps the fruits thereof— joy or sorrow. The soul is not a witness of acts... it is the soul that does acts and its, therefore, naturally engrossed by them. The soul is not God and consequently, it is not the seer of acts, but the actual doer".[56]

His belief in the traditional Hindu doctrines of Transmigration of soul and Karma was in line with his religious convictions. And reminiscent of Buddhist teachings, for him the way of emancipation was more ethical than spiritual. "Emancipation resulted only from obedience to the will of God, dissociation from sin, ignorance, bad company... the promotion of public good, evenhanded justice, righteousness..." [57]

Assuming the role of a practical religious and social reformer, Dayananda set about vigorously overhauling Hindu religious life urging Hindus to cultivate their bodily powers while returning spiritually to the true "Vedic Faith". The two great duties of the Arya Samaj, the most prominent socio-religious reform movement in India, were : (a) to preach the Vedic gospel throughout the whole world and (b) to recall India to the fore-shaken Vedic Paths.[58] Dayananda with intellectual aggressiveness countered the interpretation of European scholar, such as Max Muller, who considered the Vedas as the simple, natural, even common place, religious ideas of a primitive people and as such a valuable source for the study of religion, and also linguistics.[59] Raising the Vedas to a status higher than every existing religion and speaking of the infallibility of Vedic religion, Dayananda said that all that conforms to the teachings of Vedas : nature, attributes and characteristics of God is right, the contrary is wrong...[60]

In a bid to inculcate vigour, self-assertion and physical courage among the Hindus, Arya Samaj started some concrete programmes like 'Sudhi' and 'Sangathan'. These were the programmes started by Dayananda and his Arya Samaj for practical regeneration of the Hindus and preventing their proselytisation into Christianity. In the process, with some sort of intolerant and dogmatic disposition towards non-Hindu faiths, Dayananda sought to make Hinduism a proselytizing religion.[61]

Unlike most Hindu religious reformers, Dayananda had no penchant for defining his religious belief in the broadest possible terms, so as to give them a touch of universalism. He was conscious of the struggle between contending religions, particularly in India. "As night and day are opposed to each other", he wrote to Madame Blavatsky, the Theosophist leader, "so are all religions opposed to one another".[62] Dayananda in his book "Satyarth Prakash, vehemently condemned Bible and Koran as pretentions and held the Vedas as 'timeless, revealed truth, divine in origin'. Such an approach, as one of the supporters of the Arya Samaj records, "has met with considerable success in reclaiming Hindus converted to other faiths, and in stemming the tide of conversion of Hindus to other faiths. But its greater success lies in raising the social status of the depressed classes among the Hindus and preventing them from leaving Hinduism and joining other religious denomination".[63] Dayananda and Arya Samaj movement succeeded in fostering self-assured pride in the Hindu heritage in the mind of educated Indians. The concept of the gentle and often servile Hindu began to disappear and the stage was built for real unity of Hindu India and development of a combative nationalism. However, the crusade started by him against other religions, became a contributory factor in the growth of communalism in India in the 20th century. As was remarked by Muhammad Ali "whatever may be the inspiration of Hinduism as a religious creed, the educated Hindus made it a rallying symbol for political unity. The aspiration for self-government arrested all movements for social reform which the early impulse towards liberalism had called forth amongst educated Indians. Past history was ransacked for new political formulas, and by a natural and inevitable process 'nationality' and 'patriotism' began to be associated with Hinduism."[64]

Reform Vs. Revival

Prophets of new India, from Rammohan Roy to Dayananda Saraswati and Vivekananda led India onto the path of new awakening and regeneration. The history of Indian Renaissance makes an interesting study of the Hindu response to the Christian challenge— from resistance, through defence by imitation, to proud self-confidence.[65] Historically the social reformers and the Brahmo Movement came first who were for an all-out campaign against the ills of social life and Hindu religion. They were bent on relying more upon reason and the experience of European society and on incorporating the Western values of personal freedom and social equality and consequently, their approach towards reform was based on criticism, condemnation and abuse of Indian social customs, way of life and traditions that failed to come up to Western standards. It was a sort of negative approach. It had its unhealthy repercussions felt, particularly during the time of radical Brahmo reformer, Keshab Chandra Sen, when many Western educated Indians started hating and decrying religion, race and culture. This denationalising influence of the Brahmo Samaj was dangerous. Instead of praising our ancient seers and following our glorious traditions, members of the Brahmo Samaj expressed cynicism towards their teachings and Indian culture and civilization.

Revivalists, speaking against the indiscriminate imitation of the Western way of life wanted that the Indians must refuse to allow their country to stand at the bar of a foreign court and be judged according to foreign law. Annie Besant, the Theosophist and one of the staunch revivalists wrote, "The Indian work is, first of all, the revival, strengthening and uplifting of the ancient religions. This has brought with it a new self-respect, a pride in the past, a belief in the future... as an inevitable result... the beginning of the rebuilding of a nation."[66] In the glorification of India's past, the revivalists sounded a note of exaltation of sentiment over intellect, and that appealed to a great extent both to the conservative educated minds and the general mass.

It may be stated without the fear of contradiction that Dayananda's extraordinary claims in favour of the Vedas and his eulogies in support of Indian culture, civilization and way of life, represented a reaction against the Brahmo Samajist obsession for Westernism and Christianity. Referring to Swami Dayananda's claims, a fervent Arya Samajist makes the following statement :

> "(1) Dayananda does claim, and rightly, that in matters of religion and in the domain of spirit the Western mind has not reached either the depths or the heights commanded by the ancient Indian mind; and in such matters it has still much to learn from the ancient Indian sages (2) In matters social, the Indian soultions arrived at in ancient times are as good, as sound and as effective, at least, as are those arrived at in the West by the latest modern thought. (3) In the domain of philosophy India has nothing to learn from the West. The best of European thought does not yet come upto the level of the best Hindu thought... (4) In the realm of physical science, the Europeans are far in advance of the ancient Indians, though it may fairly and justly be claimed that most of the fundamental truths on which the superstructure of European science is raised, were known to the Indians."[67]

Swami Dayandna was highly critical of the Brahmos and questioned, "How can the principles of those who are unaware of the Vedic lore be all good?" He attacked the Brahmos as according to him, they lacked in patriotism and borrowed much from Christianity in their ways of living. The Brahmos praised Christianity and Englishmen, but condemned Hinduism and the rishis and saints of India. Instead of praising and glorifying their own country and their ancestors, they spoke disparagingly about them and appreciated everything Western. They thought that the Indians were ignorant and there was not a single learned man like the English people from the time of the very creation of the world. The Brahmos not only did not respect the Vedas — the most sacred scriptures of the Hindus, but also did not desist from condemning them. All these lapses on the part of the Brahmo Samaj were too much for a staunch nationalist like Dayananda to tolerate. However, it may be stated that most of these criticisms were not applicable to all the leaders of the Brahmo Samaj, but the Samaj was by and large identified with these concepts.

As an intellectual movement and religious organisation, the Arya Samaj of Swami Dayananda, was revivalist and purely Indian, as opposed to the rationalist and cosmopolitan character of the Brahmo Samaj. The Arya Samaj movement, therefore, had great political significance, because in a country like India, religion is very much connected with social behaviour and its socio-political institutions.

Like the Brahmo Samaj, the Arya Samaj also condemned evil socio-religious practices like idolatry, animal sacrifice, priestcraft, caste system, offerings in the temples, ancestor worship and pilgrimages and may be said to be reformist in outlook. But despite these similarities, the revivalism of Arya Samaj was evident from its insistence on the infallibility of the Vedas, faith in Karma and re-birth, sacredness of the cow, the efficacy of the homa and the importance of the Samskaras.

The reformist and revivalist zeal of Dayananda has been compared with that of Martin Luther :

> "There were many points of contact between Dayananda Saraswati and Martin Luther. As Luther, the German monk, was a child of the European renaissance, so Dayananda, the Gujarati monk, was a child of Indian renaissance. Both

> alike felt the tug of the 'zeitgeist'. Both in their different ways became exponents of the spirit. Luther attacked indulgence, while Dayananda attacked idolatry. Luther appealed from the Roman Church and the authority of tradition to the scriptures of the Old and New Testments. Swami Dayananda appealed from the Brahminical Church and the authority of Smriti to the earliest and most sacred of Indian scriptures. The watchword of Luther was 'Back to the Bible', the watchword of Dayandnda was 'Back to the Vedas'."[68]

Although Swami Dayananda was a staunch nationalist and revivalist and he was one of the most important inspirers of religious nationalism in India, he had also elements of reformism in him, which brought him closer to Rammohan Roy and other leaders of the socio-religious reform movements. The problems confronted by Dayananda were many and he wanted to solve them in the best possible manner :

> "The problem which confronted him was how to reform Indian religion, how to effect a synthesis of the old and the new, of the East and the West, in such a way as to guarantee the intellectual and spiritual supremacy of the Indian people, do full justice to the attainments of the other nations, and provide a universalistic programme of religion".[69]

It may be pointed out that Dayananda sought the solution to most of the problems, in the doctrine of the Vedas as the revealed word of God. He considered the Vedas as the fountain-head of the science and religion of all mankind and to that extent, he may be considered as a revivalist. But the modernist trends and the rationalist ideas in the philosophy of Dayandnda cannot be ignored. Both the Brahmo Samaj and the Arya Samaj as well as the other modernist and revivalist movements in India, had come under the influence of advanced rationalist ideas. Although historically speaking the Brahmo Samaj, the Prarthana Samaj and the Aligarh School appeared first and Arya Samaj, the Ramakrishan Mission and the Theosophist movement came later, "It cannot be rigidly maintained that all the 'modernist' trends appeared first and the 'revivalist' trends later."

It would be incorrect to put these movements exclusively in the modernist or the revivalist group. The Brahmo Samaj had elements of revivalism in it. It is equally true that the Arya Samaj of Swami Dayananda Saraswati spread some modernist and rationalist ideas, although it had strong revivalist tendencies.

In fitness of things it may be stated that the revivalist and often reactionary trends developed in India as a protest against the effort of the reformers to reconstruct Indian society by mechanically introducing Western ideas and institutions. In their ardent admiration for the West, the Brahmo Samajists ignored the actualities of Indian life and situation. They tried to reconstruct Indian society and reform Hinduism, without any regard for historic continuity, which alone could provide them with strength and vitality. All these activities naturally led to a violent reaction, which appeared in the form of a strong social and religious revival. In a sense, it was a historical necessity in order to bring the new thought in the country back to the realities of India's national life and history.[70] Gradually, even many ardent reformers realised the strength of tradition and the importance of maintaining continuity of social life and institutions, while introducing reforms.[71]

Footnotes

1. V. P. Varma, *Modern Indian Political Thought,* p. 29.
2. M. M. Ahluwalia, *Swamy Dayananda Saraswati,* p. 6.
3. Quoted by C. H. Heimsath, *Indian Nationalism and Hindu Social Reform,* p. 13.
4. Girija K. Mookerjee, *History of Indian National Congress* (1832-1947), p. 13.
5. *Ibid.*
6. The name of Derozio (1808-31) is associated with the Hindu College. He was accused of having corrupted the minds of the young Bengalis with his revolutionary ideas on religion, idolatry, priestcraft, free will and liberty.
7. R. Rolland, *Life of Ramakrishna,* p. 139.
8. Kenneth W. Jones, *Arya Dharma – Hindu Consciousness in 19th Century Punjab,* p. 43.
9. Bipin Chandra Pal, *Memories of My Life and Times in the Day of My Youth,* (Calcutta, 1932), p. 424.
10. C. Y. Chintamani, *Indian Social Reform* (Madras, 1892), Part II, p. 30.

11. K. P. Karunakaran, *Religion and Political Awakening in India* (Delhi, 1965), p. 60.
12. C. H. Heimsath, *op. cit.*, pp. 105-107.
13. From ISR, as quoted in S. Natarajan, *A Century of Social Reform in India*, p. 61.
14. C. H. Heimsath, p. 105.
15. M. L. Vidyarthi, *India's Culture Through the Ages*, p. 339.
16. R. S. Pareek, Contribution of Arya Samaj in the Making of Modern India, p. 42.
17. Ronaldshay, *The Heart of Aryavarta*, London, 1925, p. 45.
18. Amales Tripathy, *op. cit.*, p. viii.
19. Amales Tripathy, *op. cit.*, p. 30.
20. R. H. Pathak, Dayananda, the Man and His Mission (a pamphlet), Sarvadeshik Arya Pratinidhi Sabha, New Delhi, 1969, p. 2.
21. *Encyclopaedia of Religion and Ethics* (ed.) James Hastings, Vol. II, pp. 58-59.
22. H. B. Sarada (Ed.), Dayananda Commemoration Volume, see an article, Swamy Dayananda Saraswati — A Nation Builder, by Anand Swarup, Ajmer, 1933, p. 11.
23. De Bury (Ed.), *Sources of Indian Tradition*, Columbia University Press, 1958, p. 635.
24. C. H. Heimsath, *Indian Nationalism and Hindu Social Reform*, p. 25.
25. Anesaki, "Arya Samaj", *Encyclopaedia of Religion and Ethics*, Volume II, J. Hastings, Edinburgh (ed.) 1953, p. 58-59.
26. Quoted by Satya Prakash in his book, A Critical Study of the Philosophy of Dayananda (Ajmer, 1938), p. 484.
27. Lajpat Rai, *The Arya Samaj*, n. 6, 220-1.
28. *Satyarth Prakash* Chap. II, London, 1915, p. 310.
29. C. H. Heimsath, *op. cit.*, p. 121.
30. *Satyarth Prakash*, p. 320.
31. C. H. Heimsath, *op. cit.*, p. 94.
32. Quoted by C. H. Heimsath, *op. cit.*, p. 94.
33. Kenneth W. Jones, *Arya Dharma — Hindu Consciousness in 19th Century Punjab*, p. 42.
34. A detailed discussion of this aspect has been made in the next chapter.
35. G. P. Bhattacharjee, *Contribution of Maharshi Dayananda*, p. 7.
36. B. K. Singh, Swamy Dayananda's Contribution to Spiritual Revival in India, an article in Bhavan's Journal, Bombay, April 23, 1967, p. 31.
37. B. K. Singh, *Ibid.*, p. 31.
38. H. B. Sarda, *Life of Dayananda Saraswati*, pp. 34-35.
    Also see H. B. Sarda, Works of Maharshi Dayananda and Paropkarini

Sabha, Vedic Yantralaya, Ajmer, 1942, pp. 12-13.

39. Dayananda Saraswati, *Satyarth Prakash* (Hindi), Govind Ram Haranand, 8th Edition, Delhi, 1965, see introduction, p. II.
40. Quoted in Tarachand Gajna, An Interpretation of Dayananda (an article) in Vedic Light, New Delhi, February, 1969, p. 25.
41. According to the consensus of the scholars, the Vedas are the sources of all evidences. All the Samskars starting from birth to death have been based on the principles of the Vedas. The Vedas contain subtle as well as transcendental knowledge which are lacking in other Shastras and religious scriptures — Dayananda Saraswati, Rig Veda Vasyam (Hindi & Sanskrit) Ed. by Yudhistir Mimansaka, Part II, Ram Lal Kapur Trust, Bhahalgarh, 1973, p. 1.
42. Swami Dayananda Saraswati, *Satyarth Prakash* (Hindi), Introduction to Ch. XI, p. 225.
43. Acharya Vaidyanath Shastree, *The Veda, Why ?* (An article in Jan Gyan), New Delhi, pp. 14-15.
44. Dayananda Saraswati, *Satyarth Prakash,* p. 165.
45. *Ibid.*, p. 167.
46. Dr. Bhabani Lal Bhartiya, The Contribution of Swamy Dayananda to the Study of Vedas (An article in Jan Gyan), p. 27.
47. The rules laid down by the author of the Nirukta apply to every part of the Vedas. All the Mantras treat three classes of subjects. Some of them concern Paroksha (not sense-cognised), some with Pratyaksha (sense-cognised) and others with Adhyatmik (subjects pertaining to the self) — Swamy Dayanand Sraswati, Rig Vedadivhasya Bhumika (Sanskrit and Hindi) Vedic Yantralaya, Ajmer, Tenth Edition, 1970, pp. 383-384.
48. Pandit Gurudatta Vidyarthi, *Terminology of the Vedas,* Chicago Edition, p. 7.
49. Lajpat Rai, Pandit Gurudatta Vidyarthi, quoted in *A History of Arya Samaj,* (ed.) Sri Ram Sharma, pp. 56-57.
50. Aurobindo, *Dayananda and the Veda* (an article) in Vedic Magazine, 1961.
51. Bipan Chandra, *Modern India* (N. C. E. R. T. Publication, Delhi, 1971), p. 219.
52. Bipan Chandra, *op. cit.,* pp. 219-20.
53. Amales Tripathy, *The Extremist Challenge,* p. 31.
54. Amales Tripathy, *op. cit.,* p. 33.
55. J. Reid Graham, "The Arya Samaj as a Reformation in Hinduism with Special Reference to Caste", p. 237.
56. *Satyarth Prakash,* Translated in English by Chiranjiva Bharadvaja, 2nd edn., Allahabad, 1915, p. 275.
57. *Satyarth Prakash,* p. 279.
58. Anesaki, "Arya Samaj", *Encyclopaedia of Religion and Ethics,* vol. II,

J. Hastings, Edinburgh (ed.), 1953, p. 58-59.
59. See Max Muller, *Indian Philosophy*, Ch. II.
60. Quoted by Satya Prakash in his book, *A Critical Study of the Philosophy of Dayananda* (Ajmer, 1938), p. 484.
61. Some Arya Samajists, The Arya Samaj, p. 21; Lajpat Rai, The Arya Samaj, pp. 220-21.
62. Letter of Nov. 23, 1880, quoted in Sarda, Life of Dayananda Saraswati, p. 544.
63. Lajpat Rai, *The Arya Samaj,* n. 6, 220-1.
64. Select writings and Speeches of Muhammad Ali (ed.) Afzal Iqbal, 1944, pp. 65-70.
65. Theodore de Bary, n. 2, 603.
66. Annie Besant, *Autobiography*, quoted by Sankar Ghose, *op. cit.*, p. 77.
67. Lajpat Rai, *Arya Samaj* (London, 1932), n. 6, p. 257.
68. *Encyclopeaedia of Religion and Ethics,* (ed.) James Hastings, Edinburgh, 1953, Vol. II, n. 7, pp. 58-59.
69. *Ibid*., pp. 63-64.
70. Bipin Chandra Pal, *Swadeshi and Swaraj,* (Calcutta, 1954) p. 18.
71. K. P. Karunakaran, *op. cit.*, p. 59.

7

The Impacts of the Brahmo Samaj and Arya Samaj Movements on the Political Developments in India (1885–1920)

The Impact of Brahmo Samaj

The Renaissance and Reformation of the 19th century in India, were greatly influenced by the spread of Western education. The Brahmo Samaj played a crucial role in creating the much needed popular support for the introduction of English as the medium of instruction. Raja Rammohan Roy and his followers like Debendranath Tagore and Keshab Chandra Sen were deeply influenced by Western ideas and the religious principles of Christianity. They were thus eager to support the spread of Western education and Western ideas for modernizing the Indian society and were probably oblivious of the real intentions of the British in its insistence for the introduction of Western education. Highlighting the British intention Thomas Babington Macaulay rightly said that it was his purpose to create a class of people in India who would be, "Indians in blood and colour, but English in taste, in opinion, words and intellect".[1] Thus Western educated people believed in the legitimacy of the British Rule in India[2] and considered themselves as the chosen few to speak for all their countrymen.[3] It would not be far from truth to say that this elitist class provided the ideological base for the future Moderates of the Indian National Congress.

The British conquest generated a new vigour and dynamism in the social, intellectual and political life of India. India was not only "politically and economically unified but she also came in contact with the Western science, technology and liberal ideas".[4] Through the spread of English education, the British helped the educated Indians to develop a scientific outlook and temper which helped them in fighting against the obnoxious social evils, which paved the way for the social reformation movement.[5]

The spread of Western education created a middle class

intelligentsia, which played a significant part in the development of Indian nationalism.[6] It proved to "the body politic, what light and air are to the living organism". Writers like Voltaire, Locke, Rousseau, Robespierre, Garibaldi and Mazzini and others inspired the Indians through their writings, to cherish the ideal of political liberty. In its early days the Indian National Congress was greatly influenced by the liberal writings of Milton, Burke, J. S. Mill, Macaulay, Spencer and a host of other writers. Thus it may not be far from truth to say that India owed her democratic spirit to the parliamentary rhetoric of Bright and Gladstone. Western education inspired this small but enlightened class of people to demand increased rights and priviledges and cause embarrassment for the British administration.[7] The Indians were considerably influenced by Western education and the influence continues till today notwithstanding the termination of British Rule in India. The writings of the liberal European writers and the democratic and liberal Western philosophy greatly influenced Indian patriots and nationalists and "as in the morning of the world light travelled from East to West, so towards the beginning of the last century the returning light began to proceed from the West to the East."[8]

The early leaders of the Congress came from this Western educated class and inspite of their initial docility, created a strong national sentiment and an urge for self-government. The Indians who went to Great Britain for their higher education, came in contact with democracy, parliamentary institutions and rights of the citizen and imbibed the spirit of equality, freedom and independence. On their return back to India they found that the political scenario in the country was entirely different. It was not possible for them to lead a free life in the oppressive and depressing political atmosphere of India. Most of them took the leadership of the protest movement which proved infectious.[9] Thus the Western educated early leaders of the Congress played a pioneering role in the initiation and continuance of liberal trends in Indian politics.[10]

The legacy of the socio-religious reformers was a formidable factor in the Congress during the formative period. The cultural leaders gave greater priority to the economic prosperity of the subjects rather than their political rights and liberties. For promoting the welfare of the subjects and for implementing socio-religious reforms, they needed the support of the British rulers. It was thought that this could be made possible by making prayers and petitions to the rulers and by negotiating with them from time to time. As the socio-religious reformers depended on the mercy of the British, there was no question of confrontation with them. They always appealed for the sympathy and support of the British. On the part of the British, it was not difficult to extend support for the socio-religious reforms, particularly when there was the co-operation of the educated class. However this attitude was different from the earlier British policy of non-interference. Thus there were remarkable changes in the socio-religious spheres in India, under the changed circumstances.

A new awakening was created in India by the Renaissance and the Reformation of the 19th century. The main objective of the socio-religious reformers was to purify Hindu society and religion by destroying the socio-religious prejudices, superstitions and caste barriers. Two clear trends were noticed in the approach of the people, who wanted to emancipate India from one of the darkest pariods of her history. One group was led by Raja Rammohan Roy, which was liberal, cosmopolitan and eclectic in its approach and tried to assimilate the good aspects of other religions and cultures.[11] It was the aim of the other group of people led by Swami Dayananda, Vivekananda, the Theosophists and nationalists to revive the great Indian culture and to reform its society and religion in accordance with cultural and spiritual traditions of the country. This group was essentially nationalistic and conservative in its approach and revivalistic in its philosophy. The impact of these two groups on the Indian society was so great that even the orthodox elements were roused from their slumber. They were forced to give up their self-complacency. The cultural awakening created as a result of the Western influence was not confined only to the members and followers of either the Brahmo Samaj or the Arya Samaj. It had percolated to the other strata of the Indian society. Thus both Raja Rammohan Roy and Swami Dayananda Saraswati played a great role in inaugurating the progressive socio-religious movements in India.

During this period, the Hindu religion faced the challenge of extinction due to the proselytising zeal of the Christian missionaries, which were operating in India with the protection and support of the British rulers. It may be pointed out that the radical Brahmos and the conservative pundits, had to make a marriage of convenience and join hands to fight against the onslaught of the Christian missionaries. But they were also engaged in conflicts among themselves on various other issues. This conflict resulted in a synthesis which was represented by Pandit Iswar Chandra Vidyasagar. He stood for progress based on a synthesis of Eastern and Western cultures. He generally accepted the Western spirit of reform, but refused to break away from the Hindu society or to go too far in emulating the West, as the Brahmos were inclined to do in the beginning.[12]

This synthesis was rare phenomena during the formative period of the Indian National Congress. However, it did not become a conspicuous factor in the emergence of leadership in the Congress till it had become a sufficiently grown up organisation.

It may be mentioned that the Brahmo Samaj was openly following a policy of loyalty and extreme docility towards the Rule. It preached the idea of England's 'providential mission' in India.

Loyalty to the British Government was an integral part of Brahmo ethics. This was evident from the statement of Keshab Chandra Sen (1843-1884) who proclaimed : "It is Christ who rules British India and not the British Government".[13] Keshab Chandra Sen argued that there was the hand of providence in the British conquest of India. He considered it as a primarily moral and intellectual conquest ordained to enlighten the Indians and uplift them from their degraded conditions. Under his leadership the Brahmo Samaj tried for a synthesis of all religions.[14]

The Arya Samaj movement came as a reaction against the extreme Western orientation of the Brahmo Samaj and in many respects was its antithesis. It may, therefore, be pointed out that the Brahmo Samaj and the Arya Samaj, provided the intellectual atmosphere for the emergence of the Moderates and Extremists respectively.

It was the idea of the Brahmo Samajists to conform to Western norms and to remake India in the image of the West. They were eager to perpetuate the British Rule and propagated the concept of providential role of the British. They had definite Christian leanings and wanted to implement socio-religious reforms in the Western model. They also wanted the help and co-operation of the administration in their reform activities. The Samaj was based upon blind and almost fanatical adherence to Western methods and values. Thus the influence of the Brahmo Samaj on the first products of the Indian Renaissance was tremendous. Incidentally many of them came to hold high offices in the Congress, which to a great extent determined the character of the Congress. Due to this reason, the early Congress and its leaders were notorious for their professed loyalty to the Rule.

As against the extreme loyalty of the Brahmo Samaj to the British Rule and its Christian leanings, the Arya Samaj was a highly nationalist and revivalist organisation which was opposed to Christian leaning and blind Western imitation. It asked every Hindu to be proud of being a Hindu and to love India's culture and civilization. Its principles included among others, "to love the Vedic religion, to be proud of Aryan greatness and to make sacrifices for the country".[15] This was a vehement reaction against the Brahmo ethics which propounded that, "The spirit of Christianity has already pervaded the whole atmosphere of Indian society and we breathe, think, feel, and move in a Christian atmosphere".[16] The pursuit of the philosophy of revivalism by the Arya Samaj and its concept of sacrifice for the cause of the country and its religious dogmatism came as natural reactions against Brahmo ideology which acted as a hindrance to the development of the spirit of nationalism. It is due to the impact of this philosophy of extreme nationalism an Arya Samajist like Lala Lajpat Rai, at the height of professional success as a lawyer, could declare that, "to amass wealth was not the object of my life, to enjoy luxury was not my goal, to win official honours was not my ambition, I wanted to sacrifice myself to my people and my country".[17]

The Arya Samaj believed in the capacity of energetic action for the achievement of desired goal, rather than resigning to fatalism and predestination. As opposed to the Brahmo ideology of admiring and imitating the Western way of life and values, the Arya Samaj gave great emphasis on Aryan pride, self-confidence and self-help. It prided in the glory of ancient India and rejected the Brahmo theory that there could have been no regeneration in India without the British.

The Arya Samaj insisted that the Indians have to regenerate India's former greatness by their own efforts. It appealed to the Indians to "unfasten the claims of intellectual, moral, religious and social bondage".[18] The Arya Samaj developed as a militant organisation expressing defiance against political bondage and Indians were asked to give up their parasitical character— their helpless dependence on environment and conditions of life. The philosophy of the Arya Samaj had great appeal for the Indians as it sprang from the soil of the country and asked people to develop a sense of introspection. Even a cosmopolitan universalist like Rabindranath Tagore could not remain uninfluenced by the philosophy of the Arya Samaj. He urged the Indians to have faith in themselves and to be proud of India's past glory and rich traditions. His infectious self-confidence is evident from the following statement :

> "I shall do what can be done by self-sacrifice; I shall get what can be got by self-abnegation; I shall give what can be given by self-immolation. If this is possible, well and good; if this is not to happen, if we cannot feed ourselves without asking for services from others; if we are to remain illiterate on the closing down of schools by others; if purse strings for the service of the country are not unloosened without the incentive of Government honours, then let us take leave from the face of the earth without blaming any one. It is better to meet with doom and perdition if anything great is not achieved in our country by our own efforts."[19]

It may also be pointed out that Tagore condemned those people, who with utter disregard for the glorious traditions of India tried to make blind imitation of the West. But at the same time, Tagore was highly critical of the orthodox Indians who were conservative and reactionary in their attitude and refused to accept that the real principle of life was "to think and doubt, accept and reject, progress, change and evolve". This note of self-confidence expressed by Tagore was characteristic of the Arya Samaj philosophy. In the course of time pride in India's past traditions and heritage not only counteracted against blind imitation of the West, but also gave rise to intense nationalism, which was not prepared to compromise Indian interests at any cost.

It would amount to gross generalisation to say that the Reformists and Revivalists, in terms of their ideological orientations and commitments constituted two clearcut groups, completely separated from each other. All the Western Reformists did not plead for the wholesale imitation of Western life and culture. They shared some of the ideas of the Revivalists regarding the future development in India. On the other hand the Revivalists were not less influenced by the British institutions, the English education and their concepts of liberty, equality and rights. Most of the Revivalist leaders were the products of English education and owed their progressive ideas and intense patriotism to the British contact. The serious minded Western Reformists, shared the feeling of the Revivalists and argued that Western things should be looked with the eyes of the Indians and those aspects should be borrowed from the West, which could be made applicable to the Indian conditions. Thus the difference between the Reformists and the Revivalists in most cases was a difference of degree rather than of kind. However, the Reformists and the Revivalists differed in the degree of emphasis on the usefulness of the Western models, for the reconstruction of the contemporary Indian society and various other institutions.

The revivalist philosophy of the Arya Samaj and other organisations like the Ramakrishna Mission and the Theosophical Society, greatly influenced the ideas and the political programmes of the Extremists. But it cannot be denied that leading extremists like Lala Lajpat Rai, Bal Gangadhar Tilak, Bipin Chandra Pal and Aurobindo Ghosh, were all the products of English education. They were not less influenced by the Western ideas than the Moderates, who were influenced by the reformists ideas of the Brahmo Samaj. The love of the Extremists for their Motherland and their determination to fight against oppression, exploitation, injustice and racial discrimination, owed their origin to the British liberal traditions and the rights of the governed inherent in their democratic institutions. The Extremists were also influenced by Western thought, literature and personalities. The only difference was that the Extremists did not want to be completely uprooted from their own traditions and in reforming the Indian society, they wanted to refer to India's past as much as possible.

It would, however, be unfair to claim this as a distinctive feature of the Extremists as Moderates like Justice Ranade also did not like to be completely uprooted from the Indian soil. Referring to the unavoidable impact of traditions, he made the following observation :

> "You are unconsciously influenced by the traditions in which you are born, by the surroundings in which you are brought up, by the very milk which you have drunk from your mother's breast or influenced by those things in the world which you cannot disown".[20]

Although the political methods, provided some distinctiveness to the Moderates and the Extremists, there was no difference in their objectives relating to the reconstruction of socio-political institutions. Both the Moderates and the Extremists have submitted to the impacts of Western influence — the former consciously and the latter unconsciously. Lala Lajpat Rai said, "Western civilization is a gigantic force and we cannot protect ourselves from its advancing march".[21] Referring to the influence of Western ideas on the Extremists and the Moderates or the Reformers, B. C. Pal said that "whereas the Reformer was trying to consciously control and regulate his social evolution after the manner of Europe, the reactionary is unconscious of the domination of these alien ideas".[22] Further, he observed that, "Both the reformer and the reactionary are thus, found at the final analysis, to be equally inspired, the one consciously and the other unconsciously, by the spirit of Europe. Both have, more or less, imbibed the European temperament".[23] In an article entitled Reform or Revival, Lajpat Rai, referring to the impact of the Reformist and Revivalist schools had observed that, "On our part we here in the Punjab are prepared to take our inspiration from both these sources though we prefer to begin with the latter and call in the assistance of the former mainly to understand and explain what is not clear and ambiguous in the latter..."[24]

The Western impact was no doubt the animating force both for the Moderates and the Extremists, but despite this similarity there was a vital difference in their political method and their general attitude towards the British Rule. While the Moderates believed in the fair-play and sense of justice of the British and argued that the interests of India and Britain were allied, the Extremists attributed all the evils to the British Rule and insisted that the Indian and British interests were antagonistic. The ideological conviction of the Moderates led them to accept the methods of prayers and petitions and this almost became an overriding obsession with them. Thus the Moderate leaders who followed the policy of 'mendicancy', were greatly influenced by the Brahmo ideology of accepting the British as friends and collaborators.

There were other factors which were responsible for making the early Congress a harmless social organisation. The social factors which were highlighted during the 19th century both by the Reformists and the Revivalists played their role in making the Congress a docile organisation.

It was pointed out by I. Ramsay MacDonald, that the history of the Indian national movement was the history of the Indian National Congress. However, it may be noted that he has not taken into consideration the various social organisations which were in existence in India, and which were actively working for socio-religious transformation, prior to the emergence of the Congress. As social reform was inseparably linked with religious reforms, most of the enthusiastic reformers like Raja Rammohan Roy, guided by Western influence, tried to bring reforms in Hinduism. The concept of social service is also an integral part of the Indian tradition and the ancient Indian scriptures have always given importance to social service.

The social-service organisations which existed in India before the emergence of the Indian National Congress influenced this organisation and during the initial stages of its development it was not a political organisation in the strict sense of the term. It borrowed the ideas of the social organisations, which were already working for ameliorating the conditions of the people. Due to this the Congress very soon became popular. As it co-opted the organisational ability of the leaders of the social organisations, it reached the grass-roots in a remarkably short period of time.

It is needless to say that these social factors were responsible for making the Congress a docile and loyal organisation, as for fulfilment of the social goals it was not necessary to adopt a hostile stance against the government. The goals could only be achieved by seeking the support and co-operation of the government. Thus the humble prayers and petitions of the Congress have to be assessed in the perspective of the social factors which were responsible for its emergence.

English education had freed the minds of educated men from the bondage of superstition and harmful practices. They were not prepared to accept anything as sacred merely because it had the support of religion or traditions and customs. They started to question the validity of every custom and practice. Everything in order to be accepted, had to pass the tests set by rational mind. The English educated intelligentsia was convinced about the need for rapid transformation of the social order. Thus there was a rapid growth of social organisations, which tried to bring up the society to modern conditions of life. They tried to liberate the people from their socio-religious bondage and remove the barriers to their progress.

Social democracy in terms of removal of social superstitions and various social evils and provision of equality of opportunity for all dawned in India much prior to political consciousness. The predominant social urge of the 19th century became an integral part of the nationalist movement in India.[25] In the words of Lala Lajpat Rai :

> "We want to preach the gospel of social democracy. We know that we cannot fly the flag of socialism... (but) the present constitution of society is wrong and unjust. It is cruel and barbarous. We want equal opportunity and equal justice for all".[26]

In order to promote greater social unity and cohesion, the social reformers fought against the caste system. They fought for the progressive forces of liberty and democracy. Thus the Indian National Congress which had a social background, provided justifiable grounds for the policy of moderation pursued by the early Congress. Prominent Congress leaders of this period felt that the Indians must have proper training before they could demand political democracy. They also believed in the essential goodness of the British and their sincerity for promoting the good of the Indians.

It is interesting to note that during this period the British were also equally eager to satisfy the aspirations of the loyal Indians, in order to curb all future resistance to their authority. Precisely for this reason, the formation of the Indian National Congress, was encouraged by the Rule. This was reflected in the following speech of A. O. Hume :

> "Western education and Western ideas have let loose forces which unless guided and controlled might sooner or later involve consequences which

> are too disastrous to contemplate and it is precisely to limit and control these forces and direct them, while there is yet time, into safe channels that this Congress was designed."[27]

The rapport between the Moderate leaders and the British was based on their faith in British goodness. Pattabhi Sitaramayya has rightly observed that :

> "The Congress at that time honestly believed that the English Constitution was the bulwark of popular liberties everywhere and the English Parliament was the mother of democracy all over, the British Constitution was the best of all constitutions... That the press and the forest laws should be relaxed, the police should become friendly to the people, that the taxes should be moderate, that the military expenditure should be curtailed..."[28]

The formation of the Indian National Congress was thus encouraged by the British and in the beginning it was certainly not a consummation of political forces in the country. Its organisers never envisaged that it might have to act as an effective political organisation for demanding political rights and liberties of the people.

Lord Dufferin gave the permission for the formation of the Indian National Congress. He was aware of the spread of social consciousness as a result of the 19th century reform movements, and by his favourable gesture, he wanted to meet the challenge of the elite by confining their work to the sphere of social uplift of the people. Such an action was considered necessary as a subtle imperial strategy. In October 1884, Wilfrid Blunt wrote, "Today their motto is 'Reform', let us not drive them to make it 'Revolution' tomorrow".[29] This strategy was also explicit in the warning of Sir Henry Harrison in 1886 : "Repress the educated natives, their ambitions and their aspirations and you turn them into a solid phalanx of opposition against the Government; gratify their amibitions, and you make them the allies of the Government".[30]

This shrewd action of appeasement of the elites on the part of the Government, resulted in the containment of the educated class, who might have otherwise gone politically astray and would have posed serious problems for the administration.

Due to the tremendous educational and cultural impact of the West, the educated Indians had a psychological weakness for the British and when they got favoured treatment from the Government, they became the loyal admirers of anything British or Western. The immense faith that the educated people had in the British Government is evident from the statement of Dadabhai Naoroji, one of the most prominent leaders of the early Congress:

> "I for one, have not the shadow of doubt that in dealing with such justice-loving, fairminded people as the British, we may rest fully assured... have always believed that the time will come when the sentiments of the British nation and our gracious Queen's Proclamation of 1858 will be realised".[31]

The thirteenth president of the Indian National Congress, (1897), C. Sankaran Nair also made a similar observation eulogizing the British :

"Just look for a moment at the training we are receiving. From our earliest school days the great English writers have been our classics, Englishmen had been our Professors in Colleges, English history is taught to us in our schools. The books we generally read are English books which describe in details all the forms of English life, give us all the English types of character".[32]

In this manner, the early Congress consisting of a small elitist minority, greatly influenced by Western education and culture and absolutely loyal to the Rule, was never considered to be a dangerous organisation. The Government supported the Congress and was friendly, because it was engaged mostly in the work of social uplift and did not have any political aspirations. They had mutual appreciation and co-operation.

In his introduction to G. A. Natesan's 'Indian Politics' (1897), W. C. Bonnerjee highlighted the Congress objective in the following words :

> "Mr. A. O. Hume, C. B., had in 1884 conceived the idea that it would be of great advantage to the country if leading Indian politicians could be brought together once a year to discuss social matters and be upon friendly footing with one another... He did not desire that politics should form part of their discussion for there were recognized political bodies (like the British Indian

Association) in Calcutta, Madras and other parts of India".[33]

It is interesting to note that the persons who became the Presidents of the Congress from 1885 to 1905, the year of Bengal Partition, were either Englishmen or their staunch Indian supporters. A. O. Hume, an Englishman, was the founder of the Indian National Congress. His loyalty to England was unquestionable and he could never have dreamt of making India free from British control. He organised the Congress to play the role of a safety-valve organisation. He succeeded to a great extent in paralysing the development of a wider and more militant movement during the initial stages of the formation of the Congress.

In a bid to explain the origin and objectives of the Congress, Hume said, "begetting hold of the great lower middle class before the development of the reckless demagogues to which the next quarter of the century might give birth and carefully inoculating them with a mild and harmless form of the political fever, we are adopting the only certain precautionary method against the otherwise inevitable ravages of a violent and epidemic burst of disorder."[34]

Thus it is evident that the founder of the Congress, A. O. Hume, was keen to check the spread of extremist ideas and to limit and control forces which Western education and ideas had let loose in India. Some years later it was observed by Stanley Skinner that, "It is these newly created educated communities alone that are responsible today for all the present political agitation and unrest throughout the whole of India."[35]

A. O. Hume took all steps to prevent Congress from playing a political role detrimental to the interest of the British Government. He resisted the Congress attempt for passing proposals for the abolition of Arms Act, which would have enabled the Indians to own and possess arms. He argued that the memory of the Mutiny (the First War of Indian Independence), would never allow him to support such a resolution.[36]

A look into the list of Congress Presidents, during the formative years, would reveal, that besides its founder who was an Englishman, out of the eighteen persons who held the office of the President, four were Englishmen— George Yule (1888), Sir William Wedderburn (1889), Alfred Webb (1894) and Sir Henry

Cotton (1904). All these Presidents, obviously had absolute loyalty for the British Government in India in their own interest. It is but natural for them to expect the perpetuation of the Rule. It is needless to say that in steering the Congress through a course of carefully planned action, Hume's main concern was to keep the Congress away from political agitations. Even most of the Indians who became Presidents of the Congress during its formative years, true to Macaulay's predictions, were Indians in blood and colour but English in taste, opinions, morals and intellect.

Surendranath Banerjea was the best specimen of this type. He was a dismissed civil servant with marked Anglophilism. He was aptly described by Jawaharlal Nehru as, "a queer mixture of the East and the West, out of place everywhere, at home nowhere".[37] By his training, temperament and education, he was pro-British and loyal to the Rule. He was greatly influenced by Keshab Chandra Sen and propagated the philosophy of the Brahmo Samaj.[38] He also received all cordiality and help from the Brahmo Samaj when he along with his family was socially ostracized. He had great admiration for the British institutions and British culture and religious inclinations towards Christianity. He was attracted towards the Brahmo philosophy due to its similarities with his own emotional commitments. Brahmo influence on the Congress can also be inferred from the fact that the President of the 14th Session at Madras, Anand Mohan Bose, was also a Brahmo Samajist. Most of the Presidents of the early Congress either manifestly subscribed to the Brahmo ideology or were its tacit supporters. They were quite eager to maintain best possible rapport with the British and made strenuous efforts to avoid causing any displeasure to their British masters.

For a period of seven years (1885-1891), the Congress was over enthusiastic in passing resolutions to prove before the alien rulers that it was a loyal organisation. Its sole aim was to convince the British Government, that it would not cause it any harm. The Congress was ignored by the government due to its extreme docility and servile attitude. This is evident from the fact that in 1891, Surendranath Banerjea posed the question : "Shall the Congress exist as it has existed in the past, or shall it pronounce its doom?"[39] This move was supported by Ananda Charulu, the President the Congress and he suggested to shift the venue of the Congress Meetings to London. But it was not the sign of a revolt, rather it was an attempt to come closer to the British. Charulu wanted the Congress Session to be shifted to London where it could be held, "with the Congress banner over our heads emblazoned with the figure of the Union Jack".[40] He made an appeal to Congressmen to convince the masses that the British Rule was not foreign and "ask them to look upon our British Rulers... as taking the place once held by the Kshatriyas and as being therefore, part and parcel of the traditional administration".

It may be noted that during its formative period, loyalty to the British Rule was one of the important qualifications for a person to become the President of the Congress. On the occasion of the election of Dadabhai Naoroji to Parliament, A. O. Hume wrote a letter to the Government saying that he approved the policies and actions of Congress Presidents like W. C. Bonnerji, Manmohan Ghosh, Surendranth Banerjea and Pherozeshah Mehta, because they were loyal to the British Government and as such enjoyed its confidence. He further argued that the election of people like Dadabhai Naoroji to the British Parliament would provide additional strength to the Congress as it would secure the blessings and the support of the government.[41]

The President of the Sixth Congress Session, Pherozshah Mehta, proclaimed the commitments of the Congress to the principles of moderation, loyalty and constitutional methods. This Congress creed was also reaffirmed by Congress President Lal Mohan Ghosh when he said, "Our motto is reform not revolution".[42]

The early Congress could not rise above, the Brahmo reformist zeal and the resemblance between the programmes of action of the Brahmo Samaj and the Congress, was but natural. The Congress during this period was viewed as an organisation for promoting social uplift with the support and co-operation of the British. Its professed objective was to promote friendly relations among the people of the educated class. There was no question of demanding political liberty or complete emancipation from British control and the latter objective was never specifically proclaimed officially till 1930.

W. C. Bonnerjee, the first President of the Indian National Congress had outlined the basic principles of the Congress movement in the following words :

> "Indeed the principle on which the Indian National Congress is based is that British rule should be

> permanent and abiding in India and that given this axiom it is the duty of educated Indians to endeavour to the best of their power to help their rulers so as to improve her material prosperity and make the people of all classes and communities happy and prosperous and contented as subjects of the 'British Empire'."[43]

The Impact of Arya Samaj and other Revivalist Organisations

The Arya Samaj movement had a greater and more effective political impact than the Brahmo Samaj, though both the movements were intellectual in character. The Arya Samaj succeeded in shaking the whole structure of Hinduism and infusing into it new blood and vigour which the Brahmo Samajists never achieved.[44] The radicalism in the Indian freedom movement may be traced to the political impact of the Arya Samaj which was started as a Hindu Protestant Reformation Movement but made significant contribution to the growth and development of the ideology of political extremism and spiritual nationalism.

Amaury De Riencourt, rightly observed that, "There is little doubt to-day that the great revolt in Bengal in 1905 was largely the indirect result of the Arya Samaj's religious nationalism, and that Dayananda's organisation was the first real concrete nucleus of political nationalism".[45] The Arya Samaj was responsible to create a new awakening among the Hindus by shedding off their self-imposed isolation and baneful socio-religious prejudices. It made the people conscious that "there was fire within the great body of Hinduism which, if struck by a competent hand could be coaxed into a blaze of life and energy. The concept of the gentle and often servile Hindu began to disappear."[46]

The Arya Samaj was the spiritual progenitor of the Extremists and it provided a spiritual justification to politics for exacting maximum sacrifice and dedicated service from the people for the cause of the Motherland. The people were filled with the sense of self-confidence and were infused with the spirit of pride in their glorious heritage and traditions. This kind of political and religious revivalism led to the development of political extremism.

Bal Gangadhar Tilak tried to bring a spiritual revolution in the country through the Ganesh Festival. He also promoted cultural regeneration among the Hindus in Maharastra, through the Sivaji Festival. Aurobindo made a powerful spiritual appeal through the Bhawani Mandir. Lala Lajpat Rai and Bipin Chandra Pal, two other prominent extremist leaders, drew immensely from the philosphy of the Arya Samaj.

No doubt, the religious ideas of the Arya Samaj, inspired the Extremist leaders, but it would be far from truth to say that these ideas were perverted to achieve political objectives. Spiritual or religious ideas, developed a sense of community consciousness among the Hindus and opened before them certain new dimensions, which had been blurred earlier due to apathy, ignorance and a sense of diffidence. What has been mentioned by P. C. Chakravarty about Aurobindo, holds good about the other Extremist leaders of India. According to Prof. Chakravarty, what Aurobindo "really attempted through the Bhawani Mandir was not to pervert religious ideals to political purposes, but to transform patriotism into a religion and to provide a spiritual foundation for our political struggle. He was convinced that the goal he had in view could not be achieved by a mere group of leisurely politicians and speech-makers; it could be attained only by a band of political Sanyasins, who would completely dedicate themselves to the service of the Motherland, suffer, and, when necessary, sacrifice themselves in her cause".[47]

Due to the spread of a new consciousness based on religious and spiritual revival in India, there was a significant regeneration of socio-political institutions from within the general body of Hindu traditions. The overemphasis on spiritual and cultural revivalism was a psychological reaction against spiritual and cultural starvation, which the Indians suffered in the hands of the British masters. Jawaharlal Nehru has highlighted the degenerating impacts of British Rule in India in the following words :

> "The most obvious fact is the sterility of British Rule in India and the thwarting of Indian life by it. Alien rule is inevitably cut off from the creative energies of the people it dominates. When this alien rule has its own economic and cultural centre far from the subject country and is further backed by racialism, this divorce is complete, and leads to spiritual and cultrual starvation of the

subject people."[48]

The rise of extremism in politics was closely connected with religious and cultural revivalism and was a reaction against Western reformism of the Brahmo Samajists. Raja Rammohan Roy thanked the Supreme Disposer of the universe for "having unexpectedly delivered this country from the long continued tyranny of its former rulers and placed it under the Government of the English, a nation who not only are blessed with the enjoyment of civil and political liberty, but also interest themselves, in promoting liberty and social happiness, as well as free inquiry into literacy and religious subjects, among those nations to which their influence extends."[49]

This Brahmo Samajist view was reiterated by most of the Moderates. The Western Reformists and their successors— the Moderates, tried to reconstruct India in the image of the West. These people faced the fundamental challenge from the Revivalists and their intellectual successors— the Extremists. Aurobindo bitterly reacted that, "If India is to model herself on the Anglo-Saxon type, she must first kill everything in her which is her own."[50]

Indian politics was marked by discernible trends of political extremism towards the end of the 19th century and the beginning of the 20th century. There was severe criticism of the Western Reformists and the Moderates for their policy of extreme softness, moderation and loyalty towards the British. Their admiration and imitation of the West were looked down. The extremists discarded the myth of 'Providential Role' of the British, spread by the Moderates and exploded their faith that Indian and British interests were complimentary to each other. The argument of the Moderates for the perpetuation of British Rule, which they had inherited from the Brahmo Samajists, was brought under fire. The extremists were convinced that the interests of an Imperial Power and its subjects were bound to be antithetical to each other. This view of the Extremists was later shared by Gandhi, Jawahralal and Subhas, though they had differences in their methods and approaches, quite characteristic of their respective personalities. Gandhi became a dynamic activist and while imbibing revivalistic principles pursued the effective strategy of non-violence. Nehru also became a votary of non-violence under the influence of Gandhi and tried to make a harmonious blending of revivalism and reformism, by taking the best elements from the Western and Eastern civilizations. Subhas Chandra Bose, on the other hand while sharing the rational approach of Nehru, considered non-violence only as a policy of expediency and in the true Extremist tradition, did not give up his faith in violence as a political method.

The philosophy of the Arya Samaj, inspired the Extremists to a great extent. The Arya Samajist call to revive the pristine purity of Vedic Hinduism was a symbolic manifestation of Hindu yearning for unity and the reassertion of India's strength and vitality, which was lost due to the degenerating impacts of alien rule. The Indians became inspired by a new sense of self-conscious nationalism with complete devotion for India's traditions, religion and culture. Thus the political concepts of moderation and extremism were produced as a normal part of the social milieu in which policies itself has its being."[51]

Political extremism became more prominent since the beginning of 20th century. The Indian National Congress drifted towards a policy of vigorous and scathing criticism of the British Government. In addition to the spread of new consciousness, there were certain acts of omission and commission on the part of the Government which accelerated the development of political extremism. During this period even some Moderates had to change their opinion and they became critical of the steps taken by the Government.

The Indian Councils Act of 1892 was extremely disappointing and even the Moderates were highly critical of the Government for its niggardliness in terms of reform measures. Tilak and other Extremists blamed the Moderates for the gross negligence of Indian demands by the British. Tilak thought that the Moderates' policy of prayers, petition and appeals gave the impression to the British that the Congress was spineless and its requests could be turned down. The Congress policy under the Moderates was interpreted by the British as a sign of weakness. Tilak, therefore, argued that the Congress should adopt stronger measures for the realization of its demands.

The Moderates and the Extremists were sharply divided as regards their attitude towards the problems of India and the methods of solution of these problems. Their concept of nationalism, nature of state and political obligations were different. In 1908, Gopal Krishna Gokhale said that, "It is no use trying to overthrow the present administration, before we have something to put in its place".[52] This was challenged by a sharp reaction from Aurobindo Ghosh : "Nations that became free did not first convince themselves to be helots and then seek freedom. They denied they were servile, they laid down they were free, would become free, and became free".[53] Thus the Moderates and the Extremists stood for different political programmes, political methods and goals. This is, however, a broad classification of the methods and the approaches of the Moderates and the Extremists as it is erroneous to make a generalization of the objectives, goals and programmes of action. Moderation and Extremism were not extremely distinctive and identifiable characteristics and it would be wrong to put either the Moderates or the Extermists in one particular category. As some Western Reformers had elements of revivalism and Revivalists had elements of reformism so also some Moderates subscribed to limited political extremism as required by particular situation, and some Extremists advocated moderation if that was the need of the time. In this connection Tilak's observation has got great relevance : "The Extremists of to-day will be Moderates of tomorrow, just as the Moderates of to-day were the extremists of yesterday".[54]

The 'mendicant policy' of the Moderates continued as the official policy of the Congress for quite some time, though the extremists ideas had become sufficiently organised by the end of the 19th century. The Extremists did not become vocal and active in the political sphere till the year 1905. Lord Curzon decided to partition Bengal in this historic year in the truth of opposition from the people of Bengal and other parts of India. The mass upsurge which resulted from this unpopular act of the British Government, swept away the Moderates and paved the way for the consolidation of political extremism in India.

The Extremists were no longer satisfied in demanding socio-economic and political reforms and aimed at Purna Swaraj or complete independence, however vague it may be. They wanted the Indians to launch a new programme of action of active and passive resistance for the purpose of achieving their goals. The extremists provided a new dimension to India's struggle for freedom by redefining the strategy in terms of sacrifice and revolution. The old 'mendicant policy' of the Congress was rejected by the new generation of leaders like Bal Gangadhar Tilak, Lala

Lajpat Rai, Bipin Chandra Pal and Aurobindo Ghosh. It was made amply clear by Aurobindo in his following observation :

> "There was a little too much talk about the blessings of the British Rule, and the inscrutable providence which has laid us in the maternal, or more properly the step-maternal bosom of just and benevolent England. Yet more appaling was the general timidity of the Congress, its glossing over of hard names, its disinclination to tell the direct truth, its fear of too deeply displeasing our masters".[55]

The methods of peaceful and constitutional agitation followed by the Moderates was found to be far short of the demands of the time and could not withstand the onslaught of the Extermists, who vigorously advocated the policy of 'purification by blood and sacrifice'.

It may be argued that there was a historic justification for political extremism at the beginning of the 20th century, which marked a sharp contrast with the 19th century in terms of consolidation of national aspirations and the spread of a new awareness among the people of India. The 19th century Renaissance both directly and indirectly contributed to the growth and development of this new awareness and assertion of the newly manifested Indian identity. For making the callous British Government conscious of the demands of the people, the method of political extremism was considered inevitable.

There was a realization that the British Government would not voluntarily surrender power and give freedom to the Indians, unless forced by circumstances or organised mass revolt. Tilak aptly observed that, "political rights will have to be fought for. The Moderates think that these can be won by persuasion; we think that they can only be obtained by strong pressure".[56] The extremely soft policy followed by the Moderates was interpreted as cowardice and treacherous with the growing demand for political freedom and the consequent British policy of oppression and repression. The Moderates' demands for reform of administration and repealing of unpopular laws, had lost their relevance. The methods of prayers and petitions had become outdated and the Moderates faced severe condemnation. Lala Lajpat Rai rightly observed that, "Prayers to the ruling nation may be useful to you in proving the uselessness of appealing to the higher sense of man in matters political where the interests of one nation clash with those of another". [57]

Though the Arya Samaj was socio-religious and cultural organisation, it was suspected of active political participation.[58] The Extremist leaders drew heavily from its political ideology and were prepared for making maximum sacrifice, including the sacrifice of life for the cause of the Motherland, which was endowed with divinity and sacredness. It was attributed with a unique personality which was all pervading and all sustaining. Interpreting the political views of Swamy Dayananda Saraswati, the founder of the Arya Samaj, Lajpat Rai said that, "Foreign Government, perfectly free from religious prejudices, impartial towards all the natives and foreigners—kind, beneficient and just though it may be—can never render the people perfectly happy".[59]

Dayananda, the founder of the Arya Samaj was of the view that 'Good Government is no substitute for self-Government'. In his writings Dayananda had stated as follows :

> "Let foreigners not rule our country,
> May we not lose our independence".[60]

Lala Lajpat Rai, an Extremist political leader of great eminence, was himself an ardent Arya Samajist. He has made the following analysis of the political role and impacts of the Arya Samaj on political life in India.

> "There is, of course, no doubt whatever that the Samaj doctrine has a patriotic side... The Arya doctrine and the Arya education alike sing the glories of ancient India, and by so doing arouse the national pride of its disciples, who are made to feel that their country's history is not a tale of continuous humiliation. Patriotism and politics are not synonymous, but the arousing of an interest in national affairs is a natural result of arousing national pride. Moreover, the type of men to whom the Arya doctrine appeals is also the type of men to whom politics appeals, viz., the educated man who desires his country's progress, not ultra-conservative with the ultra-conservatism of the East, but to a greater or lesser extent rerum novarum cupidus et capax. It is not, therefore, surprising that there are politicians among the

> Arya Samaj. But is is impossible to deduce from this that the Arya Samaj as a whole is a political body".[61]

The British Government suspected the Arya Samajists for their political opinions and activities and carefully watched the activities of the Samaj during the Extremists' agitation of 1907-1910. People were forbidden to attend the meetings of the Samaj and suspected Arya Samajists in the service of the Government were dismissed for the simple reason that they were either members or active members of the Samaj. In some place, census was made to identify the Arya Samajists and the names of such persons were entered in police registers as suspects.

The Arya Samaj became politically active, specially after the deportation of Lala Lajpat Rai, when many Arya Samajists, openly condemned this action of the Government and expressed sympathy for the deported leader. Arthur Grey in his opening speech quoted extensively from Dayananda's magnum opus, 'Satyartha Prakash', to prove the complicity of the Arya Samajists in the Patiala Sedition case. On January 6, 1910, Arthur Grey made the following statement :

> "He (Swami Dayananda) points out that not only is the religion (Christianity) abominable in itself but those who practise it and profess to practise it are the rulers over India and who are in the habit of showing partiality to the followers of that religion and are in the habit of judging unjustly between the natives of this country and their own country... On page 186 (Satyartha Prakash) there is a whole chapter on the manner in which a country should be governed and the kind of people who should govern it... On page 187, he says : 'Let no man abide by the law laid down by men altogether ignorant of the Vedas...' Again on page 188 he says : 'If it is necessary a man should use his influence and the whole of his power to destroy a sovereign who does not happen to be acquainted with the intricacies of the Vedas."[62]

In the same speech Arthur Grey asked : "... is there no significance in the fact that in the last anniversary of the Arya Samaj appeared an appeal calling for funds to defend the alleged seditionists and the name of Lajpat Rai as their political leader."[63]

Despite the fact that during the viceroyalty of Lord Harding, the Government gave the Arya Samaj, a clean chit saying that it was not a subversive organisation, many Arya Samajists, took active part in political movements in the country. It is also true that some Arya Samajists co-operated with the government in various fields. "The charge that the Arya Samaj, as an organisation, was committed to political movements of an anti-government nature was baseless, but the total effect of its propaganda in relation to the raising of national pride was conducive to the strengthening of a political movement aimed at the liberation of the Indian people from a foreign government."[64]

The Extremists imbibed their spiritual nationalism from the Arya Samaj movement and deified the Motherland by equating it with mother and the Mother Goddess like Durga, Kali and Bhavatarini. The rise of extremism was, thus, an unavoidable historical phenomenon in a subject country that was aspiring for political freedom.

The Political Impacts of other Revivalist Organisations on the Development of Radicalism

The religious movements in India, were no doubt primarily concerned with social and religious questions. But they also had great political significance, because they influenced the thinking processes of large sections of people in India. The Revivalist movements influenced the Hindus to go back to their historical and religious past to find out the inner source of strength for themselves and to assert their self-confidence. They insisted the revival of Hinduism, to make it a vital and powerful force in the regeneration of socio-political institution in the country. Thus apparently religious organisations like the Theosophical Society and the Ramakrishna Mission had two aspects to their political impact : One connected with their active role in politics and the other their ideological legacy. The second impact i. e., the idological legacy was of greater importance as it determined and guided the course of political radicalism or extremism in India.

The Theosophical Society

It was founded in New York in 1875 by Madame Helena Blavatsky and Colonel H. S. Olcott. It was introduced into India towards the end of the 19th century. Though born abroad, the

Theosophical Society was largely based upon Hindu ethics and religious doctrines. It made extensive translation of Hindu scriptures into English and created a new awareness among the foreigners as well as the English-educated Indians about the richness of India's literary and cultural traditions. The educated Hindus who were suffering from a sense of diffidence revived their faith in their sacred scriptures and literature.

Annie Besant who was a prominent theosophist played a great role in influencing political developments in India. She established direct link between Theosophy and political Home Rule. She argued that British Rule was oppressive and hindered the spiritual regeneration of the Indian society. Annie Besant, by highlighting the glory of India's heritage, rich culture and traditions, aroused the pride of Indians in their ancient past.

There was a criticism that by eulogizing the religious traditions and customs of Hinduism, the Theosophical Society promoted superstitions. As a reply to this Annie Besant writes :

> "How far... would this revival of religion— which is everywhere granted as the work of the Theosophical Society—tend to superstition ? Are religion and superstition identical ? If so, then Theosophy must plead guilty to reviving superstition. But we Theosophists strenuously deny the identity, and we proclaim religion— man's search for God— as the one sure foundation for national prosperity and stability; while superstition and scepticism are alike the foes of religion, both in ignorance are alike destructive to national life.

Religious revivalism is bound to give rise to the problem of superstition, because all principles of religion cannot be justified on the basis of rational principles. Religion belongs to the domain of the heart and intense emotions and very often acts as a fertile ground for the growth of superstitions. Even Annie Besant admitted : "I am, however, willing to grant that wherever there is a revival of religion there will be some recrudescence of superstition. So in relighting a smouldering fire, there will be some smoke. But the remedy for the smoke is to blow the fire into flame; then the smoke will vanish and the fire will burn bright and clear. As Theosophy spreads, the smoke of superstition will vanish, and the fire of knowledge will blaze up. But if you refuse knowledge, the smoke will continue, for men would rather have a smoky fire than none."[65]

The supporters of the Theosophical Society claimed that the body of truths on which it was founded formed the basis of all religions and it "cannot be claimed as the exclusive possession of any".[66] But gradually it was identified with Hinduism and Buddhism. It gave universal importance to Indian philosophical speculation and greatly enhanced its popularity in India. The religious principles of Hinduism and Buddhism formed its main basis.[67] It is interesting to note that both the founders of the Theosophical Society joined Buddhism. Madame Helena Blavatsky explained with great pride to Annie Besant : "I wanted to show that, I thought a religion of the East was rather better than the religion of the West".[68]

At a time when Christian missionaries and some of their Brahmo supporters were singing the glory of Christianity and asking the Hindus to change their religion, as according to them it was the den of superstition and evil practices, the praise of India's religious and cultural heritage made by a group of foreigners, had profound impact on the educated Indians. The Indians once more, began to pride themselves on their past. They developed a commitment for their own culture, religion and their own country.

Inspite of its various contributions to national life, the Theosophical Society, has been subjected to criticisms regarding its pessimism and its contempt of the ordinary life and finite existence. "They have thought it possible to arrive by a leap at truth, when in fact nothing has really been secured by this intuitive method and everything has to be begun over again. It has lowered the dignity of the virtue by making it a means and not an end. In condemning action and individualising salvation, it has shown itself dangerously anti-social."[69]

The Theosophical Society was also highly elitist and its activities were confined to a small group of educated people. It scarcely touched the masses of people and hence was not very popular like the Arya Samaj of Swami Dayananda which had a mass appeal in some parts of India. The leaders of the Society had the fear that if the masses were involved in the process of change, then it might lead to revolutionary upsurge. This apprehension was clear from the statement of Annie Besant :

"We have scarcely touched the masses of the people, and in truth our work lies more with the educated; for the religions can deal with the uneducated, if the advanced classes be enlightened and spiritual. Better to work among those who influence the masses, than in the masses themselves, as regards reform and change. Changes should always begin above and work downwards; then they influence powerfully and healthily; but changes which begin in the masses tend to bring about revolutions rather than reforms".[70]

This elitist character of the Theosophical Society distinguished it from other revivalist organisations like the Arya Samaj and the Ramakrishna Mission. The narrow social base of this organisation was responsible for its relative weakness in terms of its impacts on political developments in India. It was more of an intellectual movement rather than a socio-political movement. However, many English and Indian Theosophists worked hand-in-hand in founding the Indian National Congress, which spearheaded the national movement in India in later years. The first meeting of the Congress was held at Adyar, under the shelter of the banner of Theosophy, where many Indian Theosophists were present along with A. O. Hume. Thus the Indian National Congress took its birth at a convention of the Theosophical Society."[71]

The influence of the Theosophical Society was thus limited, but there is "no doubt that in a limited field it contributed to the growth of nationalism in India by instilling among educated Indians a pride in the country's past and religious heritage".[72]

Ramakrishna Mission and Swami Vivekananda

For a proper assessment of the impact of ideological legacy of the Revivalist movements on radical politics in India, it is necessary to analyse the fundamental principles and the organisational functioning of the Ramakrishna Mission and its founder-Swami Vivekananda. Sri Ramakrishna was a saint and he had nothing to do with politics. But his religious ideas and yogic exercises were greatly responsible for regenerating the faith of the Hindus in their own religion and culture. Sri Ramakrishna was a devotee of Goddess Kali and practised a career of astounding spiritual disciplines and attainments. He was the apostle of divine realization. By his own example he proved that Hinduism was not a dying religion and this came as a shock to the English-educated Indians who were deprecating their own religion and culture. Under the influence of the propaganda of the Westerners and the Christian missionaries, they were thinking that Hinduism was a dead religion. These people were looking towards Christianity and other religions for spiritual inspiration. Sri Ramakrishna generated new life and dynamism into the Hindu society by asking people to rise above distinctions of caste or creed, superstitious ceremonies and baneful rituals. He proved that Hinduism was an inexhaustible fount of true spirituality.

Sri Ramakrishna's preachings attracted many young disciples, who were the products of Western education. Most of these educated people had lost faith in their own religion and traditional culture. They used to look down Indian values and almost everything that was Indian, was down-graded. They were leading a life of cynicism and extreme spiritual despair. These people were able to banish their spiritual bankruptcy due to the inspiring influence of Sri Ramakrishna and their personalities were transformed.

Sri Ramakrishna was a devotee of Goddess Kali who is also known by such terms as Bhawani, Bhawatarini, Jagadhatri and Durga. These deities became the favourites of many Hindu leaders who were struggling to make India free from the bonds of enslavement, if necessary by the use of force. Motherland was identified with this Mother Goddess and patriotism was equated with divine worship. This kind of spiritual identification between the Motherland and the Mother-Goddess made it a religious duty on the part of the Hindus to sacrifice everything for the cause of the Motherland. Such religious orientation of politics paved the way for the growth and development of political radicalism and even terrorism.

Sri Ramakrishna's worthy disciple, Narendranath Dutta, who later became famous the world over as Swami Vivekananda, spread the ideas of his 'Guru' with the spirit of a missionary and brought radical transformation in the attitude of the Hindus. Vivekananda was, temperamentally, educationally and intellectually different from his master, but he was so profoundly influenced by him that he became his spiritual heir after his death in 1886.

In 1893, Vivekananda attended the Parliament of Religions

held in Chicago. Within a shortspan of time he established himself as an outstanding religious preacher. He was described by the New York Herald as "undoubtedly the greatest figure in the Parliament of Religions" and further it added that, "After hearing him, we feel how foolish it is to send missionaries to this learned nation".

He gave new interpretation of meaning to the sublime doctrines of Vedanta and preached to the West the true message of Hinduism. A new sense of pride in their own religion and culture was created among the educated Indians, after the tremendous success of Vivekananda in the U.S.A. It was amply made clear by the great saint, that in the sphere of science and technology the West might have achieved greater progress and development, but in the sphere of spiritual attainments, India still occupies the highest place and would continue to be the eternal Guru. "Vivekananda's re-interpretation of Hinduism to bring it into harmony with modern requirements developed the idea that though India should learn practical knowledge from the West, she must teach the materialistic West, her ancient and sublime religious wisdom".[73]

Swami Vivekananda made the people conscious of their social and economic degradations, by undertaking wide tours throughout the length and bredth of India. He pointed out to them that they had forgotten their sublime culture and heritage and indulge in baneful practices like casteism, oppression of women and wasteful ceremonies and rituals which have brought disrepute to the good name of Mother-India.

Vivekananda like many of his contemporaries, popularised the concept of Motherland, which inspired a new concept of nation. Aurobindo rightly stated that a nation should be organised not on the basis of common self-interest but on the basis of a common feeling that "We are all the sons of one common mother".[74] Vivekananda contributed to the development of the concept of a nation as a 'cultural unity', in contradistinction to the Western concept of nation as a 'geographic unity'. This concept of Motherland with distinct cultural identity became the sole motivating and animating force and commanded the greatest service and sacrifice from her own, which was bright and brilliant with all divine qualities. In the words of Aurobindo : "Your common Mother that is not merely the soil. That is not merely a division of land, but it is a living thing. It is the mother in whom you move and have your being".[75]

The Extremists like Bal Gangadhar Tilak, Aurobindo and later Subhas Chandra Bose used this concept as their slogan for enlisting mass support in their struggle against British imperialism. The mother and the Motherland were interpreted to be one and the same. Conceptually they were interpreted to be inseparable from each other and both superior to Heaven. Motherland became an incarnated symbol— a living and animating force. The people were inspired by such a concept to make maximum sacrifice for the cause of the Motherland.

There was a profound resurgence in the Hindu society as a result of the teaching of Swami Vivekananda. He wanted the reforms to start from the very heart of traditional Hinduism. Unlike the movement of the Theosophical Society, the reform movement started by Vivekananda, touched the masses of people and started a new awakening in India. It helped the educated and the illiterate alike in shedding off their sense of diffidence and cynicism. They started thinking with new vigour and dynamism. It has been rightly said that :

> "Awakening can take place only on the plane on which consciousness still dwells. This explains that the most powerful agent of metamorphosis in depth could only be the profound philosophic bent and religious feeling which is so much part of India that its disappearance would destroy the very soul of that great country."[76]

The ideas of Vivekananda and his speeches explaining the pristine glory of Vedantic philosophy filled the hearts of the English-educated Indians with a tremendous sense of self-confidence and produced deep political repercussions. The Extremists were greatly influenced by his speeches and writings. Even the terrorists drew great inspiration from his writings. In the words of Dr. Karan Singh : "If Rammohan Roy can be described as the intellectual progenitor of the liberals, Vivekananda is the spiritual progenitor of the Radicals".[77]

Vivekananda's philosophy inspired the Extremists to a great extent in their struggle against the British. The fundamental importance of religion in India's national life was accepted by them. The primacy of spiritual regeneration over social reform became the basis of national reconstruction. The Extremists also accepted Vivekananda's doctrine that India had a predestined role to give spiritual light to the whole world. The Extremists worked for reviving the spiritual consciousness of the Hindu community.

It has been aptly observed that Vivekananda, "gave his countrymen an added sense of dignity and pride in their own culture. His zeal to serve the downtrodden masses opened a new dimension of activity to Indian nationalist leaders, whose Western outlook had heretofore isolated them from the vast majority of their countrymen".[78] The barriers that isolated the common mass from the educated few were destroyed as a result of the message of Vivekananda. It promoted a common consciousness among the people, irrespective of the consideration of caste, sex, colour or economic status, that they were the sons and daughters of one common mother— Mother India. Vivekananda did not mince words when he wanted to chide the Indians who blindly and foolishly imitated the West :

> "When I see Indians dressed in European apparel and costumes, the thought comes to my mind, perhaps they feel ashamed to own their nationality and kinship with the ignorant, poor, downtrodden people of India... Oh Indian ! with this mere echoing of others, this slavish weakness... will you attain by means of your disgraceful cowardice, the freedom deserved only by the brave and heroic ?... You the brave one, be bold, take courage, be proud that you are an Indian and proudly proclaim, "I am an Indian, every Indian is my brother".[79]

It will not be out of place to mention that there was a complete metaporphosis in the political climate of India as a result of the inspiring and highly nationalistic speeches of Vivekananda. In this connection, Riencourt's observation needs to be quoted :

"The greatest leaders of the early twentieth century whatever their walk of life— Rabindranath Tagore, the Prince of Poets; Aurobindo Ghosh, the greatest mystic philosopher; Mahatma Gandhi, who eventually shook the Anglo-Indian Empire to destruction— all acknowledge their overriding debt to both the Swan and the Eagle, to Ramakrishna, who stirred the heart of India, and to Vivekananda who awakened its soul."[80]

All the Extremist leaders of India drew heavily from the preachings and the philosophy of Swami Vivekananda.

The Rise of Extremism in Indian Politics

With the rise of extremism there was a radical change in the British policy towards the Congress— the friendly attitude was substituted by hostility. The Congress was no longer treated as a harmless organisation. The Government treated the Congress as a potential danger to the perpetuation of its power. For suppressing the Congress, rigorous methods were adopted. The Government issued a circular in 1890, prohibiting government officials from attending its meetings.

On their part the Extremists also pursued a more or less uncompromising stand towards the Government. The Indian National Congress was satirically called as the 'Indian Unnational Congress'.[81] The Moderates were looked down contemptuously by the Extremists. The Moderates were considered responsible for the sorry state of affairs in India. This is evident from the following statement of Aurobindo :

"I say of the Congress, then, this— that its aims are mistaken, that the spirit in which it proceeds towards their accomplishment is not a spirit of sincerity and whole-heartedness, and that the methods it has chosen are not the right methods, and the leaders in whom it trusts not the right sort of men to be leaders;— in brief, that we are at present the blind led, if not by the blind, at any rate by the one-eyed."[82]

Aurobindo repudiated the Moderates' arguments for gradual political development as impracticable and unacceptable. The examples of France and Ireland were cited by Aurobindo, where political discontent resulted in abrupt culmination of political emancipation.

> "Rather we know that the first step of that fortunate country (France) towards progress was not through any decent and orderly expansion, but through purification by blood and fire. It was not a convocation of respectable citizens, but the vast and ignorant proletariat, that emerged from a prolonged and almost coeval apathy and bloted out in five terrible years, the accumulated oppression of thirteen centuries".[83]

Despite the many pitfalls and lapses of the early Congress, which was greatly influenced by the Brahmo Samaj, it has to be admitted that it did a great deal of spade work for spreading national awakening and political education among the masses. In the words of Pattabhi Sitaramayya :

"We cannot blame them for the attitude they adopted as pioneers of Indian Political reform, more than we can blame the brick and mortar that is buried six feet deep in the foundation and plinth of a modern edifice. They have made possible the superstructure, storey by storey by colonial self-government, Home Rule within the empire, Swaraj and on the top of all complete independence."[84]

The political inspiration provided by the Arya Samaj, is evident from the fact that as early as 1881, the doctrines of Swadeshi and Boycott were advocated by Lala Sain Das, the President of the Arya Samaj. These doctrines were advocated by Tilak in 1896 in Maharashtra. Swadeshi was the direct corollary of the Arya Samajist principle of self-reliance and it received the whole-hearted support of the members of Arya Samaj during 1905 to 1907. The successful use of these methods became popular after the partition of Bengal was announced on July 20, 1905 which became a legal fact on September 29, 1905. As a result of this unpopular action of the Government, the whole nation was galvanised into a mood favourable for the spread of extremist ideas. There was mass upsurge and the long accumulated socio-economic and political grievances, provided a strong ground for the movement of resistance against the British Government. "It evoked an unprecedented wave of protests which unleashed the Swadeshi and Boycott movement and harboured the formation of the New Party in the Congress."[85] This New Party was the Extremist Party, which acquired unprecedented popularity with the people as against the Moderates who started losing the support of the people after the Bengal partition of 1905.

There was a unique political development in the year 1905, and the Moderates and Extremists joined hands to oppose the Bengal Partition decision of the Government. Surendranath Banerjee, one of the most prominent Moderate leaders expressed the bitter feelings of the people of Bengal in the following words:

> "The announcement fell like a bomb-shell upon an astonished public... We felt that we had been

> insulted, humiliated and tricked. We felt that the whole of our future was at stake, and that it was a deliberate blow aimed at the growing solidarity and self-consciousness of the Bengali-speaking population. Originally intended to meet administrative requirements, we felt that it had drawn to itself a political flavour and complexion and if allowed to be passed it would be fatal to our political progress and to that close union between the Hindus and Mohammedans upon which the prospect of Indian advancement so largely depended."[86]

Despite their ideological and methodological differences, the Moderates and the Extremists collectively opposed the partition of Bengal by the British Government. Moderates like Ananda Mohan Bose, Lal Mohan Ghosh, Rabindranath Tagore and Surendranath Banerjee organised a meeting in Calcutta's Town Hall on 16th October 1905, which was observed as the day of mourning. They passed a resolution condemning the Government decision and appealing the people to vehemently protest against the dismemberment of the Province. In the whole country there was the common demand for more vigorous political action.[87]

This gigantic movement gave a unique turn to the psychology of the entire nation, which was favourable for inacceptance of the methods and the principles of political extremism in India. "Almost overnight the ground was cut from under the feet of the Moderates, and mass opinion— not only in Bengal but in other parts of India such as Maharashtra and the Punjab where political consciousness was well developed—veered strongly in favour of the nationalist creed".[88] Even Moderates like Surendranath Banerjee, appealed to the people to take recourse to the methods of Swadeshi and Boycott. He asked them to use only Swadeshi articles and to abstain from the use of foreign goods.[89] This was a definite victory of the Nationalists as the Moderates accepted their methods of mass movement to which they were opposed earlier.

Aurobindo has aptly described the tremendous impact of the Bengal Partition of 1905, on political developments in India in the following words :

> "We in India fell under the influence of the foreigners' Maya which completely possessed our

> souls. It was the Maya of the alien rule, the alien civilization, the powers and capacities of the alien people who happen to rule over us. These were as if so many shackles that put oui physical, intellectual and moral life into bondage. We went to school with the aliens, we allowed the aliens to teach us and draw our minds away from all that was great and good in us. We considered ourselves unfit for self-government and political life, we looked to England as our exemplar and took her as our saviour. And all this was Maya and bondage... It is only through repression and suffering that this Maya can be dispelled and the bitter fruit of Partition of Bengal administered by Lord Curzon dispelled the illusion. We looked up and saw that the brilliant bird sitting above was non else but ourselves, our real and actual self. Thus we found Swaraj within ourselves and saw that it was in our hands to discover and to realize it."[90]

The schism within the Congress on ideological and methodological issues became distinct after 1905 and the Extremists got a tremendous boost. This was indicated in the 'Punjabee' as follows :

> "The hour of the inevitable parting of the ways has come for our National Assembly. It should either decide to take advantage of the new spirit and launch out a bold policy or sign its own death."[91]

The proposal to pass a resolution of welcome in honour of the visiting Prince of Wales, further heightened the schism between the Moderates and the Extremists. Gopal Krishna Gokhale and Surendranath Banerjee pressed for the resolution. But Tilak, Lajpat Rai and other Extremist leaders opposed the passing of such a resolution. Lajpat Rai pointed out that the visit of Prince of Wales staged "a gala show which aimed to divert the public from the political unrest."[92]

In 1905, there was a compromise in the Congress, between Gokhale on the one hand and Lajpat Rai and Tilak on the other, who agreed to abstain from the Congress meeting, during the passage of the resolution of welcome to the visiting Prince of

Wales. However, the resolution was vehemently opposed by J. N. Roy and R. Ray, two young Bengal nationalists, who were forcibly removed from the Congress session. The Extremists were eager to avoid a split in the Congress in the national interest, but the Twentyfirst session of the Congress in 1905, marked the beginning of the split, which became open in 1907.

There was a tremendous increase in the prestige of the Extremists and Lord Curzon, through his despotic and unpopular acts greatly contributed to the disastrous moral break-down of the Moderates. This was made amply clear by Ras Behari Ghosh in his undelivered Congress Presidential address of 1907 : "And lastly, we charge him with having set Bengal in ablaze. It is Lord Curzon and Lord Curzon alone who is responsible for the rise of the New Party, for he drove the people to despair and to madness".[93]

Gokhale also expressed his bitter feelings against the Government for the moral break-down of the Moderates and the rise of the new party of the Nationalists within the Congress. He criticized the British Government for its utter disregard of public opinion and reckless contempt for the cherished feelings of the Indians.

The Moderates had to change their political strategy in order to face the challenge of the Extremists. In 1889 the Congress goal was defined as merely good government, but now it was substituted by the goal of self-government.[94] This spirit also characterised a shift in the methods of the Moderates. Most of the Moderates accepted both Swadeshi and Boycott as methods of protest, though some among them like Gokhale had reservations with regard to the latter. On the other hand the Extremists vigorously campaigned for the acceptance of both the methods as the weapons of the Congress movement. Lajpat Rai wanted that, "The Bengal spirit of protest has to be commended to other provinces of India. If the other provinces will follow their example, the day is not far distant when England will grant our rights."[95]

The Congress was still dominated by the Moderates and there was no official Congress resolution accepting the methods of Swadeshi and Boycott. However, the anti-partition agitation gathered momentum throughout the year 1906 and the differences between the Moderates and the Extremists became further acute. Boycott became a more effective weapon than Swadeshi and the two methods were frequently resorted to by the Congressmen in their fight against the British. It was a tremendous victory for the Extremists, when in 1906, the Calcutta Congress passed the four famous resolutions on Swaraj, Swadeshi, Boycott and National Education. These were precisely the programmes of political action advocated by the Extremists.

Spiritual nationalism provided a religious fervour to the anti-partition movement of 1905. The revivalist ideas and symbols became extremely popular. People were required to make maximum sacrifice for the cause of the Motherland. Bankim Chandra Chatterjee popularised the revivalist ideas and symbols through his writings. Bankim's historical novels in general and his 'Anandamath' in particular, greatly inspired the Nationalists or the Extremists. The song 'Bande Mataram', became the battle-cry of the people in the whole country. The concept of 'The Mother' was popularised by Aurobindo Ghosh and the Motherland and the Mother Goddess, were treated to be one and inseparable. The attribution of divinity and living-personality to one's own country, by identifying it with the mother and the Mother Goddess inspired the people with patriotic and religious devotion. The Congress under the Moderates with its principles of constitutional agitation, prayers and petitions was unable to rouse such intensely emotional feelings.

The movement of the Nationalists and their acceptance of revivalist symbols, became further strengthened, with the visit of Tilak to Bengal in 1906, for the celebration of the tenth-anniversary of Shivaji Festival. The anti-partition movement became more radical and effective as a result of the inspiring speeches of Bal Gangadhar Tilak. Shivaji Festival became an important political festival throughout the country and was merged with the 'Bande Mataram' movement. Far reaching political consequences were produced as a result of the fusion of these two movements.

At the initial stages, the anti-partition movement was not a militant movement. The agitation took recourse to the non-violent methods of Swadeshi and Boycott. But police applied brute force as it was done at Barisat in 1906, to break peaceful processions and meetings and the people were forced to believe that the British would only understand the language of force and violence. In sheer despair youngmen took to the bomb and the revolver.[96]

The cry of revolution reverberated in every corner of India in 1906. "Even within the left camp further extremism developed by 1906 and it was taking the shape of terrorism".[97] In this year Gopalkrishna Gokhale told Morley that the goal of the Congress was self-government within the empire and he urged upon him to make a bold declaration on granting self-government, so as to regain the confidence of the loyal Indians. This Congress goal was dismissed by the Extremists as unsuitable for the needs of the time. They insisted that the British would have to hand over power when "the force of circumstances, compelled it to do so inspite of itself."[98] The frustration of the Moderates was further worsened, when Morley refused to undo the partition and make any statement on self-government. Even the peace-loving Indians became terribly annoyed with the Government and believed that, "only military power, actual or potential, could drive out the British."[99]

In December 1906, the Twentysecond Session of the Congress was held at Calcutta. In this session there was an open split between the 'Old Party' of the conservative Moderates and the 'New Party' of the Nationalists or the Extremists, who were more radical in their policies and programmes. The Moderates and the Extremists became organised and were out for a trial of strength.

Dadabhai Naoroji was prevailed upon by the Moderates to come from England to preside over the Congress Session and forestall the move of the Extremists to propose the name of Tilak for Congress Presidency. It is interesting to note that for the first time the word 'Swaraj' was uttered in the Congress Session, but the Moderates tried to dilute its meaning by giving ambiguous and confusing interpretations. The rift between the two parties was intensified due to this kind of interpretation. On the formulation of resolutions on Swadeshi and Boycott, in the Subjects Committee Meeting, veteran conservative leaders like Pherozeshah Mehta, Dinshaw Wacha, Gopalkrishna Gokhale, Bhupendranath Basu, Madan Mohan Malviya and Surendranath Banerjee were opposed to radical leaders like Tilak, Bipin Chandra Pal and Lajpat Rai. There could be no agreement on what should be the official stand on Boycott. The gap between the Moderates and the Extremists was widened and it became evident to all concerned that there was no possibility of resolving this conflict. More and more people gave the slogan of inevitable revolution and stern measures against the British. The Yugantar wrote : "War or a revolution is far better than death in peace."[100]

The Extremists urged upon the Indians to draw inspiration from the Japanese victory over Russia in the Russo-Japanese War. For the first time in the history of India the 'Sepoy Mutiny' of 1857 was interpreted as 'the first Indian War of Independence".[101] It was also written in the same vein in the New India that, "Absolute national autonomy is the goal. The nation must succeed in gaining it, or must perish in the attempt. Revolution is inevitable."[102]

The Extremists' political creed was gradually acquiring greater acceptability. The popularity of the symbols and the radical ideas of the Extremists provided them with mass support and strengthened their position in the Congress. It was decided to hold the Twenty-third Session of the Congress at Nagpur, which was an Extremist stronghold. The Moderates wanted the Session to be shifted to Surat, to counteract the influence of the Extremists. Prior to the Congress meeting the Extremist leaders like Tilak, Bipin Chandra Pal, Lajpat Rai and Aurobindo Ghosh, canvassed for wider support for the 'New Party'. The Extremists condemned the Moderates in strongest terms and held them responsible for most of the sufferings of the Indians. Tilak was forthright in saying that politics did not know benevolence and there was no instance in history of an empire willingly and voluntarily surrendering power to the subjugated people.

Four days before the Congress meeting at Surat on 23rd December, 1907, Tilak made an emphatic declaration :

> "We are against the policy of mendicancy. Many young gentlemen in Bengal have gladly suffered for this attitude. No one has any authority to make the Congress recede for its ideal. We do not come here to embarrass the Moderates; but we are determined not to allow the Congress to retrograde. If they are not prepared to brave the dangers, let them be quiet, but they should not ask us to retrograde. We have come here to fight out constitutionally; we will behave as gentlemen even if our opponents do not do so. Our opponents create rowdyism, when they fear defeat. We are fighting against foreign autocracy. Why should

> we allow this home autocracy? The Congress is an organisation of all people and the voice of the people should predominate. The policy of the Moderates is destructive. I don't want you to follow it; we want to progress".[103]

There were wild rumours about the Congress Session scheduled to meet on 27th December, 1907. Tilak managed to get a draft copy of the Congress Constitution, a day before the meeting and was shocked to note that there was a change in the Congress stand from the one that was taken at Calcutta Congress a year before. There was a clear indication of retrogression on the part of Congress. The Extremists wanted to stop this, if necessary by making a compromise with the Moderates. They proposed that they would withdraw their opposition to the election of the President of the Congress, if the Moderates assured that there would be no backsliding on their part. This offer was turned down by the Moderates as they were not prepared for any compromise with the Extremists. They wanted to completely banish the Extremists from the Congress and destroy the resistance to their stand for all times to come. The Surat Congress met in an atmosphere of tension and excitement.

The name of Lala Lajpat Rai was proposed for presidentship of the Congress by the Extremists, inspite of his unwillingness. He said that, "I will be the last person to allow myself to be made the reason or occasion of any split in the national camp".[104] Aurobindo Ghosh was more uncompromising among the Extremists and to challenge the activities of the Moderates he gave the call for a separate "Nationalists' Conference". This conference was held in Haripur, at the outskirts of Surat on 23rd December, 1907. Resolutions were passed in the Nationalists Conference supporting 'total boycott' and 'complete independence'.[105]

The Nationalists became organised and consolidated after the Haripur Conference. But they were also divided into two distinct groups. Tilak and his supporters were opposed to cause any split in the Congress.[106] However, they were determined to prevent the Moderates from taking any retrograde step. On the other hand Aurobindo Ghosh and his followers were determined either to capture the Congress or to wreck it completely.[107]

Aurobindo attached greater importance to the inner struggle of a subjugated people demanding independence than the appearance of fictitious unity and was of the view that in the struggle between the Moderates and the Extremists, "one or the other must be crushed or prevail before true unity of a regenerated nation can replace the false unity of acquiescence in servitude."[108]

In such a surcharged atmosphere of mutual suspicion and distrust among the Moderates and the Extremists, the name of Rash Behari Ghosh was proposed for Congress presidentship. There was pandemonium when Surendranath Banerjee stood up to second the proposal. He was shouted down by the Extremists and due to this disturbed situation the meeting was adjourned. Due to the highly uncompromising attitude of the Moderates, attempts to bring an understanding between the two groups failed.

There was shouting and pandemonium, when the Session began the next day and amidst shouting the motion of the President's election was declared to have been duly carried out. Tilak opposed this undemocratic stand and requested for permision to address the delegates. But when his requests were repeatedly turned down, Tilak ascended the platform without any regard for the rulings from the chair. He insisted to exercise his right to speech. The session was dissolved due to the use of force from both the groups.

In a way this split had become inevitable due to the different ideological commitments of the Moderates and the Extremists. One can mark the distinct impacts of the ideologies of the Brahmo Samaj, and the Arya Samaj on the Moderates and the Extremists, respectively. Despite some dilution in the political stand of the Moderates since 1905, the basic tenets remained unchanged. Similarly, though the Extremists some times made compromises with the Moderates to avoid a split in the Congress, their radicalism, intense hostility towards the British and commitment to Indian values, basically remained the same.

The Surat split and the expulsion of the Extremists from the Congress only served the purpose of the British. Government persecuted the Extremists who were ousted from the Congress.[109] It was realised by Tilak and Lajpat Rai that in a subjugated country like India any weakness in the Congress organisation would serve the interests of the Imperialist rulers. Hence they appealed for patching up all differences in a bid to forge unity in the Congress in the larger interest of the country. Tilak personally thought that the split in the Congress was "accidental and unexpected".[110] But the Moderates were determined to oust the Extremists and thought that the split was complete and final. The psychological fear of being outmanoeuvred by the Extremists made the Moderates more rigid in their determination.

This, however, did not come as a surprise for the Extremists like Aurobindo Ghosh, who accepted it as natural. He thought that the split would bring greater dynamism to the national movement and serve the larger interest of the country. He argued that extremism was the demand of the time and in due course it was bound to get popular acceptance. Aurobindo Ghosh tried to expedite the split in the Congress without consulting Tilak, as the latter stood for maintaining the unity of the party. He confessed : "Very few people know that it was I, who gave the order, that led to the breaking of the Congress".[111]

After the expulsion of the Extremists from the Congress, the convention of the Moderates met on December 28, 1907. Tilak was held responsible by the Moderates for the split in the Congress : "Tilak had been feeding the flames which have burnt the Congress to ashes. He is not a patriot, but a traitor to the country, and has blackened himself. May God save us from such patriots".

The convention of the Moderates was subsequently known as the All-India Conference. The Extremists accepted the challenge of the Moderates and meeting under the Presidency of Aurobindo Ghosh, they reiterated their faith in the 1906 resolutions on Swadeshi, Boycott, Swaraj and National Education. Tilak tried to galvanize the freedom movement, after the Surat Session of the Congress, by undertaking whirlwind tours of the country. He succeeded in spreading the fire of patriotism in every nook and corner of the country. He appealed to the people to be prepared for maximum suffering and sacrifice because these were the essential requirements for bringing Swaraj. His voice thundered the slogan : "Swaraj is my birthright; I will have it". The Government became panicky due to the severe challenge posed by extremism and it applied all possible methods for suppressing the Extremists. Government passed several new laws and suitably amended the Penal Code in order to deal effectively with the Extremists and their supporters in the country.

The Government followed a new strategy since 1908. Its policy of repression was followed by socio-political reforms for the purpose of winning the support of the Moderates.[112] For one of his articles exonerating the murderers of Mrs. and Miss Knennedy, Bal Gangadhar Tilak was sentenced to six years imprisonment. Sentence of imprisonment was also passed against Bipin Chandra Pal and Brahma Bandhab Upadhyay for their seditious writings. Aurobindo Ghosh was imprisoned from May 1908 to May 1909, for his article on the Muzaffarpur murder case.

After the expulsion of the Extremists from the Congress, the first Moderates' Congress met in 1908 and expressed its "most sincere and grateful thanks" to Morley and Minto for the reforms introduced by them.[113] These reforms were later incorporated in the Government of India Act of 1909. The Congress again went back to its traditional role of making petitions and prayers. Terrorism had become very rampant in the country since 1907. The Moderates condemned terrorism.[114] They also appealed to the Government to repeal all the repressive laws passed by it.[115]

The Congress became dull and inactive with the expulsion of the Extremists. "Having discarded the extremists, and having enforced the disciplinary rules of its constitution, the Congress became an inanimate body. Furthermore, the Indian Councils Act of 1909 deprived the Congress of its main demand— the representation of the Indians in the Councils— and thus took the wind out of its sails".[116] The Congress suffered a loss of prestige as the radicals were expelled and it reverted back to its servile stand on national issues. The Moderates expressed pious hope that the British would grant self-government. Bhupendranath Basu said : "We desire self-government not by revolution but by gradual evolution and we are prepared to advance steadily and surely, though it may only be slowly".[117]

The rise of extremism was arrested for the time being due to the imprisonment of most of the Extremists and repressive measures against them by the Government. The Extremists had to change their political strategy to some extent due to the repressive measures taken by the Government. Aurobindo Ghosh appealed to the Indians that in their struggle for freedom, they should have no hatred for the government of the country established by law.[118] He gave up his uncompromising policy and moderated his theory of revolution by advocating co-operation with the Government on the basis of progressive steps towards Swaraj. Bipin Chandra Pal reinterpreted his concept of Passive Resistance and said that it was directed only against the autocratic bureaucracy and did not oppose the British Government's right to rule.[119]

Lajpat Rai was released as he wanted to keep away from political activities and devote himself entirely to three issues : famine relief, Hindu-Muslim relations and untouchables. Morley wrote to Minto at the time of the release of Lajpat Rai : "If Lajpat opens fire again, we shall certainly support you to the uttermost in again putting his fire out by a douche of deportation".[120]

The Congress policies underwent a seachange, after the release of Tilak from the Mandalay Jail in 1914. Gopal Krishna Gokhale started a negotiation with Tilak to avoid any further confrontation between the Moderates and the Extremists. But this move could not proceed ahead due to the strong resistance of Pherozeshah Mehta..In the year 1914, the British Government was deeply engrossed in the First World War and it badly needed the support of the Indians in its war-efforts. Enthusiastic support was given by the Congress to the British Government and many Congress leaders openly addressed public meetings for encouraging the people to join the British Army.

During the First World War, even Gandhi asked the Indians to support the British Government and make all possible sacrifices, with the hope that the Government would take progressive steps in the direction of realization of Swaraj by the Indians. However, developments during and after the war betrayed the fond hopes of Gandhi and other Congress leaders.

There was a rapid change in the Congress policy in 1916. The nonfulfilment of the promises by the Government, the bitterness caused by the War and its manysided effects, completely transformed the attitude of the Congress towards the British. The Moderates were also disorganised and became practically leadersless in 1915 after the death of prominent leaders like Pherozeshah Mehta, Gopal Krishna Gokhale and Subramanya Iyer. It was no longer possible on the part of the Moderates to keep the Extremists away from the Congress. Extremist strength in the Congress was swelled and the fencesitters joined the rank of the Extremists. The number of delegates who attended the Congress Sessions from 1908 to 1914 was very small. But in 1915 it increased suddenly and 2,259 delegates attended the Congress. Suitable changes were made in the Congress Constitution to facilitate the re-entry of the Extremists into the organisation.

Despite the absence of Tilak in the Bombay Congress of 1915, the Extremists achieved great success due to the Home Rule agitation of Annie Besant. The speeches and writings of Annie Besant and the movement started by the Theosophical Society helped revivalist trends and greatly consolidated the position of the Extremists. The Moderates had not only become leaderless, they had also lost the moral courage. It was not possible for them to talk any longer in the political language of the Moderates. Political moderation was the product of a particular period of time and in the second decade of the 20th century it had lost its relevance. Under the leadership of Surendranath Banerjee, the Moderates made the last attempt to check the ascendancy of radicalism, by opposing the activities of the Home Rule League, But they failed miserably as there was no popular support for them.

The Extremists shattered the stronghold of the Moderates in 1916 and exercised full control over the Congress. A call for dynamic action was given by Tilak, Bipin Chandra Pal and Annie Besant. They demanded Home Rule for the Indians. Under the leadership of the Extremists, in 1916, the Congress "became the national forum and constituted the vanguard of militant nationalism".[121] Referring to the transformed mood of the people Lala Lajpat Rai said, "India of 1917 is different from India of 1907. In 1907 we were fighting for crumbs. In 1917 we no longer pray for concessions but are demanding rights".[122] Thus there was undisputed control of the Extremists over the Congress in the Calcutta Congress of 1917 and the Bombay Special Session of August 1918, called for discussing the inadequacies of the Montagu-Chelmsford Reforms. Tilak, Gandhi and C. R. Das provided new leadership and dynamism to the Congress. Now it was the turn for the Moderates to leave the Congress. Under the leadership of Surendranath Banerjee, they convened on 1 November 1918, a separate All-India Moderates' Conference.

The Congress attitude towards the Government became more stiff after the First World War as there was no indication of the Government becoming more responsive to public demands or public welf re. The Government continued with its autocratic and repressive policies. The Government of India Act, 1919 with its system of Dyarchy led to serious complications and resulted in deadlocks between the Reserved and Retransferred halves of the

Government. It was still an unrepresentative Government with large powers in the hands of the officials. Added to all these, there was the Jallianwalabagh Tragedy, which created acute bitterness in the minds of the Congress leaders. The Martial Law in the Punjab and the unjust and highly biased findings of the Hunter Committee disillusioned Gandhi and the other Congress leaders. Gandhi lost all faith in the good sense and fair play of the British Government and decided to start the non-violent non-cooperation movement.

Though Gandhi was a pacifist and the votary of non-violence, under his leadership, the Indian politics in general and the nationalist movement in particular assumed a kind of dynamism and radicalism, which was not known before. The non-cooperation movement was proposed to be a revolutionary step aimed at completely paralysing British administration in India. For the first time in its history, the Indian National Congress, decided to follow a policy of direct action. It was the aim of the Congress under the dynamic leadership of Gandhi to put maximum pressure on the Government so as to compel it to concede to genuine Indian demands and give up the policy of bureaucratic highhandedness and despotism. As far as his faith in the greatness of Indian traditions and Indian values were concerned, Gandhi was a revivalist. He advocated the spiritualization of politics and accepted the concept of 'Ram Rajya' as an ideal model to be emulated by the Indians. Though he gave a modernist interpretation to religion and made it broad-based and tried to tailor it to the requirements of secularism, to a great extent he was a revivalist with a flair for social reform. Gandhi was certainly a radical compared to the earlier leaders of the Congress. But he was less progressive and radical compared to leaders like Jawaharlal Nehru and Subhas Chandra Bose.

Though Gandhi had accepted Gopal Krishna Gokhale as his political mentor or 'Guru' and was talking the language of the Moderates, he gave up this stand quickly and devised the language of gentle firmness. He abandoned the old method of co-operation with the Government and faith in British sense of Justice and goodness. Through the non-cooperation movement, he decided to create a mass base for the Congress and to involve the whole nation in the movement. Tilak had propagated this strategy of mass participation in the freedom movement. But the real credit goes to Gandhi for mobilizing the support of people for the struggle against the British. By 1920, the Moderates were completely eliminated from the Congress and the Extremists were in a majority and it may be stated without the fear of contradiction that Gandhi's programme of direct action against the British was possible only due to the support of the Extremists.

But Gandhi's programme of action was characterized by an ambivalence that was unique to the history of the Indian National Congress. Despite his dynamism, he was sceptical of extreme radicalism and very often behaved as a reactionary, preventing all progressive actions and political programme. He, therefore, intermittently staged a come back to the programme of social reform and Harijan uplift, when he had problems with the Congress organisation.

Thus the impacts of the social reform movements had far reaching consequences and the Indian National Congress could never make itself free from these impacts, even when it was engaged in a life and death battle against the British Government in India. The Congress continued its social bias even after it had developed as a fully matured political organisation. Abolition of untouchability, establishment of cottage industries and rural reconstruction work constituted the programme of the Congress during very peak periods of the struggle for freedom. The legacy of the political ideologies and traditions of the Brahmo Samaj may be noticed in these reformist programmes. This Congress obsession for social reform, at times even at the cost of political progress was vehemently criticized by Subhas Chandra Bose and other Leftist and radical leaders. But the Congress had never been able till today, to rise above its reformist obsessions.

Footnotes

1. *Speeches of Lord Macaulay* (ed.), G. M. Young, (London, 1935) p. 359.
2. Leonard A. Gordon, *Bengal: The Nationalist Movement* 1876-1940, Manohar Book Service, Delhi, 1974, p. 15.
3. *Ibid.*, p. 16.
4. G. P. Bhattacharjee, *Contributions of Maharshi Dayanand Saraswati*, Arya Samaj Mandir, Calcutta, pp. 1-2.

5. V. B. Kulkarni, *British Dominion in India and After*, Bharatiya Vidya Bhavan, Bombay, 1964, p. 77.
6. Hari Hara Das, *Subhas Chandra Bose and the Indian National Movement*, Sterling Publishers Private Limited, New Delhi, 1983, p. 1.
7. A. C. Mazumdar, *Indian National Evolution* (Madras, 1917), p. 354.
8. *Ibid.*, p. 377
9. G. N. Singh, *Landmarks in Indian Constitutional & National Development*, Vol.1, (Delhi, 1959), p. 109.
10. Leonard A. Gordon, *op. cit.*, p. 15.
11. Subhas Chandra Bose, An Indian Pilgrim (An Autobiography of Netaji), Calcutta, 1948, p. 17.
12. S. C. Bose, An Indian Pilgrim, p. 19.
13. Keshab Chandra Sen, *The Brahmo Samaj — Discourses and Writings*, 2nd ed. Calcutta, 1917, "England and India", Speech delivered in Calcutta, 2 Feb., 1870.
14. Keshab Chandra Sen's Lectures in India, "The Future Church", *Sources of Indian Tradition* (ed.) T. De. Bary, Columbia University Press, New York, 1958, p. 621.
15. Lala Lajpat Rai, (Autobiography), *The Man in his Words*, Madras, 1921, p. 89.
16. Keshab Chandra Sen's Lectures in India, "The Future Church", *Sources of Indian Tradition*, *op. cit.*, p. 623.
17. Lala Lajpat Rai, *The Man in His Words*, p. 95.
18. Lala Lajpat Rai, *The Arya Samaj*, p. 174.
19. Dr. Sachin Sen, *The Political Thought of Tagore*, Calcutta, 1947, *op. cit.*, pp. 230-231.
20. M. G. Ranade, *Miscellaneous Writings*, p. 158.
21. Lala Lajpat Rai, *The Man in His Words,* Ganesh & Co., (ed.), Madras, 1907, p. 248.
22. B. C. Pal, *Soul of India, op. cit.*, p. 76.
23. *Ibid.*, pp. 76-77.
24. Lala Lajpat Rai, *The Man in His Words,* p. 28.
25. R. P. Dua, Social Factors in the Birth and Growth of the Indian National Congress Movement, Delhi, 1967, p. 4.
26. Lala Lajpat Rai, India's Will to Freedom, Madras, 1921, p. 37.
27. A. O. Hume, The Indian National Congress : Its Origin, Aims and Object, Allahabad, 3 April, 1888, Fract, 658.
28. Pattabhi Sitaramayya, *The History of the Indian National Congress,* Vol. 1, Padma Publications, Bombay, p. 34.
29. Fortnightly Review, 1884, p. 459.
30. Quarterly Review, 1886, pp. 112-113.

31. *Speeches and Writings of Dadabhai Naoroji,* G. Natesan & Co., (ed.), Madras, pp. 66-67.
32. Congress Presidential Addresses, *op. cit.*, p. 363.
33. Extract from Indian Politics, p. 185 A.
34. A. O. Hume's Speech, "The Indian National Congress : Its Origin, Aims and Object", Allahabad, 3 April, 1888.
35. Home Dept. (Political), Government of India Proceedings, August, 1907, No. 33, p. 2.
36. Hemendranath Das Gupta, *The Indian National Congress*, p. 169.
37. Jawaharlal Nehru, *Autobiography*, London, 1942, p. 353.
38. S. N. Banerjea, Speeches, "Indian Unity".
39. Report of the Seventh Indian National Congress, Nagpur, 1891, p. 11.
40. *Ibid.*, p. 7.
41. Bengalee, 3 November, 1894.
42. Report of the Sixth Indian National Congress, Calcutta, 1890, p. 8.
43. Extracts from Indian Politics, 185-A.
44. Dr. Karan Singh, *Prophet of Indian Nationalism,* p. 30.
45. Amaury De Riencourt, *The Soul of India,* p. 236.
46. Dr. Karan Singh, *Prophet of Indian Nationalism,* p. 30.
47. P. C. Chakravarty, *Sri Aurobindo and the Indian Freedom Movement* (Loving Homage), pp. 270-271.
48. Jawaharlal Nehru, *The Discovery of India,* p. 619.
49. *Raja Rammohan Roy : His Life, Writings and Speeches*, (ed.) G. A. Natesan & Co., Madras, p. 48.
50. Aurobindo Ghosh, *Ideals Face to Face,* May, 1908.
51. George H. Sabine, *A History of Political Theory*, (London, George G. Harrap & Co.) 1957, p. 7.
52. Quoted by W. C. Blunt, My Diaries, London, 1919, Vol. II, p. 229.
53. Aurobindo Ghosh, "On the Present Situation", Speech at Poona on 19th January, 1908.
54. Bal Gangadhar Tilak, '*The Tenets of the New Party*', Speech at Calcutta, 2 January, 1907.
55. Aurobindo Ghosh, New Lamps for Old, No. 4, Indu Prakash, August 7, 1893.
56. Quoted by M. A. Buch, *Rise and Growth of Militant Nationalism,* p. 45.
57. *Ibid.,* p. 144.
58. K. P. Karunakaran, *op. cit.,* p. 84.
59. Lajpat Rai, *Arya Samaj,* London, 1915, p. 176.
60. Dayananda Saraswati, *Aryabhinaya* (Lahore, Samvat, 1994), p. 214.
61. Lala Lajpat Rai, *Arya Samaj,* p. 193.

62. Munshi Ram and Rama Deva, *The Arya Samaj and its Detractors*, (Dayanandabad, 1919), Appendix 9.
63. *Ibid.*, 12.
64. K. P. Karunakaran, *op. cit.*, p. 87.
65. Annie Besant, *The Work of Theosophical Society in India*, Madras, 1909, pp. 13-14.
66. Annie Besant, "Theosophical Society", *Encyclopaedia of Religion and Ethics*, Vol. XII, n. 7, p. 304.
67. Paul Oltramare, "Theosophy", *Encyclopaedia of Religion and Ethics*, Vol. XII, pp. 313-14.
68. Annie Besant, *Birth of New India* (Madras, 1917), p. 355.
69. Paul Oltramare, Theosophy, *op. cit.* p. 315.
70. Annie Besant, *The Birth of New India*, n. 16, pp. 351-352.
71. *Ibid.*, pp. 358-359.
72. K. P. Krunakaran, *op. cit.*, p. 72.
73. S. N. Hay, Sources of Indian Tradition, (Columbia), p. 658.
74. Speeches of Aurobindo, *op. cit.*, p. 140
75. Speeches of Aurobindo, *op. cit.*, pp. 33-34.
76. A. De Riencourt, *The Soul of India,* p. 227.
77. Dr. Karan Singh, *The Prophet of Indian Nationalism*, p. 36.
78. S. N. Hay, *Sources of Indian Tradition,* p. 647.
79. The Complete Works of Swami Vivekananda, Almora, Vol. IV, pp. 412-413.
80. A. De Riencourt, *The Soul of India*, p. 250.
81. Aurobindo Ghosh, B. C. Chatterjee, p. 46.
82. New Lamps for Old, No. 3, Indu Prakash, August 28, 1893.
83. New Lamps for Old, No. 4, Indu Prakash, Sept., 18, 1893.
84. Pattabhi Sitaramayya, *The History of the Indian National Congress*, p. 99.
85. Daniel Argov, Moderates and Extremists in the Indian Nationalist Movement, p. 109.
86. Surendranath Banerjee, A Nation in the Making, pp. 187-188.
87. For details see "The Genesis of Partition and the Anti-Partition Agitation (1901-1905)", by Professors Haridas and Uma Mukherjee. Also see, "Genesis of the Partition of Bengal (1905)" by P. C. Chakravarti, (Article), Modern Review, April, 1959.
88. Dr. Karan Sing, *Prophet of Indian Nationalism*, p. 62.
89. S. N. Banerjee, *A. Nation in Making,* p. 228.
90. Sri Aurobindo, Speeches, *op. cit.,* pp. 36-37.
91. *Punjabee,* 18 December, 1905.
92. Lajpat Rai, Autobiography,
93. Dr. Karan Singh, *Prophet of Indian Nationalism,* f.n. p. 63.
94. Report of the Twentyfirst Indian National Cognress, Benaras, 1905, p. 13.

95. *Ibid.*, p. 72.
96. Subhas Chandra Bose, *The Indian Struggle*, Calcutta, 1948, p. 418.
97. Haridas and Uma Mukherjee, *The Origins of the National Education Movement*, p. 74.
98. Lajpat Rai, "The Swadeshi Movement", *Indian Review*, May, 1906, p. 356.
99. N. C. Chaudhuri, *Biography of an Unknown Indian,* p. 245.
100. *Yugantar*, 17, June, 1906.
101. *Ibid.*, 16th December, 1906.
102. *New India,* 10th November, 1906.
103. The Surat Congress — A Unique Collection of Letters, Articles and Reports, G. A. Natesan (ed.), Madras, 1908.
104. Lajpat Rai, *Indian Review*, December 1907, p. 960.
105. Bengalee, 25th December, 1907.
106. The Surat Congress — A Unique Collection of Letters, Articles and Reports, Madras, 1908.
107. Aurobindo Ghosh, Sri Aurobindo on Himself and on the Mother, Pondichery, 1953, p. 47.
108. Aurobindo Ghosh, Bande Mataram, 27th October, 1907.
109. Lajpat Rai's Speech at the All-India Swadeshi Conference Surat, December, 1907, The Indian Nation Builder, p. 348.
110. H. Nevinson, *The New Spirit in India*, p. 243.
111. Aurobindo Ghosh, Sri Aurobindo on Himself and on the Mother, p. 81.
112. Morley, Recollections, Vol. II, Book V, pp. 266, 282 & 319.
113. Report of the Twenty-Fourth Indian National Congress, Madras, 1908, Resolution II.
114. *Ibid.*, Resolution III.
115. *Ibid.*, Resolution X & XI.
116. Daniel Argov, *Moderates and Extremists in the Indian Nationalists Movement*, p. 141.
117. 'The Indian Political Outlook', Indian World, January, 1908, p. 5.
118. Aurobindo Ghosh, An Open Letter to His Countrymen, Calcutta, 1909, p. 1.
119. 'Swaraj', *Indian Review*, April, 1909, p. 294.
120. Mary : Countess of Minto, India, Minto and Morley, 5th November, 1907, p. 163.
121. Daniel Argov, *Moderates and Extremists in the Indian National Movement*, p. 159.
122. Lajpat Rai, An Open Letter to the Right Honourable Edwin Samuel Montagu, New York, 1917, p. 12.

8
Conclusion

In the preceding chapters a detailed analysis has been made about the socio-political and economic ideas of Rammohan Roy and his contributions to the Indian Renaissance and the Reformation movement of the 19th century. Rammohan was a modern man in the true sense of the term, he was the "freed individual, who had achieved full emancipation of his spirit". Swami Vivekananda described him as "the first man of new, regenerate India".

Raja Rammohan Roy (1772-1833) was the pioneer of religious reforms in India.[1] He argued in favour of the introduction of English education in India and to reconstruct Indian society and culture on the Western model. Inspite of Western influences on Indian political thinking and culture, the manner of India's contact with Britain was unfortunate as it produced "much bitterness, frustration and struggle".[2] India's contact with the West gave rise to many problems and also created its own solutions. Indian public mind was filled with suspicions about their own political, social and religious ideas and institutions and the example of the progressive movements in the West served as ideal for the Indian Reformists to reconstruct India on the Western model.

This resulted in the inevitable reaction. The Indian Revivalists condemned the Western Reformists for their admiration and imitation of the West and for the denationalising consequences of their efforts. They eulogized the glorious past of India, its traditions and the pristine purity of the Vedic religion and drew heavily from the ancient Indian philosophy.

Raja Rammohan Roy was the leading personality among the Western Reformists who vehemently criticized polytheistic, idolatrous and ritualistic Hinduism. He argued in favour of a synthesis among the religious values of Hinduism, Islam and

Christianity in his efforts to develop a theory of universal cosmopolitanism. He was against the socio-religious prejudices and superstitions and wanted to purify Hinduism by removing these evil practices. With this purpose he founded the Brahmo Sabha in 1828 and eighteen years later Debendranath Tagore developed it into the Brahmo Samaj. The Raja and most of his followers, notably Keshab Chandra Sen, were deeply influenced by Christianity, Western culture and ideas.

Rammohan represented the new spirit of India with a rationalistic mind and a passionate love for reform. Inspite of his great love for Western culture and civilization Rammohan wanted to recapture and restate the true principles of Hinduism, although he was a suspect in the eyes of the Hindus due to his inclinations towards Christianity. He argued that Hinduism should be made free from unnecessary rituals, polytheism and idolatry. He extensively quoted the Upanishads to support his advocacy of ethical monotheism. Rammohan's attempt to reinterpret Hinduism was aimed at defending it against the debasing propaganda of the Christian missionaries and preventing large-scale conversion of Hindus into Christianity.

In the beginning Rammohan had "a feeling of great aversion to the establishment of the British power in India".[3] However, afterwards he reconciled himself with British rule. He believed that political progress could be achieved by co-operating with the British rulers and by operating within the British system.[4] Rammohan Roy's spirit animated the national movement in India at least upto the First World War and as distinguished from the other revolutionary movements in Europe and Asia, the Indians desired not the termination of the British rule, but the enhancement of privileges and advantages for the Indians under that system. In the 19th century, most of the educated Indians believed that it was the British administration in India which alone was capable of providing unity, security and social progress. The educated Indians were also beneficiaries of the British rule. Trained and educated in British schools and holding occupations under the British Government in India, they felt that their existence as individuals or as a group and the protection of their interest depended on the continuance of the system.

Roy spoke about national unity and political progress, but all these ideas were to be materialised within the British system. He set the standards of liberalism and individualism in the 19th century. He was in favour of synthesis among all the religions and preached universalism and cosmopolitanism. Saumyendranath Tagore has aptly described the contributions of Rammohan Roy in the following words :

> "The foundation of modern India that Rammohan laid was a great synthesis–a synthesis among three conflicting cultures, three conflicting civilizations — the Hindu, the Muslim and the Christian. Rammohan was the first to evolve a concord and convergence among the three, thus ushering in the modern age which is characterised by the evolution of a composite nationality and a synthetic civilization in India. Indeed, he went farther. On the same lines of convergence, and through the experiences of his universal personality, he saw in the clarity of his synthetic vision, the solution of the larger problem of international culture and civilization. Rammohan understood as no body else had done before him, that human progress lies not in separation among nations but in the fraternity of interdependence of individuals and nations evolved through rational synthesis of culture and civilizations. To this synthetic vision of Rammohan in the spheres of religion and culture, the Indian Renaissance of the 19th century owes its origin and birth. Indeed there was not a single aspect of India's life — political, social, economic, religious and cultural — which was not shaken out of stupor, and rendered dynamic by the touch of this mighty personality."[5]

Roy greatly influenced the ideas and institutions of his time. Although he had many grievances against the East India Company and its administration, yet he had immense faith in the principles of British constitutional government and the Indian Moderates were considerably influenced by this most significant political legacy. In his petition against the Press Regulation to the King-in-Council, the Raja wrote, "... Your dutiful subjects consequently have not viewed the English as a body of conquerors, but rather as deliverers, and look up to your majesty not only as a ruler, but also as a father and protector".[6] In a similar manner Roy concluded his 'Final Appeal to the Christian Republic', by offering thanks to the Supreme Disposer of the universe for "having unexpectedly delivered this country from the long continued tyranny of its former rulers and placed it under the Government of the English".[7]

Rammohan Roy was a reformer and not a revolutionary. He was more interested in constructive work and reformation than in revolution and since the British rule had been firmly established in India, he wanted to utilise it, if possible in securing the good of the Indian people.[8] He gave greater importance to social reform than political freedom and insisted that reform of the society was highly essential for the gradual acceptance of Western democratic institutions in India. It was due to his ardent zeal for reformation rather than revolution, he welcomed British rule and had reliance on the British parliament for arbitration of political conflict and for the redress of the grievances of the people. From this stand point Rammohan Roy was the father of the Indian Moderates.[9] It can be stated without any fear of contradiction that upto the First World War, the Indian political leadership continued in the Roy tradition.[10]

However, in defence of the Raja, it must be said that inspite of his admiration for theBritish rule in India or his ardent support for the introduction of English education, he never denounced Indian culture or true Hinduism as expressed in the Vedanta and the Upanishads, as it was done by the blind adherents of the West.[11] He was not opposed to things Indian, but to a perversion of them and in all such controversies he wanted to remake the image of India in the light of the West[12] and reform Hinduism according to the rational attitude of the Christian missionaries. It can thus be safely concluded, that Raja Rammohan was the father of all progressive movements in modern India. "The prospect of an educated India, of an India approximating to European standards of culture seems to have never been long absent from Rammohan's mind; and he did however vaguely claim in advance for his countrymen the political rights which progress in civilization inevitably involves. Here again Rammohan stands forth as the tribune and prophet of New India".[13]

Though the radical Brahmos and the Conservative pundits were united to fight the onslaughts of the Christian missionaries on Hinduism, they were engaged in many conflicts among themselves. Out of this conflict there emerged the synthesis which was represented by Pundit Iswar Chandra Vidyasagar. "This new type of Indian stood for progress and for a synthesis of Eastern and Western culture".[14]

The synthesis was a rare phenomenon during the formative period of the Congress but it did not become a conspicuous factor in the emergence of new leadership, till the Congress had become sufficiently grown up. In this connection it has to be mentioned that the Brahmo Samaj was openly following a loyal policy towards the British rule and preached the concept of England's Providential mission in India. Although this was dangerous to the growth of Indian nationalism and patriotism, this was an integral part of the Brahmo ethics. Keshab Chandra Sen (1843-1884) one of the ardent followers of Rammohan proclaimed that, "It was Christ who rules British India and not the British Government."[15] In the British conquest of India he saw the hand of Providence and thought that it was primarily a moral and intellectual conquest ordained to enlighten the Indians and uplift them from their degraded conditions. The Brahmo Samaj under his leadership tried to synthesise Hinduism, Islam and Christianity into an Indian National Church.[16]

The Arya Samaj movement was started as a natural reaction against the Brahmo Samaj movement of Rammohan Roy. The Arya Samaj movement started by Swami Dayananda Saraswati[17] was opposed to Christian leaning and blind Western imitation and asked everybody to be proud of being a Hindu.[18] Its principles included among other things "to love the Vedic religion, to be proud of Aryan greatness and to make sacrifices for the country."[19] The revivalism of the Arya Samaj, its dedication to the cause of Motherland, intense patriotism and religious commitment were manifested as a reaction against the Brahmo ethics that "The spirit of Christianity has already pervaded the whole atmosphere of Indian society and we breathe, think, feel, and move in a Christian atmosphere".[20]

The Arya Samaj in many respects was the antithesis of the Brahmo Samaj. The Brahmo Samaj and the Arya Samaj were responsible for the emergence of the Moderates and the Extremists respectively, in the Indian National Congress. The Moderates inherited the Brahmo Samajist attitude of total faith in British goodness, their sense of justice and the providential role of British Imperialism over India. They gave more emphasis on social and religious reform and tried to achieve their goals through prayers and petitions. They were highly enamoured of the Western civilization and value system and accepted India's subjugation to British authority as desirable and perpetual. The Brahmo Samajists wanted that India should conform to Western norms and should be remade in the image of the West. Due to the tremendous influences of the Brahmo Samaj, on those who were the first products of the Indian Renaissance, many of whom incidentally came to hold high offices in the Congress, its nature was characterised by its professed loyalty to the British Raj.

On the other hand the Arya Samaj which wanted to counteract the evil impacts of the Brahmo movement, was a Hindu protestant Reformation movement. It rejected Western values and relied completely on the Vedas, which Swami Dayananda Saraswati upheld as the "repository of knowledge and religious truths — the word of God".[21] But as far as the reformist ideas are concerned we notice some similarities between the Brahmo Samaj and the Arya Samaj.

Like Raja Rammohan Roy, Swami Dayananda Saraswati also denounced the post-Vedic Brahminical Hinduism as its ritualism and exacting ecclesiasticism reduced Vedic Hinduism to a spiritless dogma.[22] He condemned caste system, superiority of the Brahmins and other evil practices like child marriage and restrictions on the widows which were foisted on the Vedic religion by Brahminical laws. Dayananda did not believe in image worship or in the caste system. Philosophically the Arya Samaj believed in the capacity of energetic action for achievement of the desired goal rather than resign to fatalism and predestination. In these respects the views of the Arya Samaj and the Brahmo Samaj appear to be identical.[23] But the differences between the two organisations, were more conspicuous rather than similarities. It may be stated that while the similarities were superficial, the dissimilarities were deep-rooted and fundamental in nature. While the Brahmo Samaj wanted to recast the Indian society on the British model and looked to the West for all kinds of inspiration, the Arya Samaj gave emphasis on Aryan pride, self-confidence and self-help. It prided in the glory of ancient India and strongly refuted the Brahmo Samajist theory that there could have been no regeneration in India without the British rule, which alone released the Indians from their old bondage. The Arya Samaj believed that the Indians could regenerate India's former greatness by their own efforts and there was no need to look to the West as an ideal model or as a source for inspiration for the purpose of rebuilding India. The Arya Samaj tried to "unfasten the chains of intellectual, moral, religious and social bondage",[24] and in the process encouraged and ignited the national movement.[25] As an organisation, although it basically worked for religious reformation, yet it expressed defiance against political bondage. Whereas the Brahmo Samaj advocated the providential role of the British and expressed the pious hope that the British imperial control over India should be permanent (or atleast for a very long period of time), the Arya Samaj gave the call to the Indians to give up their parasitical character and their dependence on environment and conditon.

The impact of the Arya Samaj on the Indian political thinking was so great and its nationalistic tone was in such a great contrast with the Western-universalism of the Brahmo Samaj, that it even attracted the attention of a cosomopolitan universalist and an admirer of the West like Rabindranath Tagore. He urged upon the Indians to have faith in themselves and to pride in the past glory of India and its rich traditions. One can easily notice the philosophy of Arya Samaj reverberating in the writings of Tagore.[26]

It is also intersting to note Tagore's scorn for those who with utter disregard for the past traditions of India tried to make blind imitation of the West. He said that India had always kept its windows open to all civilizations and impacts. She had regulated and disciplined the different races who had come here and had accorded recognition to their distinctiveness. This could achieve cohesion in the society which resulted in social and spiritual unity with one another. Tagore was representative of the resurgent generation which took pride in India's past traditions and heritage; counteracted against blind imitation of the West and promoted intense nationalism. It was not prepared to compromise Indian interests at any cost.

It has to be admitted however, that all the Western Reformists did not recommend the wholesale imitation of things Western and peculiarly enough the problems that were created in India owing to the British contact were also solved in the natural process as a result of the same contact. The Extremists who subscribed to the philosophy of the Arya Samaj, were not less influenced than the Moderates by the British institutions, English education and the concepts of liberty, equality and rights.[27] Almost all the leaders with few exceptions were the products of English education and owed immesely for their progressive ideas and intense patriotism to the British contact. The serious mined among the Western Reformists shared the same feeling with the so-called Revivalists or Extremists that India should look at Western things with the eyes of the Indian and should borrow certain things from the West to be adapted in order to be applicable to the Indian conditions. The Extremists also recognised the usefulness of some Western examples in their attempts for reconstruction of their contemporary Indian society.

Rammohan was not a revolutionary but a reformist who was committed to the cause of removing the superstitions of polytheism, idolatry, ritualism and caste distinctions. He advocated the introduction of English. He fought against the evil practices of Sati and female infanticide and spoke in favour of the remarriage of the widows. Rammohan had made significant contribution to the religious and social thought of his time and hence, he should be evaluated from the point of view of his impact on society and religion and the opinion of the generations immediately following him. Although Rammohan's religious and social reform movements did not influence the people very much and were limited to a small minority of the Hindu society, O'Malley correctly recorded in the Census Report of 1911 that, "The actual number, however, gives no idea of the extent to which the Brahmo doctrines have spread". Emphasizing the universal vision of Rammohan, Rabindranath writes :

> "Rammohan was the only person in his time in the whole world of men to realize completely the significance of the Modern Age. He knew that the ideal of human civilization did not lie in the isolation of independence, but in the brotherhood of interdependence of individuals as well as of nations in all spheres of thought and activity."[28]

Swami Vivekananda had also high praises for Rammohan Roy, as he brought India into the mainstream of the history of the world. In his own words :

> "That we did not go out, that we did not compare notes with other nations — that has been the one great cause of our downfall, and everyone of you know that the little stir, the little life that you see in India, begins from the day when Raja Rammohan broke through the walls of that exclusiveness. Since that day, history of India has taken another turn, and it is growing with accelerated motion."[29]

Rammohan did not directly take part in any political agitation and he did not make significant contribution either to the growth and development of political consciousness, seeking its culmination in the independence of India. However, he protested against discrimination and "raised a revolt against interference with independence of thought and action, revolt against social and religious tyranny, revolt against superstitious customs and inhuman practices. It was Rammohan Roy who laid the foundation of all the modern movements for amelioration and elevation of the people of India". In his advocacy of an alround regeneration of the social and national life, he laid the foundations of the future political movements in India.

Footnotes

1. For details about Roy and Brahmo Samaj, see K. C. Vyas, *The Social Renaissance in India,* Bombay, Vora & Co., 1957, pp. 9-45; D. S. Sarma, *Hinduism Through the Ages*, Bombay, Bharatiya Vidya Bhavan, 1956, pp. 65-83 and K. M. Panikkar, *A Survey of Indian History,* Asia Publishing House, Bombay, 1954, p. 213.
2. Sankar Ghose, *The Renaissance to Militant Nationalism in India,* 1969, p. 4.
3. G. A. Natesan & Co. (ed.), *Raja Rammohan Roy : Writings and Speeches,* Madras, p. 273.
4. Charles H. Heimsath, *Indian Nationalism and Hindu Social Reform*, 1964, p. 58.
5. Saumyendranath Tagore, Introduction, *op. cit.*, p. viii.
6. G. A. Natesan & Co. (ed.), *Raja Rammohan Roy, His Life, Writings and Speeches*, Madras, p. 48.
7. *Ibid.*

8. C. F. Andrews and Girija K. Mookerjee, *The Rise and Growth of Congress in India (1832-1920)*, Meenakshi Prakashan, Delhi, 1967, p. 8.
9. Sankar Ghose, *The Renaissance to Militant Nationalism in India*, p. 19.
10. Charles H. Heimsath, *op. cit.*, p. 58.
11. C. F. Andrews and Girija K. Mookerjee, *op. cit.*, p. 10.
12. *Ibid.*, p. 10.
13. Sophian Dobson Collet, *Life and Letters of Raja Rammohan Roy*, Calcutta, A. C. Sarkar & Co., p. 155.
14. *Subhas Chandra Bose, An Indian Pilgrim*, Calcutta, 1948.
15. Keshab Chandra Sen, *The Brahmo Samaj, Discourses and Writings*, 2nd Edition, Calcutta, 1917, (Speech England and India) delivered in Calcutta, 2nd Feb. 1870.
16. T. De. Bary (ed.), *Sources of Indian Tradition*, Columbia University Press, New York, 1959, op. cit., p. 621.
17. It was founded in Bombay in 1873. Its principles were promulgated in Lahore in 1877.
18. C. F. Andrews and Girija K. Mookerjee, *op. cit.*, p. 14.
19. Lajpat Rai, *Autobiography*.
20. T. De Bary (ed.), *Sources of Indian Tradition*, *op. cit.*, p. 623.
21. Dayananda Saraswati, *The Light of Truth*, Lahore, 1927 p. 678.
22. Lajpat Rai, *The Arya Samaj*, London, 1915, p. 72.
23. S. C. Bose, *An Indian Pilgrim*, f.n., p. 81.
24. Lajpat Rai, *The Arya Samaj*, p. 174.
25. Dharma Vira, *Memoirs of a Civil Servant*, Vikas Publishing House, New Delhi, 1975, p. 2.
26. Sachin Sen, *The Political Thought of Tagore*, Calcutta, 1947, *op. cit.*, pp. 230-31.
27. Chunilal Lallubhai Parekh (ed.), *Essays, Speeches, Addresses and Writings of Dadabhai Naoroji*, Bombay, 1887, p. 26.
28. Quoted by Saumyendranath Tagore, *op. cit.*, p. 98.
29. *Ibid.*, p. 99.

Bibliography

PRIMARY SOURCES

A. Writings of Raja Rammohan Roy

Roy, Raja Rammohan, His Life, Writings and Speeches (Madras, G. A. Natesan & Co., 1923)

Roy, Raja Rammohan, The English Works of Raja Rammohan Roy, (Ed.) Jogendra Chandra Ghosh (Published by Srikanta Roy, Calcutta) Vols. I, II, III, 1901.

__________________, English Works of Raja Rammohan Roy, Vol. I (Calcutta, Brahmo Samaj Centenary Committee, 1928).

Roy, Raja Rammohan, The Man and His Work, (Ed.) (Calcutta, Amal Home, 1933).

Roy, Raja Rammohan, Rammohan Roy Centenary Commemoration Volume, The Father of Modern India, Calcutta, 1935.

Tuhfat-ul-Mawahhidin (1803).

The Precepts of Jesus — the Guide to Peace and Happiness. Petitions Against the Press Regulation to the Supreme Court and the King-in-Council (1823).

A Letter to Lord Amherst on English Education (1823).

A Tract on the Religious Toleration (1823).

Rights of Hindus Over Ancestral Property according to Law of Bengal (1830).

Remarks on Settlement in India by Europeans (1831).

Questions and Answers on the Judical and Revenue System of India.

Vedanta Grantha (1815) — Commentary on Brahma Sutra (in Bengali)

Vedanta Sara (1815) — in Bengali.

Kenopanishads (1816) — in Bengali.

Isopanishads (1816) — in Bengali.

Kathopanishads (1817) — in Bengali.

Mandukyopanishads (1817) — in Bengali.

B. Reports

Indian National Congress, Annual Reports, (Printed in India from 1885).

India in 1906 (Presidential Addresses at the National Congress and other conferences held in 1906), (ed.) D. G. Khandekar, Poona, 1907.

The Congress, Conferences and Conventions of 1909; A Collection of the Presidential and Inaugural Speeches, Natesan, Madras, 1910.

Papers Relating to an Imperial Advisory Council, and Provincial Advisory Council, Enlargement of Legislative Councils, etc. (cd. 3710), 1907.

Proposals of the Government of India and despatches of the Secretary of State (cd. 4426), 1908.

Replies of the Local Governments (cd. 4435, 4436), 1908.

Press Act of 1910 (cd. 5269), 1910.

Government of India Despatch, August 25, 1911 (cd. 5979), 1911.

Report of the Royal Commission on the Public Services in India, Vol. I (cd. 8382), 1917.

Addresses Presented in India to the Viceroy and Secretary of State (cd. 9178), 1918 (includes Gokhale's Memorandum; Memorandum submitted to His Excellency by Nineteen Elected Additional Members of the Imperial Legislative Council with regard to post-war Reform, dated October 1916, etc.)

Report on Reform Proposals, Published by the Bengal Provincial Conference Committee, Calcutta, 1918.

Report on the Sedition Committee (cd. 9190), 1918.

Montague-Chelmsford Report (cd. 9109), 1918.

Report of the Indian Industrial Commission, 1916-18 (cmd. 51), 1919.

Joint Select Committee on the Government of India Bill; Report and Proceedings, 1919, Vol. I.

Indian Constitutional Documents (1858-1945), (Ed.) A. C. Bannerjee, Vol. II, Calcutta, 1946.

Indian Constitutional Documents, (Ed.) P. Mukherji, 2 Vols., Calcutta, 1918.

Indian Speeches and Documents on British Rule (1821-1918), (Ed.), J. K. Majumdar, Calcutta, 1937.

Speeches and Documents on Indian Policy, (Ed.) A. B. Keith, Vol. II, London, 1922.

Speeches and Documents on the Indian Constitution, 1921-1947, 2 Vols. (Eds.) Sir Maurice Guyer and A. Appadorai, London, 1957.

Indian National Congress

Report of the 36th Session, December, 1921, Ahmedabad.
Report of the 37th Session, December, 1922, Gaya.
Report of the 38th Session, December, 1923, Cacinada.
Report of the 39th Session, December, 1924, Belgaum.
Report of the 40th Session, December, 1925, Cawnpore.
Report of the 41st Session, December, 1926, Ghauhati.
Report of the 42nd Session, December, 1927, Madras.
Report of the 43rd Session, December, 1928, Calcutta.
Report of the 44th Session, December, 1929, Lahore.
Report of the 45th Session, 1931, Karachi.
Report of the 48th Session, October, 1934, Bombay.
Report of the 49th Session, April, 1936, Allahabad.
Report of the 51st Session, February, 1938, Haripura, Ahmedabad.
Report of the 52nd Session, March, 1939, Tripuri, Jubbalpore.
Report of the 53rd Session, 1940, Ramgarh.

C. Biographies of Raja Rammohan Roy and other Reformers

Adam, W., Lecture on the Life and Labour of Raja Rammohan Roy, Calcutta, 1879.

Ball, Upendra Nath, Ram Mohan Roy : A Study of his Life, Works and Thoughts (Calcutta, U. Ray and Sons, Bowbazar Street, 1933).

Bell, W. M., Ram Mohan Roy, Calcutta, 1933,

__________, Chaitanya to Vivekananda : Lives of the Saints of Bengal, (Madras, 2nd Edn., 1949).

Bhan, Suraj, Dayananda, His Life and Works, Jullundar, 1956.

Bomanji, Framji, Lights and Shades of the East, or a Study of the Life of Baboo Harrischander, Bombay, 1863.

Carpenter, Mary, Last days in England of Raja Rammohan Roy, Calcutta, 1915.

Chapman, E. F., Sketches of Some Distinguished Indian Women, London, 1891.

Chanda, R. P. and Majumdar, J. K. (Eds.), Selections from Official Documents Relating to the Life of Raja Rammohan Roy, Calcutta, 1938.

Chatterjee, Ramananda, Rammohan Roy and Modern India,

Calcutta, 1918.
Chaudhuri, Nirad, C., The Autobiography of an Unknown Indian, New York, 1951.
Collect, Sophia Dobson, Life and Letters of Raja Rammohan Roy, Calcutta, 1913.
Das Gupta, Hemendranath, Deshbandhu Chittaranjan Das, Delhi, 1960.
Gidumal, Dayaram, The Life and Life Work of Behramji M. Malabari, Bombay, 1888.
Gurunadhan, J., Viresalingam, The Founder of Telugu Public Life, Rajahmundry, 1911.
Iqbal, Singh, Rammohan Roy : A Biographical Inquiry into the Making of Modern India, Bombay, 1958.
Karkaria, R. P., India, Forty Years of Progress and Reform, being a Sketch of the Life and Times of Behramji M. Malabari, London, 1896.
Karve, D. G., Ranade, The Prophet of Liberated India, Poona, 1942.
Majumdar, J. K., (Ed.), Raja Rammohan Roy and Progressive Movements in India, Calcutta, 1941.
Molivala, B. N., Karsondas Mulji, A Biographical Study, Bombay, 1935.
Tagore, Soumyendranath, Rammohan Roy : His Role in Indian Renaissance, Calcutta, 1975.

D. Memoirs, Speeches and Miscellaneous Writings

An Indian, Essays on Indian Social Reform, Bombay, 1893.
Andrews, C. F., The Renaissance in India, London, 1912.
Arundale, George S., The Spirit of Freedom, Madras, 1917.
Baijnath, Rai Bahadur Lala, "Some Problems of Social Reform" (Pamphlet), Aligarh, 1891.
__________, "Suggestions for Religious Education and other Reforms in Hindu Society..." (Pamphelt), Agra, 1909.
Banerjee, Sir Surendranath, A Nation in Making : Being the Reminiscences of Fifty Years of Public Life (London, Oxford University Press, 1931).
__________, Speeches and Writings Selected by himself, (1st Edn.). (Madras, G. A. Natesan & Co., 1920).
__________, Wake up India, Madras, 1913.
Besant, Annie, For India's Uplift; A Collection of Speeches and

Writings of Indian Questions, Madras, 2nd Edn., 1917.

____________, Wake up India; A Plea for Social Reform, Madras, 1913.

Besant, Annie, How India Wrought for Freedom, Madras, 1915.

____________, Ancient Ideals in Modern Life, Benaras, 1901.

____________, The Birth of New India, Madras, 1917.

____________, Nation Building, Madras, 4th edn., 1917.

Bhandarkar, Sir R. G., "A Note on the Age of Marriage and its Consummation According to Hindu Religious Law" (Pamphlet), Poona, 1891.

Bose, Ramchandra, Brahmoism, New York, 1884.

Bose, Shib Chunder, The Hindoos As They Are; A Description of the Manners, Customs and Inner Life of Hindoo Society in Bengal, Calcutta, 1881.

Bose, Subhas, An Indian Pilgrim or Autobiography of S.C. Bose (1897-1920), Calcutta 1948.

Chakraborti, S.C., Life of Pandit Ishwarchandra Vidyasagar, Calcutta, 1896.

Chintamani, C.Y., Indian Social Reform, Madras, 1880.

____________, Indian Politics Since the Mutiny, London, 1940.

Chirol, Valentine, Indian Unrest, London, 1910.

____________, India, 1926.

Cotton, Henry, New India or India in Transition, London, 1907.

____________, Indian Speeches and Addresses (Calcutta, S.K. Lahiri & Co., 1930).

Coupland, R., India, A Restatement, (Bombay, Oxford University Press, 1945).

____________, The Indian Problem (1833-1935), London, 1943.

Das, C.R., India for Indians, Madras, 1918.

Dhar, Pt. Bishan Narayan, Young Men and Social Service, Nellore, 1911.

Dufferin, Lord, Speeches Delivered in India (1884-88), London, 1890.

Farquhar, J.N., Modern Religious Monuments in India, London 1924.

Fuller, Bampfylde, Studies of Indian Life and Sentiment, London, 1910.

Gandhi, M.K., Hind Swaraj, Madras, 1921.

____________, Speeches and Writings of M.K. Gandhi, (Madras, Natesan, 1918).

Garth, R., A Few Plain Truths about India, London, 1888.

Ghose, Aurobindo, Bankim-Tilak-Dayananda, Calcutta, 1940.

____________, The Foundations of Indian Culture, Pondicherry, 1959.

____________, The Renaissance in India, Chandernagore, 1920.

____________, The Doctrine of Passive Resistance, Calcutta, 1948.

Gokhale, G.K., East and West in India (An article in "Papers on Inter-Racial Probems", (Ed.), G. Spiller, London, 1911.

Hume, Allan Octavian, A Speech on the Indian National Congress: Its Origin, Aims, Objects, (Delivered at a General Public Meeting at Allahabad, 20th April, 1988) Calcutta.

Iqbal, Muhammed, Reconstruction of Religious Thought in Islam, Oxford University Press, 1934.

Jayakar, Mukund R., Social Reform and Social Service, Madras, 1917.

Kelkar, N.C., The Case for Indian Home Rule, (Published under the authority of the Indian Home Rule League, Poona), 1917.

Kipling, Rudyard, White Man's Burden, 1899.

Lyall, Alfred C., Asiatic Studies: Religious and Social, First Series, London, 1920.

____________, The Rise and Expansion of British Dominion in India, London, 1920.

Macaulay, Lord, Speeches with His Minute on Indian Education (Ed.), G.M. Young London, 1935.

Macdonald, J.R., The Awakening of India, 1910.

Mac Nicol, N., The Making of Modern India, London, 1924.

Majumdar, A.C., Indian National Evolution, 1917.

Malabari, B.M., Infant Marriage and Enforced Widowhood in India, Bombay, 1877.

Mc Cully, B.T., English Education and the Origins of Indian Nationalism, New York, 1940.

Mc Ston, Lord, India at the Crossways, Cambridge, 1920.

Mill, James, History of British India, 1848.

Montague, E.S., Indian Diary, 1930.

Morrison, Theodore, Imperial Rule in India: Being an Examination of the Principles Proper to the Government of Dependencies, (Westminister, 1899).

Pal, Bipin Chandra, "The Basis of Political Reform" (Pamphlet), Calcutta 1889.

__________, An Introduction to the Study of Hinduism, Calcutta, 2nd edn., 1951.

__________, Indian Nationalism: Its Principles and Personalities, Madras, 1918.

__________, Soul of India, Calcutta, 4th edn., 1958.

__________, Swadeshi and Swaraj: The Rise of New Patriotism, Calcutta, 1954.

__________, Speeches of Bipin Chandra Pal, Madras, 1907.

Paranjpye, R. P., The Crux of Indian Problem, 1931.

Parekh C.L., (Ed.), Eminent Indians on Indian Politics, Bombay, 1892.

Rai, Lala Lajpat, The Arya Samaj, London, 1915.

__________, Young India: An Interpretation and a History of the Nationalist Movement from within, London 1917.

__________, Lala Lajpat Rai, The Man in His Words, Madras, 1907.

__________, The Problems of National Education in India, London, 1920.

__________, The Political Future of India, New York, 1919.

Rama, Mahatma Munshi, Aryan Samaj and Politics, Lahore, Ist Edn.

__________, The Future of the Aryan Samaj, Lahore, 1893.

Ranade, M. G., Essays on Indian Economics, Bombay, 1899.

__________, Miscellaneous Writings, Bombay, 1915.

__________, Religious and Social Reforms, Bombay, 1902.

Ranade, Mrs. Rambi, Himself, the Autobiography of a Hindu Lady, New York, 1938.

Ratcliffe, S., William Wedderburn and the Indian Reform Movement, London, 1923.

Rees, J. D., Modern India, London, 1910.

__________, The Real India, London, 1908.

Risley, Herbert, The People of India, London, 1913.

Row, K. Srinivasa, Papers on Social Reform; Being the Speeches and Writings of K. Srinivasa Row, Madras, 1906.

Saraswati, Dayananda, Satyarth Prakash, Allahabad, 1915.

Sastri, Sibnath, History of Brahmo Samaj, 2 Vols., Calcutta, 1911-12.

Sastri, Pandit A. Mahadeva, Collected Essays of Pandit A.

Mahadeva Sastri on Vedic Religion and Social Reform, I : The Vedic Law of Marriage on the Emancipation of Women, Madras, 1918.

Sitaramayya, Pattabhi, The History of the Indian National Congress, 2 Vols., (S. Chand & Co., New Delhi, 1969).

Smith, W. Roy, Nationalism and Reform in India, 1938.

____________, Some Arya Samajists, The Arya Samaj, Lahore (1st Edn.)

____________, Tagore, Rabindranath, Nationalism, London, 1917.

Tagore, Debendranath, The Autobiography, Calcutta, 1909.

Tattvabhushan, Sitanath, Hindu Theism : A Defence and Exposition, Calcutta, 1898.

____________, The Philosophy of Brahmoism, Madras, 1909.

____________, Social Reform in Bengal, Calcutta, 1904.

Telang, K. T., Writings and Speeches, 2 Vols., 1926.

Temple, Richard, India in 1880, London, 1880.

Tilak, Bal Gangadhar, Writings and Speeches.

____________, Tilak's Speeches on Home Rule, Benaras, 1917.

Trevelyan, Charles, On the Education of the People of India, London, 1938.

Trevelyan, G. O., The Competition Wallah, London, 1866.

Vivekananda Swami, India and Her Problems, Almora, 4th edn., 1946.

____________, Selections from Swami Vivekananda, Almora, 2nd edn., 1946.

____________, Speeches and Writings, Madras, 5th edn.

____________, The Letters of Swami Vivekananda, Almora, 4th edn., 1948.

____________, The Complete Works of Swami Vivekananda, Almora.

____________, Our Women, Almora, 1953.

____________, Salvation and Service, Almora, 1949.

Whitehead, Henry, Indian Problems : In Religion, Education and Politics, London, 1924.

Wint, Guy, The British in Asia.

Zacharias, H. C. E., Renascent India, From Rammohan Roy to Mohandas Gandhi (G. Allen and Unwin, London, 1933).

E. Contemporary Newspapers and Periodicals

Newspapers

The Bengalee (Calcutta)
The Hindu Patriot (Calcutta)
The Hindu (Madras)
The Indian Mirror (Calcutta)
The Indian Nation (Calcutta)
The Indian Spectator (Bombay)
The Madras Mail (Madras)
The Pioneer Mail (Allahabad)
The Times (London)
The Tribune (Lahore)
The Voice of India (contained Extracts from Indian Newspapers), (Bombay).
Young India, (Ahmedabad).

Periodicals

The Asiatic Quarterly Review (London)
The Empire Review (London)
The Fortnightly Review (London)
The Contemporary Review (London)
The Modern Review (Calcutta)
The Indian Review (Madras)
The Hindustan Review (Allahabad)
The Indian World (Calcutta)
Harjian (Ahmedabad)
The Journal of the East India Association (London).

SECONDARY SOURCES

Ahluwalia, M. M., *Freedom Struggle in India* (1858-1909), (Delhi, Ranjit Printers and Publishers, 1956).

________________, *Swamy Dayananda Saraswati,* New Delhi, N.C.E.R.T., 1971.

Alexander, H. G., *The Indian Ferment; A Traveller's Tales,* (Williams & Norgate Ltd., London, 1929).

Appadorai, A., *Indian Political Thinking in the Twentieth Century from Naoroji to Nehru : An Introductory Survey,* (Calcutta, Oxford University Press, 1971).

Archer, William, *India and the Future,* London, 1917.

Argov, David, *Moderates and Extremists in the Indian National*

Movement, (1883-1920), (Bombay, Asia Publishing House, 1967).

Azad, Maulana Abul Kalam, *India Wins Freedom*, Calcutta, 1959.

Ball, U. N., *A Century of Service : A Survey of the Services rendered by the Brahmo Samaj*, Lahore, 1928.

Barne, M., *India Today and Tomorrow*, (George Allen and Unwin, London, 1937).

Baru, P. S., *Keshab Chandra Sen and His Work*, Calcutta, 1937.

Bary, D. C,. *Source of Indian Tradition*, Columbia University Press, 1958.

Bary, William Theodore and Others, *Sources of Indian Tradition*, New York, 1958.

Basham, A. L., *The Wonder that was India*, London, 1954.

Basu, D. D., *Ruin of Indian Trade and Industries*, Calcutta, 1935.

Beauchamp, Joan, *British Imperialism in India*, 1935.

Bevan, Edwin, *Indian Nationalism*, London, 1913.

Bhattacharya, H., *Individual and Social Progress, Principal Miller Endowment Lectures*, 1938 (Madras University), 1939.

Bhattacharya, Haridas (Ed.), *The Cultural Heritage of India*, (Volume IV), (The Ramakrishna Mission Institute of Culture, 1956).

Bomanji, Franji, *Lights and Shades of the East*, Bombay, 1863.

Bose, Sisir Kumar (Ed.), *Netaji and India's Freedom*, Netaji Research Bureau, Calcutta, 1975.

Brailsford, H. N., *Subject India* (Bombay, Vora and Co., 1946).

Brown, Ermine A., *Eminent Indians*, Calcutta, 1946.

Buch, M. A., *Rise and Growth of Indian Liberation*, Baroda, 1938.

_________, *Rise and Growth of Militant Nationàlism*, Baroda, 1939.

Burke, Marie Louise, *Swami Vivekananda in America*, New Discoveries, Calcutta, 1958.

Chakraborti, A. K., *Maharshi Debendranath Tagore* (in Bengali), Allahabad, 1916.

Chakravarti, Atulananda, *The Recovery of India*, The World Press Pvt. Ltd., Calcutta, 1972.

Chand, Tara, *History of Freedom Movement in India* (Vol. I) (New Delhi, Ministry of Information and Broadcasting, Government of India, 1961).

Chandavarkar, N. G., *The Speeches and Writings*, Bombay, 1911.

Chandra, Bipin, *The Rise and Growth of Economic Nationalism in India*, New Delhi, 1966.

Chatterji, A. C., *India's Struggle for Freedom,* Chatterjee & Co., 1947.

Chaudhury, Kali Prasanna, *Netaji and India*, Shillong, 1956.

Coomaraswamy, A. K., *Art and Swadeshi,* Madras, 1912.

________________, *Essays in National Idealism,* Colombo, 1910.

________________, *The Message of the East,* Madras, 1909.

Crawford, Arthur, *The Unrest in India,* Bombay, 1908.

Das, Babu Govinda, *Hindu Ethics, Principles of Hindu Religio-Social Regeneraton,* Madras, 1928.

Das, C. R., *India for Indians*, Madras, 1921.

Das, M. N., *Studies in the Economic and Social Development of Modern India* (1848-56), Calcutta, 1959.

Datta, K. K., *Survey of Indian Social Life and Economic Conditions in the Eighteenth Century* (1767-1813), Calcutta, 1961.

__________, *Education and Social Amelioration of Women in Pre-Mutiny India,* Patna, 1936.

__________, *Dawn of Renascent India,* Calcutta, 1964.

__________, *Renaissance, Nationalism and Social Change in Modern India,* Calcutta, 1965.

De Mello, F. M., *The Indian National Congress,* Oxford, 1934.

De Reincourt, Amaury, *The Soul of India,* (New York, Harper and Brothers, 1960).

Desai, A. R., *Social Background of Indian Nationalism* (3rd Edn.), (Bombay, Popular Book Depot, 1959).

Desai, Bhulabhai, J., *INA Defence–Subject People's Right to Fight for Freedom*, Bombay, 1960.

Desai, Neera A., *Women in Modern India,* Bombay, 1957.

Deutsch, K. W., *Nationalism and Social Communication*, London.

Digby, W., *"Prosperous" British India,* London, 1903.

Dodwell, H. H., *Sketch of the History of India from 1859 to 1918.*

Dubois, Abbej, A., *Hindu Manners, Customs and Ceremonies*, 1906.

Dunbar, Sir George, *India and Passing of Empire,* London, 1951.

Dutta, C. C., *The Culture of India as Envisaged by Sri Aurobindo,* Bhartiya Vidya Bhavan, Bombay, 1960.

Edwards, Michael, *The Last Years of British Rule* (London, Allied Publishers, 1963).

Fisher, Louis, *The Life of Mahatma Gandhi,* Jonathan Cape, 1952.

Frager, A. L., *India Under Curzon and After,* London, 1920.

Franda, Marucus, F., *Radical Politics in West Bengal,* The M.I.T.

Press, London, 1971.

Ganguli, B. N., *Dadabhai Naoroji, and the Drain Theory*, Asia, 1965.

Ghosal, U. N., *A History of Indian Political Ideas*, Bombay, 1959.

Ghose, Sankar, *The Renaissance to Militant Nationalism in India*, (Bombay, Allied Publishers, 1969).

____________, *The Western Impact on Indian Politics* (1885-1919), Calcutta, 1967.

Ghosh, P. C., *Indian National Congress* (1892-1909). Firma K. K. Mukhopadhyaya, Calcutta, 1960.

Gokhale, B. G., *The Making of Indian Nation* (2nd Edn.), Asia Publishing House, 1960

Gopal, S., *British Policy in India*, 1858-1905, Cambridge, 1965.

________, *The Viceroyalty of Lord Ripon*, (London, Oxford University Press, 1957).

Goyal, O. P., *Studies in Modern Indian Political Thought* (Delhi, Kitab Mahal, 1964).

Gordon, Leonard A., *Bengal, The Nationalist Movement*, 1876-1940 (Delhi, Manohar Book Service, 1974).

Gregg, Richard B., *Which Way Lies Hope ? An Examination of Capitalism, Communism, Socialism and Gandhiji's Programme*, Navjivan, Ahmedabad, 1957.

Gupta, Nagendranath, *Indian Nationalism*, (Bombay, Hind Kitabs, 1946).

Haithocos, John Patrick, *Communism and Nationalism in India, M. N. Roy and Commintern Policy*, 1920-1939, Oxford University Press, Bombay, India, 1909.

Hardie, Kerl,

Hertog, Sir P., *Some Aspects of Indian Education, Past and Present*, 1939.

Hastings, James, (Ed.) *Encyclopaedia of Religion and Ethics*, 1955.

Heimsath, Charles H., *Indian Nationalism and Hindu Social Reform*, Princeton, 1964.

Hoederness, Sir T., *Peoples and Problems of India*, 1911.

Iyengar, K. R. Srinivasa, *Sri Aurobindo* (Calcutta, Asia Publishing House, 1950).

Jog, N. G., *Lokamanya Bal Gangadhar Tilak*, Publications Division, Government of India, 1970.

Kabir, Humayun, *The Indian Heritage*, 3rd Edn., Asia, 1955.

Karunakaran, K. P., *Religion and Political Awakening in India,* (Meerut, Meenakshi Prakashan, 1966).

Kaushik, P. D., *The Congress Ideology and Programme* (1920-47), (Bombay, Allied Publishers, 1964).

Keith, A. B., *Speeches and Documents on India Policy,* London, 1922).

Khan, Aga, *India in Transition* (Bombay, Times of India Office, 1918).

Kriplani, J. B., *The Indian National Congress,* 1946.

Madhok, Balraj, *Political Trends in India* (Delhi, S. Chand & Co., 1959).

Mason, Philip, *The Men who Ruled India, 2 Vols.*, London, 1953-54.

Mazumdar, A. C., *Indian National Evolution, A Brief Survey of the Origin and Progress of the Indian National Congress,* 2nd Edn., Natesan, Madras, 1917.

Mazumdar, A. M., *Social Welfare in India,* 1964.

Mazumdar, B. B., *History of Indian Social and Political Ideas from Rammohan to Dayananda*, Calcutta, 1967.

Mazumdar, R. C., *History of Freedom Movement in India,* Vols. I, II and III, Calcutta.

____________, *Glimpses of Bengal in the Nineteenth Century,* Calcutta, 1960.

____________, (Ed.) *British Paramountcy and the Indian Renaissance, Part II,* Bharatiya Vidya Bhawan, 1965.

Mc Lane, John R., (Ed.) *The Political Awakening in India,* (New Jersey, Princeton Hall, 1970).

Mukherjee, Haridas and Uma, *The Growth of Nationalism in India* (1857-1905), Calcutta, 1958.

Muller, Max, *Biographical Essays,* London, 1884.

Munshi, K. M., *Pilgrimage to Freedom,* Bharatiya Vidya Bhavan, Bombay, 1967.

Nanda, B. R., *Mahatma Gandhi*, (Revised Edition), (London, Unwin Books, 1965).

Naoroji, Dadabhai, *Poverty and Unbritish Rule in India,* 1876.

____________, *Speeches and Writings* (Madras, Natesan & Co.)

Narain, V. A., *Social History of Modern India,* Meerut, 1972.

Narayan, Jayaprakash, *Towards Struggle,* (Bombay, Padma Publications, 1946).

Nehru, Jawaharlal, *Glimpses of World History,* London, 1949.

________________, *The Discovery of India* (London), Meridian Books Ltd., 1956).

________________, *Autobiography* (Bombay, Allied Publishers, 1962).

Panikkar, K. M., *Asia and Western Dominances,* London, 1959.

______________, *The Foundations of New India,* London, 1963.

______________, *A Survey of Indian History* (3rd Edn.), (Bombay, Asia Publishing House, 1956).

______________, *Commonsense about India,* (New York, Macmillan, 1960).

Parekh, M. C., *The Brahmo Samaj,* Rajkot, 1929.

Philips, Maurico, *The Teachings of the Vedas,* (London, Longman Green & Co., 1895).

Poddar, Arabinda, *Renaissance in Bengal : Quests and Confrontations* (1800-1860), (Simla, Indian Institute of Advanced Study, 1970).

Powell, Baden, *Land Systems of British India,* Calcutta, 1895.

Pradhan, R. G., *India's Struggle for Swaraj,* Madras, 1930.

Prakash, Satya, *A Critical Study of Philosophy of Dayananda,* Ajmer, 1938.

Prasad, Amba, *The Indian Revolt, 1942,* (New Delhi, S. Chand & Co., 1958).

Radhakrishnan, Sarvapalli, *Eastern Religion and Western Thought,* 2nd Ed., London, 1940.

Ramana Murthi, V. V., *Non-Violence in Politics,* (Delhi, Frank Brothers & Co., 1958).

Ramgopal, *Lokamanya Tilak,* (Bombay, Asia Publishing House, 1956).

Ranga, N. G., *Outlines of National Revolutionary Path,* (Bombay, Hind Kitabs, 1945).

Rao, M. V. Krishna, *The Growth of Indian Liberalism in the Nineteenth Century,* Mysore, 1951.

Rolland, Romain, *Prophets of New India,* London, 1930.

______________, *The Life of Vivekananda*, London, 1947.

______________, *The Life of Ramakrishna,* 3rd Edn., Almora, 1944.

Roy, B. B., *Religious Movements in Modern Bengal,* Calcutta, 1965.

Sarkar, Jadunath, *Economics of British India,* Calcutta, 1916.

Sarkar, Susobhan, *Bengal Renaissance and Other Essays,* (New

Delhi, People's Publishing House, 1970).

Savarkar, V. D., *The Indian War of Independence* (National Rising of 1857), London, 1909.

Sen, Sachin, *The Political Thought of Tagore* (Calcutta, General Printers and Publishers Ltd., 1947).

Sharma, Bishan Sarup, *Gandhi as a Political Thinker,* (Allahabad, Indian Press (Publications) Private Ltd., 1956).

Sharma, Jagdish, *India's Struggle for Freedom,* 3 Vols., (New Delhi, S. Chand & Co., 1962, 1964, 1965).

Sharma, Sri Ram, *Constitutional History of India* (3rd Edn.), (New Delhi, Orient Longmans Ltd., 1974).

Singh, G. N., *Landmarks in Indian Constitutional and National Development*, Delhi, 1959.

Sinha Pradeep, *Nineteenth Century Bengal*, Calcutta, 1965.

Smith, Donald Engene, *India as a Secular State,* Princeton, 1963.

Smith, W. R., *Nationalism and Reform in India*, New Haven, 1938.

Spear, Percinil, *A History of India,* Pelican, 1970.

Tagore, R. N., *Nationalism,* (London, Macmillan, 1917).

Tayyebulla, M., *Between the Symbol and the Idol at Last,* (New Delhi, Allied Publishers, 1964).

Thompson, E., *The Reconstruction of India,* London, 1933.

Topa, Ishwar Nath, *The Growth and Development of National Thought in India,* Hamburg, 1928.

Tripathy, Amales, *The Extremist Challenge,* (Calcutta, Orient Longmans, 1967).

Upadhyaya, Ganga Prasad, *The Origin and Scope of Mission of the Arya Samaj,* Allahabad, 1940.

____________, *Philosophy of Dayananda,* Allahabad, 1955.

Varma, V. P., *The Political Philosophy of Sri Aurobindo,* (Bombay, Asia Publishing House, 1960).

Vidyavachaspati, Indra, *Arya Samaj Ka Itihas* (in Hindi), (Delhi, 1957, 2 Vols.)

Vyas, K. C., *The Social Renaissance in India,* Bombay, 1957.

Wolpert, S. A., *Tilak and Gokhale : Revolution and Reform in the Making of Modern India,* 1962.

Young, G. M. (Ed.), *Speeches of Lord Macaulay,* London, 1935.

Index